One

Percent

To: Ms. Carolyn
With all the love, joy + peace
in the world.
Author Aerielle Tuggers

Based On a True Story

By: Aerielle Tuggers

Battle One

Chosen from the Beginning

On May 17, 2015, Jay walked across the stage and looked out into a cheering audience at such an auspicious occasion as the dean called her name. She was presented with her Bachelor of Arts degree in psychology. People gathered from wall to wall forming a sea of many colors filling the space. She could make out some familiar faces from a distance. She shook the hands of the dean and president before snapping a mental picture of what would be her highest esteemed honor and most sought after reverie. In that special moment, she paused and took a mental note of the thousands of people in the room smiling at her beaming with delight. She had graduated from the internationally recognized and highest ranked Historical Black College, Spelman College. There were so many people present to celebrate her successful milestone, yet none of them truly knew the person they were celebrating. This caused mixed emotions of pride and emptiness overwhelming her as she stared back into the crowd. She was proud because she was the first in her generation to earn a degree on both sides of her family, but also empty because two of the three people whom she had done it all for were not there to witness the spectacular feat.

To her peers who admired her, Jay was just a goofy beauty filled with knowledge, confidence, happiness and innocence. Paradoxically, this was a girl born to two parents who were drug addicts, leaving crack cocaine in her system as she traveled through the birth canal, and later sold for drugs. The scars led to an on-going battle with the deepest depression imaginable for the entirety of her life.

It was at the moment of walking across the stage during commencement services that she grasped the concept of whom and what she was. She was a miracle child who was chosen to be the first in her family destined for greatness from birth. She was chosen from the beginning exactly twenty-one years, seven months and twenty-seven days prior to that day where she earned her right of passage into societal piety and to live as if no harm had been done to her.

Her life and struggles began on a hot autumn day in September of 1993. The sun tilts over the horizon and pierces through the dark clouds, not enough to illuminate the darkness altogether but enough to provide hope that pure sunshine without the grim face of night will soon prevail. Her mother, now nine months pregnant, sits on the porch of a crack house in northern Memphis, Tennessee staring straight into the sun's gleam. She challenges herself to keep her eyes unwatery and fixed on the light without blinking as she smokes her problems, frustrations, anger and resentment away. Mad at the world, blaming the world for her misfortune yet damaging herself with each breath inhaling the medicine that she believes cures all problems. Rubbing her swollen belly, she loves this child as much as she loves herself. As she is injecting the fumes of crack cocaine into her own system, she is also injecting those same toxic fumes into the veins of her unborn child. Just so they can suffer together. Her mentality was, "I die, you die", a love so connected that they hit rock bottom together with their highs. She whispers, "See how much mommy loves you." She sits there under the sun on that porch. Having fallen more in love with the lifestyle than her husband of eleven years and wondering where he had disappeared to this time. When she was off getting high, he was somewhere getting drunk. Their codependency supported each other addictions. They were in love with each other's addictions as much as they loved each other.

No man, woman or child could match the unwavering love she had for this man. She loved the highs and lows of love that included blows to the head and blackened eyes. This love led to fighting every night over drugs she had stolen from his stash to sell. She was selfish and wanted to quench her own thirst. This made her feel invincible. She punched back with love and threw objects that abased her husband's dark skin as they ended their nights higher than the sun she was currently sitting under.

Still, she began to think of how she had ended up on this porch begging for another hit from drugs or from her husband. Was it because she grew up in a house where she was undoubtedly the least favorite child? Or was it because she did not biologically belong to the man her mother married and started a new life with? This was a well-kept secret that survived for decades. Was it because her mother was seventy-five percent Crete Indian with long silky naturally auburn-colored hair, grey eyes? She was the only one of the three children that didn't look like her mother. Instead, she had a dark complexion. Her complexion compared to that of her mother's resembled placing a light mocha coffee next to a medium-dark roast. Born in an era where colorism was abounding, her own mother quivered at her skin tone.

Was it because she had fallen in love with and married a man that no one accepted because he was the neighborhood dope man and wild Black Panther? Maybe it was because she and her husband fought so much and got police complaints so often that the cops simply stopped responding to the calls. She knew why but turned a blind eye to it; she was only living for the moment she could get high again. Instead of facing the facts, she was constantly looking for the next best thing. So, she ran. She ran from the demons compressed in her self-consciousness; she ran from herself; she ran from her husband. It was a cycle as she would return to it all days later because of the feelings of nothingness that overwhelmed her when she went without the sameness of the chaos.

She wanted her husband, even though the last time she saw him she threw a brick into her own window to get his attention, leading to another drunken fight leaving him unconscious while she pleaded for him to awake. She missed how happy they used to be. If it weren't for that last argument, he'd be right there on the porch next to her. Yelling out, "How are my girls doing?" He wanted to know how she was doing and the baby girl she was carrying. She knew early on that the little one was going to be a daddy's girl because she'd only kicked when he started talking. After all, he was the one who took the sick leave from work because of his morning sickness. She thought of how she became pregnant, and though it started out as an argument that led to bloodied walls and bruised faces, she knew this child she was carrying was created out of love. It was a dangerous love that could have killed them all, but a love nonetheless. "Well whatever, he's off getting high with the next girl now," she thinks to herself.

She's been sitting there for hours staring at the sun so inebriated that she doesn't even notice the water, so much water. Continuing to challenge God by looking directly into his light, she laughs, ignoring the water dripping droplets of blood on the porch beneath her. God proves himself all-mighty as she is inflicted with a pain like none she had ever experienced before. Sharp pains begin to surface in her lower back and spread to her abdomen. Attempting to stand, she falls back down on the stair of the porch surrendering her delusional power over to God. "Ok, you win," she screams at the sun. Her high now slowly wearing off, she feels her child moving sporadically as her hips are widening making way for a life to be born. Thinking the world is ending, she cries out loudly for her mother only to be comforted by the concrete step. Here, she is giving birth on the front porch of a crack house. Her equally drugged up friends run out of the house, throw her into the back seat of their car and rush her to the nearest hospital. Once there, they drop her off at the emergency room entrance and take off.

Completely natural for her to have and with no family or friends there to hold her hand during such a momentous occasion, she gives birth to this baby girl after eighteen hours of labor and exactly five days before her husband's fortieth birthday. Still thinking that she is going to die from the after-labor pains, she requests that upon her death her child be released to Brady, her mother. "It's a girl" she heard the doctor say, as if she was unaware of that. She held this child for the first time and in awe of this precious gift, she shouts out, "My baby is the prettiest baby in the nursery", though she hadn't even seen the other babies in the nursery. However, those moments of bliss quickly came to an end as everyone noticed that there was something terribly odd with this newborn.

The nurse snatched the baby girl away as the four minute old infant seemingly flashed a glare of hatred toward her mother for bringing her into a world of such pain. The doctor ran numerous tests and placed the newborn in an incubator in the specialized neonatal unit where she laid completely helpless and closed off from the world for the next couple of months of her new life. The small baby could not be held, breathed on, or touched due to her low immune system. Rather than spending her new life in the home of her family, the baby lies struggling for life with tubes coming from what seemed like every hole in her little body. There were tubes coming from her mouth, nose and ears. A simple cough on this new born would have been tragic and possibly ending her short life. The doctors warned of the baby's condition and that the child was not expected to make it past a week as she had been severely damaged by the cocaine, marijuana and pain medication that her mother had been addicted to for the entirety of the pregnancy. Her mother, upset and yearning for another high thinks to herself, "I'm too sober for this. If only I could get high, maybe I could process the pain." Laying there with no pill to take, no pipe to smoke, no needle to inject and no substance to shoot, she is forced to consciously think about her life and the life of her critically ill newborn.

"Maybe if I don't get too attached, I can handle losing her. I've lost every child before her, what makes her so different. I am forty-one years old; I've been married for eleven years, and we're both drug addicts. I don't need a child anyways. My husband will be disappointed, but he has two children from two previous relationships before he met me. At least he's gotten the experience of being a father and he's a good father when he's not high or drunk. He hides his addiction well from his children and his mom. With me, he is a demon. Me on the other hand, I don't deserve to be a mother. I won't even give her a name," she thinks as she tries to cope through denial. She dries her tears as she hears her husband coming in the room yelling "How's my girls?" She sighs loudly while in shock that he was there because she hadn't seen him for the last month of her pregnancy. She thinks, "Who told this idiot I had given birth, I just wanted her to die in silence; in peace."

After receiving the test results, the doctors realize why this child is sick and begin immediately detoxing her from the drugs that were running through her small veins. Still not being able to hold her, her father began glancing at all the sickly infants through the window of the Neonatal Unit. Without ever seeing her before, he pointed her out to the nurse saying "That one over there is mine." Thinking that he is mistaken, the nurse explains to him that the child that he is pointing to is not his daughter. However, the attachment he had to his child was an unusual one; one that usually only mothers would have. He began telling the nurse, "I had morning sickness with that child, she only kicked when she heard my voice not even her mother's, and I took a leave of absence from work because for most of my wife's pregnancy, I couldn't keep anything on my stomach. Despite my not carrying her in my womb like her mom and being her father, I know my child when I see her and I am telling you she's my child." After many other exchanges of words and disagreements, it was confirmed that the child was in fact his child. He named her after her mother, the love of his life. Jay was her name.

It was evident that Baby Jay was a fighter. She had been growing inside of a being that didn't even love herself. The self-hate continued through the time of Jay's conception until Jay's adulthood. It was unfathomable how the baby survived the toxic environment that the illicit substances created. Though her little body often trembled uncontrollably and her cry was fainter than the whimpering voice of a baby goat, she fought. Day after day, doctors advised her parents to prepare themselves for the worst as her heartbeat would beat inconsistently rising and then falling over and over again. With each day of hearing her father's voice saying "How's my girl", her voice got stronger and her muscles got stronger. Her eyes would open up with wonder to see her father by her side day after day. After the Department of Children and Family Services ensured that she would be in a safe environment upon her discharge from the hospital, Baby Jay was released to the custody of her father two months later (who had only sobered up long enough to get custody of her). Other than a nurse having to come out and give a daily shot in her foot to help build her immune system for two additional months, Jay had become a completely healthy and normal baby girl.

What a way to start a life. Ninety-nine percent of children born under those conditions would not survive. Of the eleven years her parents had tried to conceive and failed (either losing the child through miscarriage or birthing a still born) Jay was the one percent who fought and lived.

Battle Two

Disappear into Destruction

Normally, a parent's responsibility while expecting would include ridding themselves of bad habits, immoral behavior, corruptible mindsets and definitely any addictions that would be damaging to the child. Well, Jay's parents had certainly missed that memo. After eleven years of trying to have a child and at the ripe ages of thirty-nine and forty-one, they were still not mentally or physically prepared to be parents together. Viewing from the outside into the situation brought constant judgment from peers, family, church members and even strangers. "Why were they trying to conceive if they knew they were addicted to drugs and alcohol" or "How had they anticipated raising that child in such hostile environments" were questions which arose often. However, to walk in the shoes of Jay's parents would be an indescribable load for anyone to bear. Anyone notwithstanding Jay's parents that is.

They were still battling several addictions including addiction to each other, addiction to alcohol, addiction to marijuana, addiction to methamphetamine, and addiction to crack cocaine. The addiction included any drug that they could get their hands on. They now faced a new battle; the battle of raising a child. Although they remained in those heavily addicted lifestyles, they loved their new baby girl. For now, the new born seemed to have the life of a completely normal and healthy infant. Upon entering the house as a visitor, one would see a car seat in the middle of the living room floor, a baby swing in the kitchen along with a very expensive high chair bought by the baby's maternal grandmother Brady. Emptied baby bottles were always in the sink and tiny socks about the size of an adult's big toe lie wherever Jay had been. Even as a newborn, she knew how to rub her feet together until her socks came off. She would squirm and became irritated when they were put back on her feet. She'd start rubbing them together for about fifteen minutes before the socks fell off again. Along the walls going down the hall, the visitor would see stuffed animals that had been tossed away from Jay's boredom and left in the floor. Her bedroom was a well-lit space with pink walls and unicorns. Despite Jay never sleeping in her crib a single night because of her father's attachment to her, she had the nicest room that any infant girl could imagine.

In plain visibility, the house seemed childproofed and resembled the house of any happy parents who had just brought their infant home from the hospital. However, taking a closer look at the hidden demons floating about and hiding within the crevices of the walls would scare away any visitor. There was always a stash of drugs at the bottom of Jay's baby bag because that is one place no one expected to find anything. Attached to the bottom of the crib was a 9 millimeter gun in a holster and two very sharp razor blades taped underneath the bottle of Gerber formula. Designated diapers had bags of cocaine tucked in them. If one could get pass the overbearing smell of lemon Lysol and bleach, they would notice the marijuana stench that lingered throughout the house.

Though with a closer view, many could see that they were still addicted to the streets, almost paradoxical the love and desire to be committed for their child was also very obvious. They had become equally addicted to this infant. Until now, nothing had ever become just as important as their lifestyle. Caring for their child shared their attention along with their need to get high. Family and friends cared about the well-being of the baby. So, they visited the house, played with the baby, and bought some of the child's necessities. While there were some concern at times, reporting the parents to authorities for the child to be removed from the home was never a consideration.

A typical day in this household began with Baby Jay waking up around five-thirty in the morning, full of energy and wanting her bottle. Jay's father, Curtis, would spring out of bed, prepare the bottle, and make his regular cup of coffee before jetting off to work; her mother would normally stay home, lounge around in her pajamas and care for their child. There were instances where she loved their girl time, just the two of them. She would comb Jay's hair (reluctantly because of Jay's tender-headedness), paint her tiny finger nails and watch the dog, Duffy lounge around the baby as if he were her protector. In some moments, she seemed to be adjusting well to her new life as a mommy. Then, there were also those moments when she would be just as eager for another hit as Baby Jay was for another bottle. It was in those moments that she eluded back to the lifestyle that she'd always find her concord. Yes, of course she loved her daughter but the love that she had for her infatuations were incomparable.

Somedays, being a stay-at-home mom was difficult. Jay was not always the most pleasant baby, especially if her father was gone. She behaved horribly when her father was not around. She would cry non-stop, not eat her food (because her father wasn't feeding it to her), and only took one nap during the day before waking up fussy. Unlike her dad who would hold her all day, her mother refused to hold her while she was asleep. She was stuck in this small, two bedroom house that was dark and lonely; similarly to how she felt about her life. Not knowing how to handle the postpartum depression and not being able to see her friends

12

anymore (because her husband forbade it) caused her to feel isolated. After all, she was stuck in the house all day with a crying child that didn't sleep. She succumbed to the only escape she knew. As Baby Jay would be going on a rant, screaming to the top of her lungs for no reason at all or falling off the edge of the bed or couch from her little rolling tantrums (it seemed that she always landed on Duffy who managed to always be there to catch her), Jane would be in the bathroom trying to cope. Little did she know her husband was away trying to cope as well.

He would leave for work and come home at the same time every day. However, every break he got was spent drinking his problems away, smoking away his bitterness and shooting up his small pieces of happiness. He forbade his wife from going out the house for two reasons: First, the places she wanted to go were no place to take a child. Secondly, he didn't want to run into her while he was selling or consuming narcotics. He would come home so happy because he was still very much buzzed from the several consumption breaks he had taken at work. Nonetheless, Baby Jay would be overjoyed seeing him come into the room shouting "How's my girls." She knew then that her favorite person had arrived. Jay's mother was relieved because she could finally get away from both of them and shut herself in whichever room they were not in. His fatherly duties of feeding her, changing her diaper, giving her a bath and playing with her until she fell asleep on his chest would be implemented full force. Then, the next morning the same routine would start up again.

Fatigued by this new schedule that she is forced to adhere to because of the baby, she loves Jay but misses her old life just as much. She had become so depressed and anxious to return to the lifestyle that she had fallen so madly in love with many years ago.

She thinks to herself "I know my husband is out doing whatever he wants to do when he is not in my presence, he says he's working and to some extent that is true because he's paying all the bills. He has assured me that he is finished with that lifestyle, selling drugs, alcohol and all the unnecessary drama. But, I know him. I fell in love with the streets because he was in the streets. When we met there was an instant connection. I had been so sheltered my entire life and here was a man selling dope, making money, getting high and living in the fast lane; I was intrigued. We dated, became best friends, and got married. He became my addiction, and I became his. It wasn't long before, everything he partook in, so did I. If I haven't given up this regiment neither had he" she thought to herself. It was not hard to rationale his behavior as it mirrored her own.

Jane, sending herself into a mental breakdown, she began reflecting on everything all at once. First, she started with the worries of what her family now thinks of her, having flashbacks to the reason why she had ended up in this predicament. In her head, she heard her mother's voice replaying an argument they'd once had telling her how much of a failure she has always been. She rebuts by "I'm the first to go to college." Her mother then screaming back in her direction "But you did not finish, so your going doesn't matter." She was quick to take up for herself stating that "You know why I didn't finish" as she then fast forwarded to the devastating time when the only father she knew died during her senior year in college. She was in college at the University of Memphis, only three credits away from earning her English degree when she received the dreadful phone call from her mother at 11:52 in the morning. "Jane, your father is dead. He got killed this morning while he was at work on the construction site," her mother, Brady, cried hysterically through the phone.

She replayed the feeling of nothingness because until she'd met her husband, her father was the only one that truly made her feel loved. She reminisced about receiving that dreaded phone call informing her of her father's death and then strategically planning out the steps of how to commit suicide. In her mind, she had no one else or reason to live for. After the funeral, she drove to north Memphis to an abandoned warehouse and parked behind the building farthest from the street. She sat there staring at the moon and questioned God until finally making her decision. Screaming at God "You don't win, I control my fate. It's over, I call quits, I can't do this anymore." She takes her notepad filled with poetry and turns to a blank page to write the following message:

"To whoever finds me,

DON'T LET MY MOM SEE ME LIKE THIS
but tell her the following...

I hope you know that I love you and that this decision to end my life is no reflection of you. I want to be with daddy or anywhere other than here. I can't live without him. My entire life has been nothing but rejection and failure and now that my number one supporter is gone, there's no point anymore. I'm in too much pain. I just don't want to suffer. My biggest fear has always been of suffering, being tormented. This is torment. This is torture.

I know that this will disappoint you but, it will be no worse than the disappointment that you already feel for me. To make it easier, I have written out my obituary. In the back seat, I have laid out the dress that I wish to be buried in. It's my favorite pink dress; I've always thought that I looked really pretty in it. Don't cry too much and continue to be strong for my little brother, Tray and sister Grace. They need you now. Kiss my sorority sisters for me too. They were like family to me. I know that you weren't too fond of them but they need you too. I've never been good enough, but I'm finally free.

Love,
Jane

She had a collection of pills that she had kept over the years as she had been an avid non-believer in pharmaceutical drugs since her early childhood. Therefore, anytime that she had gone to the doctor and received any type of medication, she would throw it in a large bag that was filled with prescriptions she refused to take. Instead she would find some natural remedy to cure her sickness. However on that day, she opened up that bag. One by one, she gulped down those pills that she had been disregarding for years until she was unconscious in the driver seat of her car.

To her dismay, she woke up in the hospital two days later thinking to herself, "Damn it, I fail at everything. I can't even commit suicide correctly." The doctors called her mother, Brady in. Her mother looks at her in tears, filled with disappointment and embarrassment because now everyone knows just how mentally ill her first born daughter is. Fast forward twenty-one years later, here she is still wishing that the suicide attempt had been successful. From that phone call from her mother until this very point in her life, she blamed all of her downfall on her father's untimely death and the love/hate relationship with her husband.

Jane thought about the many acts of kindness her father had done for her over the years, like purchasing her first car with full coverage insurance when her own mother would refuse to give her a ride to or from school. Who would have imagined that exactly two weeks later, he would be killed? It was almost as if he knew that his life was coming to an end and he wanted for his eldest daughter to know just how much she was loved. She thought of how horrifying it was that twenty-one years following her father's death she was still just as low as she was the day she had tried to commit suicide. But her moments of contentment would arise as she'd realize that her father taught her the meaning of

17

unconditional love and that was a lesson that would forever be ingrained in her heart. Through all of the negativity, the countless times she'd lived up to her mother's words of being a failure, her father was the only person to still be in her corner. Even though he was gone, she still felt his love in the presence of his spirit. Sometimes, she could still feel his love through her mother, Brady. Though Brady was extremely hard on Jane and often times tore her down with her words, small acts like calling her three to four times a day to see what she was doing, whether or not she had eaten was the perfect reminder that regardless of their disagreements, Brady still cared about and loved her oldest daughter.

Now, being a mother herself she wanted to be the person to teach her child what it is to love unconditionally, only if she had the ability to actually do it. She knew that was impossible. She loved Jay but the one condition to her love was her drug addiction. Even through her addiction and absences which were sure to arise because of that addiction, she wanted Jay to feel her love. "What if my addiction kills me, leaving Jay with no mother? What if Jay grows up and wants to be like me? What if she grows up to hate me?" She asks herself in that moment. Clouded by her feelings, she becomes overwhelmed by her past mistakes, present dismal situation and dead end future.

She is then snapped back into reality by a loud knock on the door. Thinking it was the police, she puts away the blunt she was smoking as she sat in rapture, grabbed baby Jay and placed her in her crib. She answers the door only to see a woman standing there. "Where is Curtis?" the lady at the door bellowed. Not acknowledging the lady's question, Jane asks "Who are you?" "Look, I know you're his wife and all, but when Curtis comes home, tell him that I have been trying to contact him about our son

18

he needs to be taking care of", the woman says as she points to the young boy sitting in the car who bore no resemblance of Curtis. Feeling completely disrespected and feeling the need to defend her husband, without another word Jane grabs a knife lying on the kitchen counter and slashes the woman's flesh right in her abdomen. Injuring the woman only enough to draw blood, she tells her to never return to her home, pushes her off the porch and slams the door in her face. On top of everything she already had on her mind, her husband's infidelity was now at the forefront.

Not knowing the best method of coping with the information she had just received or the thoughts she was already wallowing in, she began to long for a much more intense high than what her husband had stashed in his duffle bag. She knew that she could not be at home by the time her husband arrived because her temper would override her common sense. She would end up in jail or worst because Curtis fights back and this time she just may kill him, or he'd kill her. Also making sure that she fled before this anonymous woman called the police or returned for retaliation, Jane hurriedly throws a few outfits, a bundle of diapers, wet wipes and baby formula in the baby bag. She feeds Duffy and lets him outdoors to roam in the back yard. She takes off through the back door walking down the alley way with her baby in her arms, bag on her shoulder and drugs on her mind. After a few hours on the bus, she gets off in North Memphis.

Walking around the neighborhood, she hoped and prayed that she would run into the guys she met the last time she was on that side of town. They were so accepting and gave her a feeling she hadn't felt in a long time. They were her friends and her family. She missed being in an atmosphere that she could completely be herself. To her family, she was unsuitable, because they were all about upholding a perfect image, especially her mother. To the friends she had grown up with, she was vacillating because she could not decide which route she wanted to go with her life, as she was an extremely intelligent young lady who could serve as a walking dictionary but constantly chose fighting as her first line of defense in resolving any dispute. To her husband, she was quarrelling because they loved each other to the point of insanity and fought each other like enemies before making love like soulmates. But with these guys there were no undertones associated with their relationship. It was a feeling of not being judged, questioned or shamed because they were all in the same place together. Knowing how close she is getting to her favorite spot, she begins to get goosebumps just thinking about how high she would be in a half an hour.

"Is that who I think it is," she hears a man yelling from a distance. "Big Jay and baby Jay," he shouts out to Jane. She smiles with excitement to see one of her friends that she had met not too long before her baby was born. They stand on the corner conversing about all that has happened over the past couple of months. He tells her that he was about to go "have a good time" and invited her to come along. Acknowledging the fact that her husband would be very upset with her for bringing this baby, she decides to drop Jay off at another friend's houses that lived close by. "Come with me to Ms. Williams' house so I can drop Jay off with her if she's home," she said to him; he agreed.

Ms. Williams was home and sitting on the porch. She screams out elatedly to see them coming. She grabs baby Jay from her mother and begins kissing and loving on the baby as she says, "I remember when you found out when you were pregnant with this child, now look how big she's gotten. Please let me have her.

You know I could never have children, and I always wanted at least one. So, can we please just share her? Come on Jane, I took care of you before you were pregnant and even during your pregnancy. Any drug your heart desired, I gave it to you free of charge. That's our baby. What will it take for you to let me keep her, just for a day or two, or as long as you'd like she said jokingly." Jane, now fighting temptation knows that Ms. Williams has always taken care of her. When she'd come up short on cash, when she needed a place to sleep after getting into a fight with Curtis or simply to talk all day, Ms. Williams was there. So she bargained.

If Ms. Williams agreed to front her some "rocks", she could keep Jay for a few days and she'd return with eighty bucks for her generosity. Of course, Ms. Williams agreed to this arrangement. "Of course, I'll keep baby Jay and front you what you need to make it through a couple of days," Ms. Williams shouted. Knowing that she probably wouldn't be back for a while, she kissed her baby and ran off with her friend who was irritated for having to wait for her. Jay reached over Ms. Williams' shoulder for her mother and began to whimpered because she doesn't know this strange woman her mother was leaving her with. "Will you hurry up" Jane's friend said as she got her drugs from Ms. Williams. Jane jumps in his car and prayed silently that Ms. Williams would keep Jay safe. Finally free from her spouse, her thoughts and motherhood, she disappears not to return for a couple months.

Battle Three

One Hundred Percent Best Move

This place feels so familiar and though she is now a six month old infant, the smells, the people, the screaming and fighting is so comforting. Jay is content because she has been here before; this is the very step her mother was sitting on when she went into labor and spent a lot of her pregnancy while she was away from her husband. She can finally sit up by herself, positioning herself from the front porch to see people stepping over her, guys playing crap next to her, sitting there in the residue of roaches from marijuana and used condoms yet she is so at peace as long as no one tries to pick her up. Baby Jay fits right in and with eyes wide opened she is looking directly in the face of demolition. Once again, her mother's addiction had taken over, and the worst was yet to come.

Curtis came home at his usual time only to find an empty nest. Duffy, his wife and Jay were gone. This was rather abnormal being that his wife was not allowed out of the house but at that point, he could care less about where his dog or his wife were, only concerning himself with the whereabouts of his daughter. Automatically filled with anger, Curtis began his search for baby Jay. No one in the neighborhood saw where her mother had gone and only mentioned a fight that they had seen with her and a strange woman earlier that afternoon. After some time of not knowing where his daughter or wife had disappeared to, he was finally tipped off by one of his friends. His friend explained to him one morning in passing that he saw baby Jay at one of the houses he delivered to out in north Memphis a day prior but her mother was not with her. Without any hesitation he loaded his pistol, jumped in his car and headed to north Memphis. He chalked

Duffy's disappearance up to the next door neighbors who absolutely loved Duffy. Ironically, he noticed that on the day that he last saw Duffy, the next door neighbors were loading up their belongings onto a moving truck, headed to reside in another town.

Many moons had come and gone, and with each night of not seeing her mother or father, she became more and more comfortable in the arms of whoever was passing her around until night fall. Though she was never the friendliest of babies, normally, she'd be fine until someone picked her up, then she'd sound off. But Jay became extremely frightened and her behavior showed uneasiness as the sun began to disappear and dark air covered the window. Jay knows that when night falls its bath time and horrible things had begun happening at bath time. Going from one lap to the next as she cries to be put down and left alone, everyone who was once infatuated to hold an infant becomes disgusted by the smell of this day old diaper, until Ms. Williams finally puts the pipe down and prepares the baby's bath water.

The kitchen is dark and the only visible light is the dim light that's right over the stove. Ms. Williams grabs her largest pot, fills it with water and places it over the far left burning eye on the gas stove. She stumbles around a little because she is still inebriated but she sings tunes of happiness because soon baby Jay will be asleep. Then her parental duties would be over for the night. She floats off into her own sick world, illusion-filled thoughts of what could have been and what has come to be makes her smile. She is a proud woman; proud of her flaws and embraced by her past. She loves every bit of the life she has come to know. In her mind, she has become a mother and Jay is the daughter that she wants. Ms. Williams felt that Jane would eventually come for Jay and when she does she would just buy her off again. "How happy you make me little one" she says to Jay with slurred speech and drunken breath.

Waiting until the water is boiling and bubbles from the dishwashing detergent are flowing out of the pot. She gets the little white bucket and puts it in the sink before pouring the steaming water over into the bucket. Grabbing baby Jay and taking her out of her milk stained clothes and dirty diaper, she begins walking toward the sink. Jay was already crying because Ms. Williams had picked her up but when she notices where she's going and sees that bucket with the boiling water, she begins to scream as piercingly as her little lungs would allow as this has been the routine every night. She is frightened beyond measure, thinking of the people in her life that are nowhere to be found. Wanting nothing more than to see a familiar face that will save her from the pain she endures far too often to be an infant. She begins kicking as hard as she could and squirming around trying to escape Ms. Williams' grip before she is placed in the hot water and bathed with it.

With all her might she continues to kick and scream as Ms. Williams brushes over her fragile skin with a dishrag. Ms. Williams was clearly not in her right mind as she'd whisper as if she's doing nothing harmful "Oh hush little one, it's just water, it will be over soon," attempting to comfort Jay. When she is taken out of the water, dead pieces of the skin on her tiny thighs wipe away onto the towel that she is dried off with and small pink patches cover her inner legs. The water would have been too warm for a sane adult to withstand but was harmless to someone who was stoned out of their senses from substance abuse. She couldn't feel her hands or any other body part because she was higher than an air force jet all the time, she had suffered two strokes brought on by a drug overdose years prior so often times she couldn't even control her limbs. Despite the tears of utter pain welling up in Jay's eyes, her crying so hard that her breathing was disrupted and her face had turned as red as the scalded flesh between her thighs from the tears, Ms. Williams won't stop bathing her until she is sure Jay is clean. After five minutes of bath time and completely clueless to the harm she's caused this baby, she dries her off and tries to calm her; allowing her to cry until she no longer pays attention to the soreness between her thighs and falls asleep.

Though Jay was never the quickest to fall asleep (even in the care of her parents), since she had been living with Ms. Williams, it would take even longer for her to go to sleep. She was an infant but she didn't trust. She didn't have the vulnerability of an infant. Jay's problem with going to sleep had less to do with the loud music and constant hollering from the bi-daily house parties and more to do with her primary needs during her first stage of life not being efficiently met. She was fed, burped, changed and held whenever Ms. Williams remembered to do so and sometimes in her boredom, the sound of herself crying was the only source of entertainment baby Jay had. The only thing that came on a consistent basis was that Satan-fostered bath water. It took Jay longer to fall asleep because she was still gaseous from not being burped, she had rashes from not being changed often enough and her entire body, but specifically her legs were sore and no one could comfort her like her mother or talk her to sleep like her father.

She was too young to offer self-expression in any form other than the cries that went unnoticed, but she was old enough to know that though the place is familiar, this is not where she belongs. She knows that the people that love her are not here, as she is neglected every day and boiled like an egg every night, she knows that this is not home. The faces of her parents are engrained and though she'd rarely go to strangers, she knew that if she was ever in her mother's arms again she'd never relinquish the grip she'd have on her. Never again would her mother be able to just pass her on to anyone without Jay putting up one hell of a fight.

Day breaks and Ms. Williams makes Jay's bottle, feeds her and dresses her with another one of the few pieces of clothes her mother had left in the baby bag. Preparing for her customers to begin trickling in, she plays with the baby briefly and then sits her in her normal resting spot on the porch so that she can tend to her business. Sporadically and loudly Ms. Williams hears a man irate and pointing a gun at her head first screaming, "Where is my girl, give me my child" then pointing the gun upward and sounding off two warning shots in the air. Recognizing his voice from the porch Jay begins to cry as if she's saying "Here I am dad, please come get me, these people are crazy." He rushes pass Ms. Williams and grabs baby Jay still threatening to shoot up the entire house if anyone were to try to stop him. Ms. Williams frantically panicking begins to explain, "Her mother left her here awhile back and promised she'd be back to get her within hours and never returned. Hey, I paid for this child and her mother is supposed to be giving me a little something extra when she returns so you can't leave with her unless you pay off Jane's debt and reimburse me for the product I fronted your wife. That's my child I said, I paid for her." Not even acknowledging Ms. Williams' twisted logic, and Ms. Williams not bold enough to face the barrel of his gun, he places baby Jay in her car seat without even strapping her in and drives away. Relieved that he has found his daughter, he calls the police to inform them that Jay had been found alive and well and the amber alert he had placed could be discontinued.

In the moment his mind was clouded with frustration, but he still decided not to give her away to the police. He knew that if he attempted to have Ms. Williams locked up for the kidnapping of Jay, his wife would fall somewhere in the line of fire and despite her carelessness he couldn't be responsible for throwing the mother of his child in jail. During this time of the mass incarceration of the 90's and both he and his wife having a prior record, he opted to maneuver around the justice system as best as possible. Still, he couldn't fix this, he couldn't make this right. He needed clarity, he needed help. It was time to pay his mother, Lillian a visit.

With red eyes from tears and baby Jay peacefully asleep in his arms, he stood on the front porch of his mother, Lillian's house trying to gather his feelings before knocking on the door. However, Lillian was a discerning woman, and she knew just by the feeling that had come over her that her child was somewhere nearby and in trouble. She went to the front door to see her youngest son Curtis crying and holding baby Jay. Without saying a word, she takes the baby from his arms and invites him in for a hot meal. They ate in silence for some time until all of a sudden Curtis broke down crying even harder than before. "What am I supposed to do with her? I am a man with no experience in raising a baby girl by myself. My other two children were raised by their mothers, with frequent visits and financial support from me. But I can't raise her alone. I work two legitimate jobs and have a side hustle. The lifestyle I lead is just not conducive for raising a child alone," he explains to his mother.

He drives himself into mental torture thinking to himself, "Jane is a fool, and I'm the fool that fell in love with and married her. But is she the victim? Am I the monster that created the worthless woman and mother that she is right now? I did that to her. She was no angel when I met her, but she was definitely not the devil that she is today. I was a drug dealer, and I kept her away from that lifestyle to the best of my ability, until her depression kicked in, then she got into my stash and everything went downhill from there. She wanted the life I was trying to shield her from. She never wanted children; I wanted her to have my child because she is my wife. My other children came from past relations, but never had I loved anyone until I met her. She deserved to have my child. God tried to warn us, we didn't need a child. Lost baby after lost baby but I kept going; not wanting to see my reality. Motherhood is not for her and I forced it on her. Now, we have a child together that neither of us can raise.

She left our child in the hands of some low-down, prostituting, drug dealing, sex-trafficking, disease carrying monster. She sold my child to get high. I know that our marriage is on the rocks, and that she never asked to be a mother. I understand how difficult the transition is, but damn it, we were supposed to be doing this thing together. I was never supposed to give up on her but she has given up on herself and I refuse to allow her to give up on our daughter. I did my dirt, but never would I stoop low enough for those demons to challenge my fatherhood. She will never get my child again. I don't know how I am going to do this, being a drug addict and alcoholic myself, but never again will she be trusted. Through all the times we've gotten high together, all the times I beat her ass for getting high on the drugs that were my supply to sell and trying to dissuade her from drugs altogether, of all the times that she damn near killed me for my recklessness, this takes the cake. She will never be trusted again. She will always be my soulmate, but this time, our soul ties are forever severed" he thinks.

Again with Lillian's discerning spirit, she could almost hear his private thoughts as if they were her own, and she knew her son was in no condition to raise this child alone, yet realized that he had to be held accountable for his actions. Together they came up with a solution. She told her son that she'd change her shift to the night shift to stay at home with this baby in the day while he worked, and that arrangement worked out well for a while. Curtis would drop baby Jay off with his mother at six in the morning, work his full-time job, then rush over to his part-time job and pick her up around eight at night. Lillian's night shift began at nine and ended at five in the morning and she would hurry home to be there when the baby arrived. For years Curtis wore the disguise of getting his life together in public, but in private the demons of his past attacked him and guided his feet to the path of insanity. The woman he loved would disappear for months at a time and reappear for no more than a few hours. As angry as he was with her and despite him never being able to forgive her, if there was an opportunity to be in her presence, he took it. He was still heavily addicted to drugs and alcohol, he and Curtis Jr. his oldest son's relationship was completely tarnished and his middle daughter Lea was pregnant with his grandchild at age fifteen. Nonetheless, his mother was not deceived and knew of her son's anguish without him ever uttering a word to her.

About two years into their arrangement, Lillian could see her son Curtis' distress now more than ever before. However, she wanted to allow him the chance to bring his faults to her before bombarding him with her parental guidance over his life. Shortly thereafter Curtis' situation had plummeted. He never saw his wife anymore as they were legally separated and finally moving toward a divorce. He wasn't getting any rest after bringing his now two year old energized daughter home in the middle of the night and he had overdosed several times within the past couple of months while at work, resulting in him losing one of his jobs and being evicted from his home. Knowing that he could not keep up this behavior, he decided to have a frank conversation with his mother about his life and the life of Jay.

He could no longer mask the fact that he had a serious problem that was soon going to dismantle his life and subsequently the lives of his children, especially Jay being that she was depending on him the most at her young age. He had stayed up the previous night contemplating his decisions. He was very indecisive at first about what he wanted to do, but the one thing he was certain of was that he did not want his daughter Jay to be taken away from him. He knew that going into a rehabilitation center for three months would leave her in the system and to him that was not an option. Therefore, he turned to his only source, Lillian.

One summer morning without warning, he dropped baby Jay off with her grandmother as usual, only that morning his guise was completely disenchanted. Jay toddled in happy as always to be with her "ganma and Jo Jo" (because she couldn't pronounce grandma and Grandpa James). To James' surprise, Curtis came in shortly afterwards carrying all of Jay's clothes, toys and necessities. Curtis then requested to speak to his mother Lillian and step-father James about his current dilemma. Finally being completely candid with them, he explained how he overdosed several times within the past couple of months, gone through withdrawals from trying to stop on his own, relapsing and had received his final eviction notice. He explained how he hasn't seen or been with Jay's mother in six months; he had filed for divorce of which she was not opposed to and how he had no one else to turn to. He made sure to clarify why he hadn't given Jay to his wife's family. Though they loved her, just as much as Lillian did, he said "I know that if I gave her to them, out of spite, they would try to rid me of my paternal rights. I have custody of Jay and I don't want that to change because she is my child, I am just not in the position to care for her right now. Besides, they really dislike me and blame me above all else for my wife's outcome, and that is fine because I am to blame but their hatred of me will not damage my child or keep me from seeing her."

He goes on to apologize for all of his wrong-doings toward his mother and badgers himself for his mistakes. Now that he needed his mother more than he ever had, he knew that he had to mend their broken relationship. He felt as though the limit had been reached from his mother as he was a constant disappointment to her. However, up until this point he had never cared to think about how his behavior had affected the number one woman in his life. He had put Lillian through so much. As if it wasn't already difficult enough raising two boys on her own, Curtis was the true trouble child. Lillian had lived through heartache after heartache. Firstly, getting pregnant at seventeen with Leon whose father (also seventeen) fled back to his hometown of St. Louis when she told him she was with child. Then two years later, she entered into a marriage at nineteen with an older, alcoholic and abusive man, birthing Curtis through that union. After escaping that toxic marriage, she raised her family alone on a janitorial job at an elementary school for the rest of her career.

Curtis held the countless disappointments close to his heart and continued to dwell on them as he looked into his mother's face. Leon went on to get married, attend a trade school and got a more than decent job at FedEx as an architectural designer but Curtis never focused or cared about school. Playing basketball and sneaking off with girls was all he went to school for, only keeping his grade point average at a mediocre level to appease the coaches enough to be a starter on the team. He was in a fight every other week, being sent home from school for the remainder of the day or suspended for weeks at a time. He fought girls, boys, and teachers, anyone who made the slightest gesticulation of disrespect towards him. His anger prompted multiple arrests as a teenager and his sex appeal with the girls is what led to the birth of his first born Curtis Jr. when he was seventeen. He had no fear, he had no filter, he didn't care, until now. But to Lillian there was no offense taken. She was a mother; she forgave easily, spoke calmly but with sternness, never held grudges, and above all, loved and protected her children wholeheartedly. She prayed over her children, over their lives. She prayed not for riches and gold (though those things were nice), but for their survival in a world that was not made for them and that she herself could not provide.

Surely Lillian was exasperated with the late night phone calls to come bail her son out of jail for fighting when he wasn't even supposed to be out of the house, the prank phone calls from girls claiming to be pregnant with his child and having the only ones proven to be his was Curtis Jr., Leah and Jay. Yet, she protected him. She loved him like none other and in that moment as he quivers with fright that she has finally given up on him she proves that a mother's love is unreserved. "I need you mother", he whispers.

Knowing that their lives would now be forever altered, his step-father didn't utter a word, but his mother Lillian sat there with the look of approval and bliss as they amended their agreement of raising baby Jay. Lillian decided that she would quit her job where she was working for a janitorial service at a school and become a stay-at-home "ganma" while James (an Army veteran) continued to work as a part-time car mechanic. After all, she was well pass retirement age (though she wouldn't be able to retire unless she worked three more years for the company) and only went to work to get away from her grouchy husband. She wasn't sure that with her age, no real income (other than her husband's) and poor medical condition that she'd be able to offer much. However, she also knew her son's situation would not change overnight and she would never make this baby pay for her parents' mistakes. Moreover, she loved this child, Jay spent most of the day with her anyways and she was already attached. James loved children and having a little one around permanently would not be a difficult transition for him to make either. James got along great with babies. It was the older aged children that James had a problem with.

Nonetheless, Curtis told his mother that he was checking himself into rehab for drug addiction and alcoholism that day at noon and that he was entrusting her and James with his most prized possession until he returned. He told them "I have to get clean, because if I don't, Jay won't know she has a mother or a father. I have to do this for her because the route her mother's going, she'll be dead soon and I don't know whether Jay will ever know her mother, because Jane is not allowed to have her alone, ever. I want her to know that she has parents, so I have to get clean. She has to know that she is loved." Though it hurt Lillian to the core to see her youngest child battling such a terrible illness, she appreciated the gift of being able to raise this child and being given a third chance at being a mom. She called it her third chance because she had already had two grown sons, Leon and Curtis. However, several years before Jay was born, she and her husband James had unexpectedly and miraculously conceived in her late fifties. Yet she miscarried in her second trimester giving birth to a still born. It was Lillian's first daughter and James' only biological child. They named her "Autumn" and laid her to rest without ever really mentioning of her again. Up until the point of her granddaughter Jay's arrival, she had been secretly battling depression from the loss of a child. She wanted so badly to have a girl and for James to experience fatherhood since he loved children so much, but she thought after the loss of Autumn that it wasn't meant to be, especially at her age.

Now, Lillian sits there thankfully thinking of how ironic it was that two years following the loss of her daughter, Jay was born on the twentieth day of autumn where she and her husband James were raising this baby girl. She says to her son Curtis, "Give her to me, I want her. Regardless of what happens she will know who her mother is, who you are, where she has come from. She will know her truth." From that moment onward, Lillian and James saw Jay not as their grandchild, but the daughter they never had. Not being able to trust anyone other than his mother and wanting to provide the most stable life possible, he agreed that Jay would now reside with her. Even after his return from rehab he would not move her; she had been bounced around enough. She needed stability, she needed love from her own bloodline.

Jay moving with her grandparents turned out to be the best thing for everyone involved. She brought healing to Lillian and James by giving them the opportunity to raise their one and only girl. James contributed nothing but blank stares to the conversation about him and Lillian permanently keeping Jay. Nonetheless, he was just as elated as Lillian was. Jay's presence in James' life brought about a man that Lillian had never before witnessed entirely. He loved Lillian's grandchildren so much so that most of them didn't find out until adulthood that he was not their biological grandfather (though if anyone were to look at Leon and Curtis' relationship with James, it would be evident that he is not either of their fathers). But children don't pay attention to those things. Lillian babysat at least two of her grandchildren most weekends and James would take them outside to play sports with them, give them money to go the candy lady's house, take them to stores and let them pick out toys. However, they had all gotten older now.

He was an amazing grandfather, because he only had to be that on weekends and he had been far removed from that age group of children, but now that little Jay would be around every day, all day, a lot changed for the better. The first major lifestyle change that was made was that James stopped smoking. At first, he only smoked in his back room which all the grandchildren knew not to go in his man-cave, except for Jay. Jay didn't care. If she saw him go back there she would follow him and sit there looking at what he was doing. Though smoking cigarettes was an addiction that started overseas in the Vietnam War many years ago, Jay had severe asthma and being that she followed him anywhere around the house, he had to give that addiction up. Within days of her being there, his man-cave had turned into her toy room, because she'd just leave her toys in there until she returned to play with them again. Despite all the toys that she already had, he'd still be bringing a new toy home from work every other day. Jay's presence softened him around the edges. It tuned him into his more sensitive side and regardless of how grouchy and short-tempered he was with Lillian, he adored baby Jay and she loved her "Jo Jo" just as much.

Jay's move allowed her father to get the treatment he had been so desperately seeking while freeing her mother of the responsibility that would have eventually killed her or possibly Jay or both of them. Not then being aware of the significant impact the move would have on her, Jay's moving with her grandparents ultimately saved her young life.

Battle Four

Lifetime Phobias

This cell is cold and lonely Curtis screams to the top of his voice hoping that someone will hear his bantering cry. "Help me" he shouts out to the night guards patrolling the hallways. Imprisoned by the thoughts that weight him down, he lies on the floor with his head leaning against the silicon covered walls. "I miss drinking beers with my friends on the front porch hollering at all the chicks that walked by. I miss lying out on the hood of my car selling my rocks and making fast money; my wife and all three of my children being very well taken care of, not wanting for anything. I miss the feeling of being so elevated; I thought I was walking the streets of heaven. Most of all, I miss the moments I had with my wife, with and without the drugs. We used to be so happy and regardless of what her family or anyone else thinks she will always be my first love". He thinks to himself.

Night shimmers, cold sweats, paranoia, disappointment and annoyance disable Curtis. The feelings of withdrawal have completely incapacitated him and have left him wondering whether or not his life is worth the living. He hears the voice of his mother singing songs of comfort in his ear and visualizes his daughter's face. Undoubtedly, he is in a much better place. Though he knows he is not in the best situation, he is grateful to not be in the place he once was. The drugs, alcohol, the lifestyle had become a part of his identity. Without those things in his life he was lost. However, knowing that he was on the way to recovery and reconstructing a new identity; he pushed through.

Aside from drugs and alcoholism, women were also his addiction. He had his first son, Curtis Jr. his senior year of high

37

school at age seventeen and with a woman he was infatuated with. She was lusted after by all the young boys, drooled over even by grown men that knew better. She was trouble and so was he. Little did he know that his infatuation with her was the beginning of his collapse and she sat the tone for every other failed relationship he would have in the future. Shortly after giving birth to Junior, she too decided that motherhood was not for her. She began gathering her possessions and making plans of heading to New York with her best friend to become an "escort." Upon finding out what his high school sweetheart was involving herself in, his infuriation with all women began to surface as he nearly beat her to death when finding out she was leaving and what she was leaving to do on her eighteenth birthday, leaving Curtis Jr. with his maternal grandmother to raise primarily. Throughout each future relationship, his infidelity and abuse proved to be an emptiness unfulfilled. Not only had the mother of his child abandoned the both of them to become a professional whore, but he had turned down a basketball scholarship to college to stay in Memphis and attempt to help raise a son that grew up resenting him. Other than his step-father James who he had no relationship with, he had no idea what fatherhood looked like as he didn't have the closest relationship with his biological father either. Anger was the culprit and drugs were the escape.

As the days turned into weeks and weeks into months, he was getting closer to his release date and he now learned through the recovery process that he had a defined purpose. Originally, he went through the twelve step program of recovery for his child, thinking that it would create a better life for her. He wanted his path in life to teach Jay which route not to take since he had seemingly failed at raising his other two children and Jay was the only child he purposefully brought into the world. While aiming all of his attention on the betterment of his daughter, he began to see improvement within himself. Going through life to please no one and to make decisions that would benefit him became his goal and in doing so would likewise benefit all three of his children. Through the first step of recovery in admitting that he had a problem, he had to be clear about how the problem arose in the first place. He came to realize that his addiction was not who he was, rather a mere association of his past self. His entire life, he had been hiding behind anger and guilt; anger that had gone unmanaged and guilt from the many problems he'd caused because of his anger.

The group of people he befriended became his niche and in order to be adequate within that group, he did as they did. Not ever again wanting to submit his power to an emotion or to another being, he became very strict on the company he kept and made a list of the people he must cut off in order for him to remain clean. His greatest fear was relapsing back into the life of a drug addict and alcoholic. Harshly, the first name on his list was his wife Jane.

Back at Lillian's house a series of phobias were unraveling with baby Jay as well. She was carefree but reserved all in the same breath. She was afraid but fearless, shy but unfastened. Even at such a delicate age, it was clear to her grandparents that Jay had been taunted by something or someone. Lillian began to suspect something odd when she would place Jay in the bathtub or notice how uneasy she became anytime she saw or heard running water. Every time Lillian tried to place Jay in the tub, Jay would curl her legs around Lillian and clinch her tightly, making sure not to touch the water. This had been going on ever since Jay was an infant but her reaction was seemingly getting worst. The only way Jay would be comfortable with getting in the water was if she saw Lillian get in first and placed Jay in her lap. That procedure happened every night at bath time. Lillian would run the bath water, put little floatable toys and bubble-bath soap in the water, to make it more appealing to Jay. Still, Jay would stand in the corner naked until Lillian got in first before climbing in and sitting in her grandmother's lap. Even with her grandmother's presence, she hated the water and would not play in it. After being soaped down and rinsed off, she was ready to get out. There was no splattering in the water or playing with the bubbles and if her grandmother took too long, she would begin to cry softly, to speed up the process.

During a doctor's visit, Lillian mentioned to the pediatrician Jay's ongoing fear of water which the doctor thought that type of behavior from a child to be odd. "Children generally loved to play in water and were the most adaptable to the water" he told Lillian. "Well not Jay, she wants no parts of the water, she won't even play in it when I am in the water with her. She just sits there frowning and waiting for the bath to be over." The doctor asked Lillian if there was any other abnormal behavior the toddler was exhibiting. "Yes" Lillian said. "She will not sit or play in any enclosed places like her play pin or crib." Either I or her maternal grandmother Brady will have to get in the play pin with her in order for her to be at ease. Her father sold the crib he had at his house shortly after she turned eight months because she would not sleep in it, which is partially his fault because he held her all night long, every night when she was asleep. He would say that he didn't want her to feel afraid of being in the crib by herself. Now, the only way she falls asleep is if she is next to me in bed or in my lap and the entire night she clinches onto my gown, if I move too suddenly she wakes up frightened and won't go back to sleep for hours. She is very selective to who she'll go to even if she knows them particularly well. She'll follow my husband around, bring all of her toys to him to play with her, she'll go outside and sometimes he'll even take her with him wherever he's going. But she won't stay away from me for more than two hours, before she asks to come home with her baby gibberish saying "I go home now, I go home now" and getting louder each time she says it. I've just chalked it up to her being severely spoiled." However, the doctor advised that there was much more to that situation; inferring that there was some psychological issues occurring with this in regards to attachment and warning that if she doesn't get checked out, it could lead to further issues as she matures. Of course getting psychological help for Jay was out of the question as she decided as a Christian woman to just pray over her grandchild and trusted that God would handle it.

With a few more doctors' visits the pediatrician informed Lillian of some very disturbing news about Jay that would partially explain her abnormal behavior. "After close examination of these scars on the back of Jay's inner thy (that the family had written off as birth marks), we have concluded that she had been severely burned as an infant." Confused, Lillian asks how that was possible and of course not being aware of what had happened to this baby while left in the care of her mother, the doctor could not answer but knowing the child's medical and custodial history from birth and by the look of the scars he predicted that "it probably happened between the ages of zero to eight or nine months old. She can't verbalize her feelings due to her age and most likely does not remember the exact incident, but running water triggers an uneasy response because that was probably the method used when she was burned. It is likely that after hearing or seeing running water, she was burned, which created a fear of water. The placement of the burn marks on her thy suggests that she had been

41

sat in water that was too warm for her sensitive skin and in turn generated these lifelong scars on her inner/back thy. This now explains her fear of water as well as her attachment to you and why she does not go to certain people whether she knew them well or not. She has learned not to trust even those she may know." Following the doctor's visit, she and Jay went over to Brady's (Jay's maternal grandmother) house to explain to her why Jay acted the way that she did and only interacted well with the two of them. She wouldn't even stay with her grandmother Brady for more than a few hours before she would have to be taken back home to Lillian however she stayed with her longer than she would anyone else.

Lillian and Brady were heart-broken and did their best to care for and comfort Jay. Over-doing everything; Lillian held her constantly, rocked and sang her to sleep every night, and Brady gave her anything her young heart desired and that her pockets could afford. However, they quickly observed that all the love, affection and money in the world could not undo the damage her mother had already done. One blazing August afternoon, Lillian had fed Jay and gently laid her down for her midday nap; being careful not to startle her. This was routinely the time that she would get all of the household chores done such as washing clothes, vacuuming the carpets and beginning her preparation for dinner. However, what happened that afternoon would forever be decorated in Lillian's memory and midday naps were no longer required.

Lillian had washed clothes and gone outside in the backyard to hang them on the line to dry, making sure to leave the back door opened in the event that Jay awoke from her nap, she could easily find her. Whenever Jay woke up and Lillian was not

42

next to her, she would spring out of bed and go running around looking for her "Ganma" and if she didn't find or hear her within seconds, she would begin to whimper. For whatever reason, Jay woke up extremely troubled that day. She jumped off the bed and headed for the front door rather than the back door that Lillian had left opened for her to come to. With much effort and will power, two year old Jay had unlocked and opened the wooden and the screen door, jumped off the front porch and took off down the street in nothing but her t-shirt and a diaper. As she ran, she began to cry out loudly for Lillian. "Ganma, ganma, where are you ganma," Lillian heard from the backyard.

Clothes dropping from her hands and with her arthritic knees, she headed for the front yard running as fast as her bones would allow. She is now petrified running behind Jay screaming, "Here I am Jay, here I am, just turn around". Jay so frantic, not even hearing her grandmother's voice behind her, continues running down the street and towards the woods. Lillian is just praying that she can catch her before she gets to the dead-end road where there is nothing but trees and a swamp, in which neither she nor baby Jay could swim. "Hopefully, she'll stop since she's afraid of water" Lillian thought. Luckily, a boy that lived down the street happened to be walking in the direction coming toward baby Jay. Lillian then pleading out to the boy "Catch her, stop her, please stop her." The teenager then grabbed Jay and to his surprise she was relatively strong for a toddler as she bit, kicked and hit him with her tiny fist. Finally getting her under control he turns her in the direction of her grandmother and asks "See little one, is that who you're looking for?" Still very upset, she continues to cry loudly and trembling from fury as her grandmother clutches her from the boy's arms. Jay plunges her head into her grandmother's bosom crying "Ganma you leave me, you leave me." Her words resonated deeply with Lillian's spirit as they both stood there crying she assures her "Jay, I will never leave you."

After walking back up the block and into the house, Jay wouldn't let Lillian out of her sight, still traumatized by the thought that her grandmother had left her. Hours later, James returns home from the car shop and Lillian begins enlightening him on the adventurous day she and Jay had. In the middle of telling him what happened she began to cry. James completely confused asked her why she was crying. She said while holding sleeping Jay in her arms "This child has been hurt before, badly. She is so young yet she already knows the pain of being left and or hurt by the people that are supposed to love her. When I was finally able to catch her, she looked at me with so much hurt in her eyes and she has been sitting in my lap for the entirety of this afternoon until she fell asleep, because she's afraid that I too will leave her." Unknowingly, it was a fear that would remain with Jay forever.

Battle Five

Abnormal Normality

A couple of months had gone by and it was leading up to Jay's third birthday. Brady had major plans for Jay and some other small children to surprise her with a big birthday party at "X-Cite." It was a little place similar to "Chuck E Cheese" for small children. There were play pins filled with different colored balls, race cars and lots of toys, pizza and candy. However to reserve a party room was very expensive and took about two months in advance to book. Brady had it covered. She was determined to make it Jay's best birthday yet.

Brady called Lillian one Saturday morning and told her of the ideas she had for Jay's birthday party and to get her dressed because she would be spending the weekend with her. Lillian thought the idea was absurd; to spend that amount of money on a birthday party for a child that wouldn't even remember it. "Neither of my children had birthday parties until they were five so that they could at least half way remember the hell I went through for their day. But it's your money she said jokingly" as she and Brady laughed over the phone. She got baby Jay dressed and packed an overnight bag for her (though she knew that she would be coming to get Jay when night fell). Jay was excited to see her "Bebe" she called her because calling Brady "grandma" was not allowed, as she'd always say humorously, "I look too good to be a grandma."

Jay knew when she was expecting company and she would stand in the front door looking out and talking to her "Ganma." Brady had arrived and Jay was screaming to Lillian "Bebe here." Brady came in very upset that Jay was not yet dressed but it wasn't Lillian's fault nor should it have been a surprise. Baby Jay was a

45

nudist. As Lillian would be dressing her she would be undressing herself; while Lillian is putting her pants on, she would be taking her shirt back off. Brady finally got her dressed again and loads her into her van telling Lillian "We'll see you tomorrow," Lillian shouting back "Oh you'll see me tonight, she's not going to stay with you" knowing that Jay was not going to spend a night away from her. Brady turned up her "rhythm and blues" station while Jay sat in her car seat singing along with every song and mispronouncing all the words. Brady would always play this station because hearing Jay sing along to Jay Blackfoot and Luther Vandross songs would be the highlight of their time spent together.

They'd arrived at Brady's mother's house to pick her up and come along for a day of fun. The plan for the three of them was to go shopping at the "Mall of Memphis", check out the venue for Jay's third birthday party, grab some dinner and head to Brady's bowling tournament that night because Brady was in a professional bowling league. However, the adventures ended with the first event because of Jay's behavior. Though Jay was young, her personality was already intact. She was not very social or friendly unless she was around that person often, she enjoyed being alone (with the exception of her grandmothers) and seemed to be very independent. However, Brady was not very well aware of Jay's independence at the time, but she was surely about to be enlightened.

As they were shopping, Brady's mother looked around and realized that Jay was no longer behind the wheelchair. At first she was sitting in her great-grandmother's lap because she wanted to "ride in the car" as Jay put it, then she got down and asked her great-grandmother if she could push the car (meaning the wheelchair). Of course with the help of Brady, she pushed her great-grandmother's wheelchair for about ten minutes before running off. Brady's mother sitting in her wheelchair and waiting for Brady to come out of the dressing room notices that Jay is nowhere in sight. She yells out to Brady to come out of the dressing room. When Brady comes out, she asks "Where is Jay?" Her mother cussing at her angrily saying "I don't know dummy, that's why I called you out of the dressing room. My legs have been amputated so chasing her down or looking for her isn't an option for me, now go find her" she screamed at Brady.

Brady then pushed her mother to the nearest corner so that she wouldn't be in anyone's way, and ran off looking for Jay. After a two hour search for Jay in the largest mall in Memphis, the mall was placed on lockdown, no one was allowed in or out and she still hadn't found Jay. All of a sudden, a lady in a boutique came out to greet the elderly woman who seemed to be looking for someone she had lost. She asked Brady "Ma'am, are you looking for a baby?" Brady answers with much anticipation "Yes, a little girl have you seen her?" Before the lady could tell her that Jay had been in the store alone for a few minutes but she wouldn't let anyone pick her up nor did she talk to anyone, Brady looked down and knew exactly where she was. There was a trail of baby clothing leading to Jay's location that fit the description of what Jay was wearing. First, Brady saw Jay's right shoe, then both socks, followed by her t-shirt, pants and finally a diaper. The left shoe was nowhere to be found. Jay had completely undressed and was sitting in the middle of a circular clothing rack; naked. "Bebe," she shouted as she jumped up into Brady's arms. Without saying a word to Jay, she put her clothes back on, got her mother and left the mall.

After calming herself enough to actually talk, Brady asked Jay "Why did you leave in the mall?" Jay simply responded "Looking for Ganma." Brady explained that she cannot walk away from people without telling them where she was going and from that point on she could only come out shopping if she had a stroller. Now changing the subject as she saw that Jay was about to cry, she asked Jay "Do you want to go to the bowling alley to see me play, if you do, you have to promise me you will not walk away from me?" Jay responded with excitement and broken English "Yes, I pomise." Knowing that she was going to need someone to help watch Jay while she played in the tournament, she went and picked up her two older granddaughters, Nicole and Paige who were fourteen and nine at the time. She thought they would have the energy to watch Jay and chase her down if she decided she wanted to bail again.

That evening around six they loaded the van up with Brady's bowling gear, a few of Jay's toys and some snacks and headed out to the tournament. The tournament had begun and surprisingly Jay was being well-behaved for a while, sitting there with her two older cousins. She wasn't however very fond of all the people who were trying to pick at her face and asking to hold her or to give them a hug. She wasn't even talking to her cousins; she was just sitting there trying to be left alone. Finally becoming annoyed by all the attention, she jumped out of her chair and started walking toward the door. Nicole and Paige took off after her. After she had reached the door she saw that night had fallen and began to cry. Nicole and Paige asked her why she was crying as she repeatedly whined out "I want my Ganma." Nicole carried Jay back to Brady. Brady asked "But aren't you having a good time with me and your cousins, I thought you were going to be a big girl and spend the night with me tonight." Jay becoming even

48

more upset yelled out "No, I want my Ganma." Around eight-thirty that night, Lillian received a call saying Jay wanted to come home. Lillian having known that Jay was not going to stay was already dressed and waiting for the moment Brady was going to call. "I know, I'm on my way. I told you so," Lillian said with a smirk on her face.

After a forty-five minute drive out to Frasier where the bowling tournament was being held, Lillian was greeted by a very pleased toddler running towards her. Finally, her grandmother had arrived and she was content. Lillian then asked Jay if she was ready to go home and to her surprise Jay responded "No, watch Bebe." Keeping a smile on Jay's face and taking a moment to enjoy being out of the house, Lillian stayed for the remainder of the tournament cheering Brady on and holding Jay in her lap the entire time.

Grasping the concept that it took a village to raise a child was becoming more comprehendible to everyone in Jay's life. Curtis had finalized his divorce with Jane and she didn't even fight for custody or visitation, so he was awarded full custody of Jay which he then decided to share with Lillian. Jay spent the majority of her time with her two grandmothers Lillian and Brady and saw her father three or four times out of the week following his return from the rehabilitation facility. She enjoyed trailing along with her grandpa James when he would be outside working on cars or doing yard work (despite her grass allergy). Jay was comfortable with any of the above-mentioned and would sometimes interact with strangers if someone she knew was nearby and stayed within her peripheral. But regardless of where she was or who she was with, when night fell she had to be taken home to her grandma Lillian. Other than her mother, she knew that she was very much loved by her family and they provided for her as much of a normal life as they could. Still, there was a void in Jay's life that could not be filled.

Battle Six

Never Alone

She waits patiently at the door, excited and dressed to
perfection. Jay had spoken with her mother earlier that day and
she'd promised that she was coming to get her and take her out for
dinner as a late birthday present around five that same afternoon.
After getting off the phone with her mom, she picked out her
favorite outfit and asked Lillian to help her get dressed. "I want to
be pretty for mommy," she exclaimed to Lillian. She had just
turned three and hadn't seen her mother in about seven months,
however very aware of whom her mother was, she was anxious to
finally be reunited. She pranced around and refused to eat because
her mommy was taking her out. After getting dressed and standing
in the kitchen watching Lillian prepare dinner, she stood in the
front door looking through the glass for about three hours until
nightfall. Though she wouldn't have gone with her mother
anyways because it was now night and she had a fear of being
away from her grandmother at night, she was still very
disappointed. James closed the door and asked her to come and sit
with him. Wanting no consolation from her grandfather, she stood
there in the middle of the floor crying.

Lillian rushed over, picked her up and placed her in her lap.
After some time passed, Lillian sat there with her and began to cry
as well. James, not wanting to deal with the array of "female
emotions" he called it, went into his man cave to watch baseball.
Whenever Jay would cry, so would Lillian which is the reason why
Jay got very few spankings from Lillian. Regardless of why Jay
was crying; whether it be a well-deserved whipping or because she
had been let down by her mother, Lillian would cry too. She could
not stand the sight of Jay in tears ever, as she would say "She's

cried enough and I'm not going to be the one to ever make her cry."

She sat there holding baby Jay and with tears in both of their eyes, Lillian began to pray. Lillian understood her granddaughter's pain as she too grew up without her mother. Her mother had died giving birth to her younger sister Mickey when she was only two years old. She had no memory of her mother; the way she looked, the way she smelled; nothing. She grew up wishing for her mother's presence and crying often because she wanted a mother. Feelings of resentment and hatred rang over her towards her younger sister Mickey for her short lifespan as Mickey died of pneumonia at the age of three when Lillian was just five. So, she knew the torment of wanting a mother, of waiting for a mother, calling for her, knowing that she'll never come.

After she completed her prayer, she stood Jay up and said to her "I am going to teach you a song that I want you to sing whenever you get sad. Whenever you begin to feel low or alone, I want you to sing this song. And I want you to always remember that as you sing this song, where ever I am, I will be singing this song too, even if we're not together. You are never alone." Jay agreed. They sat there singing ♪*If it had not been for the Lord, on my side, tell me where would I be, where would I be*♪. Not knowing then the impact that song would have on herself or Jay, she had implanted a seed that would forever be inside her granddaughter. Lillian saw Jay's reaction to learning new songs and at an early age, Jay loved to sing and she sounded surprisingly good. She began to sing with Jay every day, all day. Lillian taught her a number of songs throughout her lifetime, but nothing would ever compare to that very first song, that would always remain in her spirit.

A few weeks later, Lillian went to choir rehearsal like she did every Saturday morning, only that day she had to bring Jay because Brady was out of town at a bowling tournament. As everyone was sitting in the sanctuary waiting on all of the members to arrive, Jay began to sing loudly and carelessly over everyone's conversation *"If it had not been, for the Lord on my side, tell me where would I be, where would I be."* Astonished by how well the child sounded and how clearly she was articulating her words, the choir director turned on the microphone and handed it over to Jay. Knowing exactly how it operated (as she had watched her grandmother sing in church every Sunday), she stood up directly in front of her grandmother, placed the mic up to her mouth and continued to sing. As tears rolled down Lillian's face, she became overwhelmed by how much this baby had gone through and how true the words to that song was in regards to Jay's life. They had only sung that song a few times through on that one day, and there it was weeks later and baby Jay was singing it as if she had learned it that day.

The very next day, Sunday morning, Lillian called everyone and invited them to church because Jay would be singing publically for the first time. Aside from being the youngest and smallest person in the choir stand, Jay fit in perfectly right next to her grandmother on the soprano row. She couldn't see over the banister because she was too short but she could definitely be heard. When it came time for Jay's solo, her grandmother stood her up in the front of the church and whispered to her "Do you remember what I said about this song?" "Yes, I am never alone" Jay said. The choir director gave her the microphone and Jay began to sing. Everyone that knew the background of that song had begun to cry; James, Brady, Curtis and especially Lillian. Curtis was so shocked and overcome with emotion that he stood up and walked

53

to the middle of the church in tears, and remained standing there until she was finished. At the end of her performance she received a standing ovation and even strangers were in tears by the voice of this three year old child. Curtis ran to the front of the church and picked her up into his arms and thanked his mother Lillian for the woman that she had been to his daughter.

Jay was naïve to the reasons why everyone was so emotional but she learned that she enjoyed singing and above all else, she had a gift. That day, she had touched so many people's lives without realizing the act that she had done. Her father had never heard her sing before, and to hear his child sing those words with such conviction and as if she really knew the meaning behind the words served as reassurance for him that everything would be okay. However, even in her young age, she knew what the song meant and would always mean to her. She knew the feeling of disappointment and betrayal and had cried many tears because of those feelings. She also knew that if she sang that song, she would never be alone and that her voice would reach her grandmother's ears regardless of how far apart they were. Jay could feel her grandmother's exuberance when she sang and Lillian would always be the only audience she needed.

She now attended choir practice every Saturday with Lillian and the congregation was truly enlightened every time young Jay would sing. Soon after becoming so engrossed in the choir, James began to take her to Sunday school with him. Unsure of how she would react by being with other children, since she was only around elders all the time, he sat in with her for the first couple of Sundays. However, Jay was adapting well to the social environment without being very social with the other children. She got along well with everyone but stuck closely by her Sunday school teacher. Comprehending the material more relatively than most of the other students, she became the permanent "teacher's helper" of the primary Sunday school class. She was learning to read and could hardly write, but she listened diligently and spoke very well. She could repeat anything that she was told and could also present the meanings associated with what she had learned.

It was evident that she was not only being educated about spirituality at church, in her Sunday school class but at home as well. Lillian was an extremely spiritual woman who believed that anything a child needed to learn was necessary to be started at home which is how she guided Jay towards having a strong spirituality as well. She would often tell Jay, "You have to know God for yourself, you have to gain knowledge for yourself, don't depend on the other fella to tell you." Jay wouldn't completely understand that until reaching adulthood, but as a child she imitated the actions of her grandmother. She saw her grandmother pray every night, so she prayed every night. Her grandmother went to church every Sunday, so she went to church every Sunday. Her grandmother had the voice of an angel as she sang in church and that was the voice that she copied.

Jay was a concoction of all of the people in her life from her youth up to adulthood. Her presence had gladdened so many people and with each person that invested their time in her, they were becoming a part of her. She would continue to carry an unfulfilled space in her heart but even with that voided space, she knew that she would never be alone.

Battle Seven

Lineage Born Fighters

Too many unfamiliar faces smiling at her she thinks "Welcome to the class, how are you today" the teachers says enthusiastically to her. Wanting absolutely nothing to do with her or the other children in the classroom, she clinches her father's leg and begins to cry angrily "Don't leave me, I want my grandma" (as she can now pronounce "grandma"). Lillian and Brady had purposefully told Curtis to take her for her first day of kindergarten because if either of them were there and tried to leave her, she would throw a tantrum that they wouldn't be able to handle. Ms. Pam assures her that she would be fine and that she would have plenty of fun in the kindergarten class with her and the other students despite her being younger than everyone in the class. Jay had just turned four rather than five but upon Brady's demand, that she is too smart to be in pre-school, she was given a standardized test by the Dioses of Memphis for private school entrance. Not only did the board decide to promote her to kindergarten early but they granted her a scholarship that helped with the private school tuition.

Brady was adamant that Jay would be attending a private school until she graduated from high school. In fact, all of Brady's grandchildren were in a private school by the age of four, though somewhere along the line between kindergarten and high school graduation they had strayed far from their upbringing. Education was always a privilege that was not priced in Brady's mind. She believed in education and appearance above all else as she'd say often to each of her grandchildren "You should think, act and look like you have a family that cares about you. You are not a thrown away and forgotten about child, so you will never look like you're

56

thrown away." For that reason, Jay was the best dressed toddler in her elementary school and her reading and writing was as astonishing as her daily wardrobe. Regardless of how advanced those tests showed her to be or how well-dressed she was every day; Jay was not amused to be in school and away from her grandmothers for most of the day. Jay really didn't understand why she had to go to school anyways. In her mind, Lillian and Brady were her teachers and she didn't understand why she had to go to a place with people she didn't know or care to get to know just to continue learning.

Finally after days of the same behavior, she is convinced through candy that she is in sufficient care and that her father can leave her there. Ms. Pam (her kindergarten teacher) soon became one of Jay's favorite people. Just as she was in her primary Sunday school class, she clung to Ms. Pam; sitting with her and the other teachers at the teacher's table rather than with the other children. She did not take naps during nap time because she didn't like sleeping around people that were unfamiliar and still was not having much interaction with the other eleven children. She thought nothing of abnormality in regards to socializing chiefly with adults because that's what her life consisted of at home.

She was being raised as an only child and loved being with the grown-ups she knew. The only interaction she had with other children came when Lillian's oldest granddaughter Lenzie (Leon's only daughter) got pregnant with Kenya during her junior year of high school. Lillian kept Kenya so that Lenzie could still enjoy her weekends as a teenager. Though Kenya was three years younger than Jay, she served as Jay's first consistent interaction with another child despite them only being around each other on the weekends. Jay had nieces and nephews by her older brother Curtis

Jr. and her sister Lea. Curtis' youngest child at the time was seven and Lea's first born was a year younger than Jay but until early adulthood she never really had a relationship with any of them.

Prior to starting kindergarten, Jay was used to helping her grandmother Lillian snap peas and clean collard greens from the field. She'd bring her Barbie foldable chair to the kitchen and watch Lillian as she cooked; learning about spices, temperatures and measurements. Then, her grandmother would make her pick two books, newspaper articles or Bible scriptures to read aloud. Lillian didn't care about the subject as long as Jay was reading for comprehension. After Brady would get off work, she'd come by and pick Jay up, take her to the park or another fun outdoor activity just to get her out of the house. She'd typically take Jay shopping, to the library, to get ice cream or junk food and then they'd go back to Lillian's for dinner. Again, she'd have to read aloud for Brady before she was allowed to open her junk food and eat it. And the rest of their time they'd be watching "CNN", "CNBC", "Lifetime" or "BET" until whichever sports game that was in season came on and James changed the channel. Then Brady would leave to go home for the night though she'd still call and talk to Jay on the phone every couple of hours.

However, being in school was a bit different. In school children there were hyper and noisy (which is normal for young children) but Jay had been trained that too much noise or movement gets her in trouble when dealing with older adults, especially with Brady. The only noise Brady tolerated was the jarring sounds of the bowling pins falling down at the bowling alley when she played in a tournament and music, she loved music. Other than that, Brady would constantly say to Jay as a reminder of her intolerance "Old people don't like a lot of noise, so you'd better watch yourself." Thus, even as a kid, she herself hated loud noise and unnecessary movement. Brady didn't do loud laughter or crying either. If Jay laughed too loudly, Brady would begin mocking her and end by saying "Shut up, you sound like a hyena." If she cried too loudly, she'd mock her again and say "Shut up, nobody cares about all those tears."

Her grandmother's friends would often joke about how they knew Jay was being raised by her grandparents. They said, "When you take a normal four year old in the store and tell them to get whatever they want, they'd typically get a doll and some candy, but not Jay. She doesn't prefer candy. If you tell Jay to get what she wants, she hands you a bag of pork rinds and a root beer or Coca-Cola. That child has been here before and she definitely has an old soul." So, it was clear that she was going to be a loner.

In the beginning of the school year, she was often teased for always being with the teacher rather than playing with the other kids. The other students would say things in an attempt to make her feel badly about herself, frequently talking about how skinny she was (because she never ate at school), her large teeth and being a teacher's pet. She had complaints from the teacher, not of unruly behavior but of extreme reservation. Even as the youngest in her class other students would be sitting on the carpet or playing with items in the classroom at play time, Jay would be in a corner looking out of the window silently counting the cars that drove by or reading one of the children books at the back circular table. Instead of giving the students their expected reaction to their fictional superiority, she learned to defend herself mostly with her actions and infrequently with her words. She became a fighter at an early age which stuck with her as she transitioned through each phase of her life. Being in school was definitely bringing out the

Curtis and Jane in her. Though Jay took ninety-five percent of her looks and temperament directly from her mother, one component that is calculated in the five percent that she took from her father was his anger issues.

The first encounter occurred during recess one afternoon (her least favorite part of the day, because she was forced to go outside with a bunch of children she did not like). That day she did as she would routinely do during recess; walk away from her class to her favorite tree that was about fifteen yards away from the playground and climb to the top of it. She enjoyed sitting at the top of the tree, softly singing whichever song her grandmother had just taught her and watching everyone else run around playing games. Her song would often be interrupted by her own laughter at how stupid she thought her classmates were for running around and falling just to get up, run and fall again. She would sometimes sit there naming what person looks the most similar to what animal, she whispered to herself things like "Joseph looks like a giraffe, Amy looks like a Lizard." That is mostly how she remembered whichever animal she had learned about each day; by associating one of the kids with the animal they resembled.

However, that specific day, a little boy noticed her in the tree and decided to bother her. He climbed up the same tree and sat next to her on a branch as she continued to sing and ignore his presence. Finally, as his white skin began to flush red from anger, he interjected her song by suggesting "Hey, you're a little girl, you shouldn't be climbing trees, you should be down there playing the mommy or the maid with the other little girls. You're a stupid black girl. Climbing trees is for boys." Completely insulted and without saying a word, she raised her foot to his head and kicked him out of the tree. As he began to bellow out from having a broken arm, Jay climbed down and walked away as if she had done nothing wrong. Fortunately for her, none of the teachers or students had seen what had happened because she was in the most secluded area on the field and far enough away from the playground. They only heard him crying. Ms. Pam ran over to the scene to find him lying there alone and asked him why he was crying. Following his explanation of who had kicked him out of the tree, Ms. Pam screamed out loudly across the field "JAY, COME HERE."

As she sat there with the mangled student and Ms. Pam she was asked "Did you kick him out of the tree?" Jay simply responded, "Yes." When she was asked for an explanation on why she had done it, she responded with no remorse "Because he called me a stupid black girl," which in her mind had justified her action. Had he left her alone and not offered his futile opinion of what she as a black girl should be doing, she wouldn't have kicked him. She was never the problem child; she was always the opposite until she was bothered. In each event that didn't involve her people of choice, she just wanted to be left alone to do whatever it was that she was there to do and then go home once her required tasks had been fulfilled. Yet, an apprehension of a life-long stigma was made that day for the very first time. She was a black girl and he was a white boy.

On that day, she was introduced to a phenomenon that she'd involuntary have to deal with for the rest of her life. According to that little boy (and so many others in the world that she would come to meet), there were certain parameters that she fit into and other boundaries that due to her race and gender that were not to be crossed. Obviously, Jay knew that there were some students in her class and throughout the elementary school that did not look like her. Her teacher and most of the teachers there did not look like her, however most of the children in her class and throughout the school did. Regardless of skin color or gender, she dispelled the same displeasure of being bothered towards everyone in her presence.

Her punishment was a phone call to both of her grandmothers and not being able to participate in recess for two weeks, which was not very much of a punishment. She was fine with no recess because that meant she wouldn't have to be outside with those kids that she hated anyways. She was hoping that her punishment would be more along the lines of just staying at home with her grandparents for a couple of days, but that would have been too good to be true. Two weeks later she cried when her punishment was over and she was told that she had earned her privileges to rejoin her class for recess.

When she got home the afternoon of the incident, her grandmothers Lillian and Brady asked her about what had occurred at school that day as both of them had received a phone call from the principal. Still, with no remorse for what she had done, she explained exactly what had happened. "He called me a stupid black girl grandma and he told me that I should only be playing with dolls like a mommy or a maid Bebe" she said to them. Due to the fact that the little boy had started it, Jay did not get in trouble. Lillian and Brady always told Jay that she would only be disciplined if she was the person who picked or started a fight, but if she was defending herself then there would be no consequences for her retaliation. Her grandmother's motto was "Do no harm, but take no shit." They all sat there and laughed as Lillian said jokingly "I bet that's the last time he calls anyone else stupid, he'll be walking around school with a disfigured arm that just so happens to be in a black cast. Who looks stupid now? " Brady went on to advise Jay that the little boy's comments are the sentiments of quite a few people in the world and that as heart-breaking as it is, it will not be the last that she would hear of her character, intelligence or competence being attacked by those who do not look like her.

As both mommies and janitors/maids for most of their lives, surely Brady and Lillian too were offended by the boy's derogatory comments toward their granddaughter. Lillian said to Jay, "You are a little black girl but stupidity is the last association with that description. There is nothing wrong with being a mommy or a maid because without mommies human nature wouldn't exist and without maids, houses, businesses, corporations and even the school that you attend would rot with filth. However you are not limited to being either of those things because you are black and female. Anything he and every other boy can do, so can you if you put your mind to it. Besides being a mother is a far harder job than any job a man has done or will ever do. Blackness, though others will try to dissuade you of this, is God's blessing. Being black is beautiful; you have the blood of African royalty running through you and you are beautiful" she told Jay before becoming angry all over again that her grandchild can't go to school to learn in peace because of ignoramuses like this little twit. "People's folly comes out in their children; and I can almost guarantee that his parents do think black girls in particular are stupid and hold titles of mothers and maids exclusively. I don't care if you never become a mother but I'm determined to expose you to every opportunity that positions you to one day hire a maid, and the way that my God works, that little boy may just be the 'help' you hire" Brady added.

Though Lillian had a sweet spirit and disposition, if pushed far enough she'd quickly shift into a fighter defending herself. Brady's entire disposition was stern and hasty to anger; only warming up to a person after she has gotten to know and trust them. Though Jay's temperament was closer to that of Brady's, (being that it did not take much to upset her) if left unbothered one would think she has a sweet and quiet spirit like that of Lillian. Lillian and Brady began indirectly telling Jay about why they were such advocates for standing up for oneself and not allowing anyone to disrespect them. Jay sat there and listened as her grandparents cossetted her in what life was like for them as children. Lillian was born in the Walker Homes area of south Memphis, Tennessee on August 19th, 1930 and Brady was born in Tunica, Mississippi on August 1st, 1932 of which they both had so many experiences to share with each other about their journey. Lillian and Brady sat there that afternoon sharing two influential stories with each other in the presence of Jay that would largely influence Jay's awareness of her ancestry and hone in on where her "no-nonsense" attitude is derived.

Lillian told Brady that when she was Jay's age, she and her older siblings would have to walk about eight miles to and from school (sometimes barefoot because her father couldn't always afford shoes). She said that as they walked to school, there was a bus filled with white students that would pass them every day. As the children passed, they would spit on her and her siblings, throw objects from the bus and sometimes the driver would allow them to get off the bus and chase them down the street. Sometimes they would catch up with them, beating them until they were black and blue. She explained to Jay how she and her siblings were not allowed to go to school with white children and all of their books were second hand material given to them from the white schools.

She said that because the white kids knew that their books were going to black schools, they would write racial slurs and threats like "Blacks are stupid or I'll kill you if I catch you reading" between the lines of the pages similar to the insults the little boy had said to Jay. "I'm glad you kicked that little white boy in the face for calling you a 'stupid black girl', because when I was your age, we couldn't retaliate, whether being spat on, hit with metal objects from a bus, or blatantly punched in the face." She went on talking about lynchings and shared all she had witnessed by the time she was Jay's current age or a little older. She ended her portion of the conversation by saying she knew of a person who was lynched and she had actually seen the body of a man, hanging from a tree as she and her siblings were walking to their destination. "At some point, injustice became normal. I thank God that we've come this far; where my baby can go to school with the white boys and kick them off of trees out of retaliation to his actions without me finding her hung up somewhere by her neck, but it ain't over yet. Our plight ain't nowhere near over" said Lillian.

Brady then began to share her lineage with Lillian as she initiated her story by exclaiming to Jay "I am sharing this in your presence not to create hatred in your heart but to inform you of where you have come from. You're not too young to hear about what we've been through and the lineage that has birthed you. You're never too young because in some people's eyes, you were born adulterated because you're black. You don't live by the same standards as a white child, even at your young age and you never will. Lillian and I don't rely on your school to teach you your history during 'black history month,' we will tell you ourselves. There is no one month of your history because it was our reality every day of the year and what happened to us is also your history.

It is a history that you are not to forget regardless of how old you get, who you meet or where you go in life. You will learn your history like it's the back of your hand," she said to Jay. She started by telling her that she and her sister were mixed; Crete Indian and Black (which was obvious because neither Brady nor Brenda looked completely black). "My paternal grandparents and father are full blood Cretes and my maternal grandparents; Indian and Black, my mother is a mixture of the two."

She said that early in her childhood, she and her older sister Brenda lived in Tunica, Mississippi with their mother and grandparents (which is by far one of the most racist states in the U.S.) though Tennessee wasn't any better as it was still a part of the Jim Crow south. As she talked to Lillian and Jay listened, she said that her grandmother worked picking cotton in a field owned by this white man and that she and her sister would often go with her to help. One day, the owner came out to the field where they were and began to feel on her grandmother's rear as she was bending over picking the cotton. Her grandmother's discomfort and unconsent was evident as she fought off his sexual advances. Brady and Brenda began to cry as their grandmother was tasseling with this man and telling them to "Go home, run home." They were in utter shock and could not move. Eventually, the man became tired of fighting with their grandmother. He back handedly slapped her and told her that if he could not have his way with her, that she was fired and to get those "nigger children" off of his property. She adjusted her clothes back to their normal place and did just that grabbing Brady and Brenda by their wrists and running home. After getting them home, Brady told Lillian how badly they were scorned by their grandmother for not leaving when she asked them to. A few hours later her grandfather came home from work and her grandmother explained to him what had happened to her at the cotton field as their granddaughters watched. With a hot-head, he grabbed his rifle, got on one of the two stallions they owned and headed for the cotton field. Knowing that nothing good would transpire from this, her grandmother fell to her knees and began to pray that her husband return to their family alive.

Here he comes staggering through the door at close to midnight. "I shot him, you'll never have to worry about him again but you have to leave town now." Brady explained that she could hear her grandmother crying out and begging her husband to stay by his side or to come along with them. "No," he said, "You have to get our daughter and the grand girls out of here. They have a bounty on my head and they will find me, because I just killed a white man in front of witnesses. Head north and get far enough away to not be traced, I will stay here and face what is coming to me because if they don't at least find me, they will pursuit. If I am found with you, they will kill us all." Brady said as she began to tear up, "Grandmother got us up that night, packed up everything portable, loaded it in our little car and headed to Memphis. That was the last time we ever saw our grandfather and from that point onward I lived in a house run by women." Her mother went on to have multiple children until there were nine siblings total, all of which were being raised by their grandmother.

After Brady was of age, she and Brenda both were forced to get jobs as "the help" to assist their grandmother in taking care of their younger siblings as their mother would only come around long enough to drop off another child that she had birthed to their grandmother. "That is why all of my grandchildren will go to a private school; to have the best education possible. Education leads to opportunities. My life and opportunities as a young girl and even as a young woman was cut short because of the responsibility I had to help provide for my family. Then after finally being freed of my responsibility as an older sister, I slipped up and accidentally started a family of my own. So now, I live through each of you and you, my child, will be educated. You will be well versed, you will be successful. I work to give you and my other granddaughters the chance at life that was never made available to me and that I couldn't afford to give my children fully, Brady said."

At such a premature age, Jay knew from the stories that she had listened in on that she was being raised in the midst of resilient women. Her grandmother Lillian encountered the struggle of being mocked and humiliated by white children and adults and had actually seen the aftermath of a lynched body. Her grandmother Brady was scarred from seeing the beating and near rape of her grandmother and was forced to relocate to another town because of a bounty that was placed on her family. Lillian was the granddaughter of a slave, daughter of a sharecropper and sibling to the downtrodden whereas Brady was the mixture of the two most hated minorities in America (Indians and Blacks) who fought every day to mark and claim their territory, their bodies, and their lives.

There is no doubt about where Jay's elasticity is stemmed from. Jay had already encountered a number of painful situations and had just as many more to come. However, after becoming informed of her own personal ancestry, it was clear that the women in her family were fighters and survivors of which she too was deemed from the beginning to be nothing less.

Battle Eight

Unwanted

It was Christmas day and unlike any other night, Jay would traditionally spend the night leading up to Christmas with her Grandmother Brady because she had a chimney and Lillian didn't. Jay would say "Santa won't come to a house that doesn't have a chimney." She'd always enjoy being with Brady but for Christmas she would get to spend time with her aunt/godmother (her mother's baby sister) Grace who would be visiting from Florida for the holidays. The only time Jay didn't mind spending nights away from Lillian was on the rare occasions that her godmommy came into town. Brady's ritual for Christmas was to have all of her children and grandchildren over to eat and enjoy each other's company. Usually all but one of her children would come home and spend Christmas Eve night at her house so that they could wake up on Christmas day as a family. Tray (Brady's only son) had never really moved out of her house and Jay's mother was always the one that wouldn't show until Christmas day for a few hours. "Jay, I'm going to pick up your mother from the north side of town, would you like to ride?" Grace asked. She said yes, excited and wanting to be the first person to see her mother on Christmas day. Jay sits in the back seat eagerly, but what she was about to see and hear would forever damage her mind; creating doubt about whether or not she was ever adequate.

Disbelief fills her mind as she looks out of the backseat window at her mother running in the yard and playing with five small mixed children. When she saw that Grace and Jay had pulled up, she kissed each of the children on their foreheads and told them that she would be back. A few of the younger ones began to cry while the older ones begged to come along with her. She comforts

69

each of them and assured them that she would be returning to them that evening after spending time with her own family. "I haven't seen mommy since last Christmas. I called her and left messages inviting her to my dance recital, volleyball games, two talent show contests from this year and my kindergarten graduation a few years back. She never came. But she is here with these little boys and girls every day. It's just not fair that she gets to come home to them and not me." Jay thinks to herself as she holds back her tears. Her mother gets into the car, acknowledges everyone "Hey, my beautiful little sister Grace and lovely daughter Jay." Jay sits there, not voicing a word and listens to her mother ranting about the children she was just with. "I have been living with my friend, Sam, and those are his children. I keep them every day. They are so well behaved, and I just love them. They do well in school, and they don't give me or their daddy any problems. As you can see their mother is white. "Sam loves dem white girls and those kids are so pretty to me," she says to her sister, Grace, unaware that Jay was absorbing her words like a cotton towel absorbs water in the back seat.

For the remainder of the day, Jay walked around uneasy and hoping that her mother would just leave because her presence brought about an exasperating feeling. She said to her aunt/godmother when they had made it back to Brady's house "Auntie Grace, I wish that I were your daughter. There have been nights that I have asked God why he gave me to my mother when my mother doesn't want me and then I think of you, and you don't have any kids. You say you don't ever want kids of your own but you treat me like I'm yours." Grace simply responded, "You are my one and only godchild so this is as close to motherhood as I am going to get and your mother loves you, she is just sick right now." As a child Jay didn't comprehend what her aunt meant by "sick" but what was beginning to resonate with her was the feeling of self-hatred, resentment toward her mother and even more abhorrence filled with untrustworthiness toward other people. It's amazing how something seemingly so simple could have such a lasting impression on a child's well-being and that would require support throughout her adulthood to recover from.

For the next couple of days, Lillian noticed how differently Jay had been behaving. She was already very much reserved and shied away from interactions with most people, but surprisingly she was beginning to act this way toward everyone. Lillian could detect that something immensely powerful was controlling this child's thoughts because she would stare out into the distance completely dazed more often than normal. She could not tell what had triggered this response because she was not at Brady's house on Christmas, but she figured that she would either ask, or in time she would be made aware of the situation. One day soon after that Christmas, Lillian sits on the couch and silently observes Jay looking out the living room window. "She's been in the same spot for about an hour not answering or talking to anyone. What is she thinking about?" Lillian wanders to herself deciding not to ask in that moment.

Lillian would always ask Jay about any situation that clearly elicited a response rather good or bad, "And how do you feel about that" and Jay would then be expected to verbally express those feeling to her grandmother in a way that makes sense or she could opt to say nothing at all by saying "She doesn't want to talk about it." However, she could never respond with a head nod, or humping her shoulders. She had to speak because using body language (though a valid form of communication) was not proper communication in Lillian's house. This led Jay to be extremely in touch with her feelings. Whether or not she chose to share the truth with others, she knew exactly how she felt. Jay's young mind was very advanced. The emotions that she felt based on her observations were explicit and being raised by her grandparents definitely had an effect on Jay's perception of the world around her. She was wise; often called an "old soul." However, that garnished wisdom could be viewed as both a benefit as well as a disadvantage. It was a benefit because she was smart, excelling faster than most children her age in her problem solving skills, in class and in extra-curricular activities. Jay's ability to hold a conversation (regardless of the topic) was superb because most of her time at home was spent conversing with her grandparents. It was a disadvantage because through that wisdom, she never really viewed the world through the innocent eyes of a child. Her thought process matched her environment; deep-rooted.

"What is wrong with me? Last year she told me that she was going to be getting better and after she does, that I would come and live with her, what changed? Oh, I know what changed; she just moves in with her 'friend' and likes his kids. Does she know that I can be well behaved? I can sing and play sports. But maybe I'm not pretty. There is not a trace of white blood running through my veins (and according to my grandmothers, I shouldn't want it to be). My hair is nappy, and my teeth are big, I must not be pretty. Pretty girls' moms want them. At school, all the really pretty girls have their moms there. At ballet practice, all the girls' moms help them into their leotards and tutus, and it doesn't help that I am the only black girl at my dance studio. For Mother's Day all the other kids made these pretty cards for their moms but I never even see my mom, so I made it for my dad and my grandmas. Every mother/daughter lunch that my school has had since kindergarten, Brady has come. I love it when Brady comes but sometimes, I wish she'd bring my mom too, but I know that probably won't happen because Brady and my mom can hardly stand each other. Maybe it's me; I'm just not good enough. The people that want me are my grandmas, James, Auntie Grace and dad; but not my mom. And, what did Aunt Grace mean by "sick." My mom's not "sick" at all. Whatever, I know who my real mama is; Grandma Lillian, she is my mother. Going forward, I'll call her mama" Jay thinks before enacting on her thought.

Snapping out of her hour long daze and surprisingly turning around to see her grandmother already staring at her, "Mama, can I have a cheese toast and French fries for dinner," Jay asks Lillian. "What did you just call me," Lillian asked. "I called you mama," Jay repeated. With the sternest voice she had ever used when addressing Jay, Lillian yelled "I AM NOT YOUR MOTHER!" Don't you dare give that title to anyone other than your mother, do you understand me?" Completely confused and broken-hearted, Jay responds, "No ma'am, why not?" as she began to tear up. Seeing Jay begin to cry prompted tears to form in Lillian's eyes as she thought about how to explain her reasoning to her granddaughter without making her cry more.

"You only get one mother and no matter what she has or has not done, she will always be your mother. The only thing as a human that she was obligated to do was to bring you into this world so she has done her due diligence, and for that reason alone, no one else gets to be called your mother. If you choose not to call Jane 'mother' that's fine, but don't you ever give her title away. I lost my mother to at age two, as she died giving birth to my younger sister. I don't even remember what she looks like, but I had a mother and no other woman no matter how significant they were deserved my mother's title. Yes, child I understand the pain of not having a mother, but at least you know who yours is. Brady and I are your grandmothers, James your grandfather, Grace your aunt and godmother, Leon your uncle and godfather, Curtis your father and Jane your mother. Don't you ever forget us. And yes, I will make you a cheese toast and some potatoes for dinner," explained Lillian.

Though Lillian meant what she said whole-heartedly, Jay's interpretation at the time was immature and further supportive of the thoughts she had been having since Christmas day. Taking her grandmother's words personally, she thinks, "Now, not even my grandma wants to be my mother, which is odd because she's always told me that she sees me as her child. At least her mother was dead, mine is alive and lives in the same city less than thirty minutes away and I only get to see her at Christmas." Indignantly, Jay goes to her room and plunges her face into the pillow crying out to God to let her die. There were so many perturbed thoughts in Jay's mind.

As a young child, these experiences had begun deteriorating her innocence. After that Christmas, she no longer believed in Santa and was beginning to even doubt the existence of God. Santa Claus was now a thing of the past because every year since Jay could remember, she had asked Santa for her mother to be a part of her life. At the same time, she prayed to God every day because that is what Lillian had taught her to do. She prayed for her mother, she prayed to be a normal child with a normal life. She prayed that her mother would come home, yet her prayers went unanswered. Year after year she became more and more disappointed especially this year. She was aware that there were times she would be treated differently because of her skin color in comparison to white people but now a brand new phenomenon

74

introduced itself. Darker skinned black people can also be treated differently than lighter skinned black people, even by other black people. In reality, her mother, Jane, had meant no harm by saying how much she enjoyed caring for her friend's children. Also, she was unaware that Jay had even overheard her speaking with those children before she had gotten into the car that day. Be that as it may, Jay's interpretation, though misguided by emotion and misunderstanding had some validity. "Hmmm, maybe the closer a person's skin is to white, the better they are treated, and the more they are loved. I am fair skinned but nowhere near white" she thought to herself.

On top of the disappointment she was already facing within a few months, another part of her normal life as a child began to fade away. In less than a year, she had been diagnosed with astigmatism and her eyesight had already decreased by sixty percent. Her left eye was twice as weak as her right eye and her right eye's vision was still extremely poor. For a while, the optometrist struggled to find a solution to correcting her eyesight or to at least stop the regression. Finally, she is given a prescription for glasses and contacts and though her eyesight didn't get better, it remained stagnant as she wore that exact same prescription for the following fifteen years.

The glass lenses were as thick as four quarters being wedged between your thumb and index finger, which only added another factor to her being a target to getting picked on in school. This also explained her increased anxiety toward going to school. It was almost guaranteed that she'd be headed to the principal's office by the end of the day. Still, not a trouble maker per se, students thought she was an easy target for bullying because of her being so small and though they often tried and failed, they would wait until they found something new to pick on her for, but still, they were mistaken at every attempt. If one of the students said anything derogatory towards her because of her bony legs, big teeth and now, her thick glasses, she'd generally punch them in the mouth or the throat. Students at her elementary school enjoyed picking on other kids, especially if they were loners, and they were very persistent even if the student defended themselves. So on a few occasions, Jay had to remind them, that she was not to be bothered, ever. They'd normally never get the opportunity to physically harm her because as soon as they'd approach her talking badly about her and she felt threatened, when they got within arms reach, she'd attack them like a lioness protecting her young. They learned over time, that their best bet was not to even speak to Jay. Because she was beginning to be thought of as mean, most children steered far from trying to be her friend and though being mean wasn't necessarily the association she wanted attached to her name, she chose to be that over being bullied. After all, she already harbored horrible feelings about herself, taking those jabs from someone else was a threat to her sanity.

Emily, the one friend that she had at school was starting to drift away as well because her grandmother didn't want her being friends with a black girl, she realized when Emily had finally come home with Jay for a sleepover. Emily's mother loved Jay but Emily's grandmother (whom Emily and her mother lived with) was a blatant racist. She was forced to give that friendship up on the day that James dropped Emily back off at home. As Emily and Jay skipped up the driveway, hugged and said goodbye, Emily's grandmother watched scornfully through the screen door. Upon escorting Emily to her door, James carrying the little girl's overnight bag, sleeping bag and toys, Emily's grandmother opened the door and told James to drop everything on the porch. He told her that he could bring the stuff in because it was a little heavy but she responded that "niggers weren't allowed in her house." Needless to say, that was the end of that friendship.

When Jay got home she cried "I don't understand. Why I am here, everyone leaves me, the people that I love don't love me and I don't love myself, please God just let me die."

She doesn't know it now but the feeling she was experiencing at eight years old was a battle that she would forever face. To be alone, motherless and unwanted were three adjectives that described her life until redefining the descriptors of which became a mission later on in life.

Battle Nine

Blessed Curse

A few years had passed and with each year, Jay looked more and more like her mother. Not that she needed another reminder, she walked into Brady's kitchen to see who was at the front door after hearing someone entering the home. It was her aunt Brenda (Brady's older sister). "You are the spitting image of Jane," her Aunt Brenda says to Jay. Brady spatting out before Jay could reply "Yes she is, Jay is just like my daughter. She loves to read and write poetry but the negative is that she has the exact same attitude, too. Between her mother Jane and her father Curtis, she doesn't have a chance at being sane. And with that attitude she's going to end up just like her mother, you mark my words. Honestly, it gets on my nerves, it's like Jane's been reincarnated and we don't need another Jane in the family" says Brady. Jay becomes vexed by her grandmother's comments and responded brusquely to her Aunt Brenda and Grandmother Brady. "Thank you!" responds Jay. Brady then declaring, "See what I mean, look at that nasty ass attitude, I hate it! She's cursed with her mother's spirit." Jay clearly irritated goes into her room, closes the door and calls her Grandmother Lillian to come pick her up, "Please come get me grandma, I hate being over here," she says to Lillian.

After being picked up without warning, Brady calls Lillian to express her frustrations with the both of them. "I do not appreciate how Jay will call you without even telling me that she is ready to leave. Simply because Jay is upset with my directions, you just do whatever she says. We are the parents; Jay is the child. She does not have an opinion nor does she get to feel any type of way about what I say to or about her. The only reason she prefers to be with you all the time over me, is because you allow her to do as she pleases. When she gets with me, she becomes upset because I make her follow the rules," Brady says to Lillian.

Then, Lillian responds, "Well excuse me if I am fabricating but talking about her mother (your own daughter) to her face and declaring detriment over her future isn't making Jay change her attitude. If you talked about my mama all the time and I just have to sit there and take it, I'd have a bad attitude towards you too. That's common sense Brady. Further, she does not prefer me over you, she's a pre-teen, she equally dislikes us both, I promise. Hell, she just turned eleven. That's what pre-teens do. She's getting to that age; it's all a part of her growing process and you have to let her go through it or you'll ruin her.

She spends most of her days with you and nights with me when she's not in school, and for you to spend so much time with her, you should know that she's not a bad child at all. She doesn't get in trouble here because she listens to me and she does as she is told the first time I ask, but then again, I actually know how to 'talk' to her rather than at her. Most of the time, I don't listen to you either Brady, because you don't know how to 'talk' to people. I don't share your belief that she doesn't have an opinion and that she doesn't get to feel a certain way when you (or anyone else) offends her. You don't have the right to tell someone whether or not they can be offended. What the hell do you mean by that, she's a human being not one of your damn expensive psoralen dolls, she has opinions and feelings just like you. I may get irritated at times with her behavior and her attitude but I'll handle them appropriately. However, 'appropriately' never includes talking negatively about her parents or speaking badly about how her life is going to end up. You are not God and you cannot judge your daughter, Jane or my son, Curtis. Yes, Jay is spoiled and I taught

79

her my phone number when she was three years old. I promised her that if she ever called me, I'd come to wherever she was and bring her home and I don't make false promises. She never has to be anywhere she is uncomfortable, even if that means with you," snaps Lillian.

Brady then becoming extremely upset declares, "Well, screw ya'll, since you think you're so much better at raising her, and she loves you so much more, then I'm done. You can now pay for her ballet, tap dance and gymnastics classes, school clothes, tuition for her private school education, books, hair and any other expense that needs to be taken care of. How's that damn-it" she shouts through the phone before hanging up in Lillian's face.

Knowing that Brady will soon get over it (as she always does), Lillian hangs up the phone and goes on with her evening. That was not the first nor the last argument had between them and they still remained best friends and co-parents. A couple of days after any argument they were back on speaking terms.

A few days have passed and Jay keeps seeing something very odd in her undergarments. After the third day she calls out to her grandma because she is becoming very creeped out by whatever this is. "Grandma, come here please!" she shouts out to Lillian from the bathroom. "What is it child?" she says as she opens the bathroom door to see Jay sitting with bloodied underwear. "Oh, Lord, that time has come." Lillian said under her breath as she walks out of the bathroom. Jay looking confused barks, "Wait, come back." Lillian responding, "Oh hush, just sit there for a minute, I'll be back." Lillian picks up the phone, ending their three day silent treatment and calls Brady. "What do you want?" Brady answers as Lillian snaps back, "Girl, get over yourself. I need you to go to the store and bring me some feminine products and sanitary napkins, Jay got her 'Aunt flow' today and the last time I had a cycle, Jay's existence hadn't even been thought of. So I don't have any here."

Completely forgetting that she was angry, Brady begins to laugh and say "Well, you've had one more recently than I have, it's been close to twenty-two years since my last cycle, but I'm on my way, I'll be there in a few." Jay was still sitting there as five minutes turned into thirty minutes, panicking. She hears a knock on the door; Brady had arrived carrying three bags full of feminine care products. Jay comes out of the bathroom as Brady is organizing all of the products in a pretty display on the couch for Jay to choose from. "Pick the ones you want," says Brady to Jay.

Feeling overwhelmed by how many options she had and not having a clue how to use any of them, Jay just picks the pink ones because pink is her favorite color. "Now what do I do with it?" Jay asks Brady as Brady tells Lillian to show her. Lillian demonstrated how to properly put on the pad, how to dispose of it and gave her tips on the proper hygiene as Brady begins packing up the rest of the items to return them to the store. Brady then gets a phone call from her second oldest grandchild, Paige. She was headed to the hospital in labor with her first son. Brady says to Lillian disappointedly, "I'm headed to the hospital, my second great-grandchild is making his entrance into the world. Now is the perfect time to explain to her what can happen now that she can get pregnant, so that she doesn't end up going into labor on the day of her high school graduation like her older cousin Paige. Maybe we can see Jay walk across the stage to get her high school diploma and bring graduation gifts instead of baby gifts to a hospital." It was clear that Brady was disappointed with the choices that her two older granddaughters had made. She was hoping that Jay made better choices.

Nicole (Brady's oldest grandchild) had birthed her first child during her senior year of high school and Paige (Nicole's little sister) was currently in labor on her high school graduation day. Incidences that Brady was clearly not happy about given her view of the importance of getting an education and not having children until you can take care of them. Brady knew pursuing college as teenage mothers would be challenging and once you'd reached the point of having a child, Brady considered you to be an adult and she made it clear that she would help with the child, but the handouts to you (the adult) were over, no more helping you. It was then, that Brady had given up on them, as her favorite line to use on teen moms in their family was expelled to Paige over the phone "Well, your life is over now, it's no longer about you and from this point onward it won't ever be about you again, you wanna be grown, it's time to spring into mommy mode young lady, you can't be no baby when you got a baby."

Lillian sits on the couch with Jay as James excuses himself to his man-cave from the conversation as he knew what was about to take place. "Jay, you got your cycle today. It will come once a month and that is a good thing. You will have a cycle from this point until about age fifty but that now means you can have a baby if you have sex. If you do not get a cycle and you've had sex, you're pregnant. Do you understand?"

That was the most horrible explanation of what was going on with her body but having to have this conversation with a child (or at all) was new to Lillian. After all, Lillian had raised two boys and weirdly enough, she didn't get her first cycle until a month or two before she became pregnant with her first child at seventeen.

This is probably one reason to why she conceived so early; she was ignorant to sex education and to the functions of her own body. Lillian didn't get the best explanation of sex or a cycle either because that lecture was given to her by her father who was a man, that knew nothing about women's bodies other than how to impregnate them. He just took her to the store and bought her pads. Her older sister showed her how to put a pad on and that was the end of that conversation/demonstration. Lillian didn't learn about women's health until after she had become pregnant with her son. Back in Lillian's days, children didn't ask questions and adults explained nothing to children. It was a respect thing. Thus, she pretty much gave Jay the same talk her dad had given her and showed her how to use the pad just as her older sister had once showed her.

Still, without full comprehension of what a cycle was and why she had to have one, Jay responds "Yes ma'am" to her grandmother's inquiry about her understanding; not really wanting any further details. She only knew that having a cycle was connected to sex and a baby. However Jay was completely unnerved by the thought of having children especially at age eleven. A lot was changing about her; she was now in a training bra and had gotten what she thought to be a curse that would remain with her for the majority of her life.

Though one major life altering event had taken place, there were three more events that occurred the year of 2004 that would leave their trace on her for the rest of her life. She almost lost both of her grandmothers, Brady and Lillian. Brady had had several heart attacks that had gone unnoticed for some time, and Lillian had an extremely high blood pressure seizure and the third life altering event was that she had witnessed a murder. These events had all happened within a span of a month.

Though they were parents in Jay's eyes, she was born late in their lives, her grandmothers were aging and their health was beginning to reflect their age. Her grandmother, Brady, would take her to school every day and drive her to all of her extra-curricular activities which included swimming lessons, basketball games, volleyball tournaments, and ballet/gymnastic/tap dance recitals. Jay's Aunt Grace and Grandma Brady funded all of those expenses. One day, her Grandmother Brady was taking her to school and walking her to her first class which was slightly annoying to Jay. Jay would say, "I'm in the sixth grade. I don't need you to walk me to class anymore. No other kid's parents walk them into class." However that day, Jay would regret turning her grandmother away. Brady heard her words that morning and surprisingly said "Fine, walk yourself to class," as she hugged her and kissed her goodbye. Jay was shocked that she could walk from the car to class by herself because Brady always walked her to class and spoke to her teacher every morning for about seven or eight minutes. Knowing that something had to be wrong, she went to her class with her grandmother on her mind for the rest of that day.

Hours later, school had ended and to her surprise, her father, Curtis, was there to pick her up. This was unusual because normally Brady would come to take her and pick her up from school and stay at Lillian's house until she had finished all of her homework. Jay gets in the car and worriedly asks her dad, "What's wrong, why are you here, where is Bebe?" "I picked you up because your grandmother Brady is in the hospital and Lillian is there with her. Brady had a heart attack this morning shortly after she dropped you off at school. So that's why I am here to pick you up from school. We are on our way to the hospital to see your Grandma Brady. Jay began to cry at the thought of losing her grandmother Brady. When they arrived at the hospital, an emergency procedure had already been completed. Her aunt Grace had made it there from Florida, and the entire family filled the ICU waiting room. When the doctors told the family that two people at a time could come in the room to see her, Jay was the first in line. Despite the hospital policy of there being only two guests per room during visitation hours, there were three guests at all times with Brady because Jay would not leave the room (literally lying in the bed with Brady) until the visitation hours were over. To Jay's amazement, she walked in the room to Brady sitting straight up and talking as if she were completely healthy. The doctor explained to the family that Brady had had several heart attacks without even knowing it, and was actually having another one that morning while walking Jay to her class. That was the real reason she had allowed Jay to continue to her class alone, she made it out of the car and to the entrance of the school but was out of breath so she told her to go on to class as she returned to her car and drove herself to the emergency room.

After four days in the hospital, Brady was released and back at home performing the duties of her usual routine; back at work, bowling and helping to take care of Jay. Though it seemed to be a happy time for Jay, she found herself back in the emergency room waiting area by the end of that week.

Saturday of the same week that Brady was released from the hospital, Jay and Lillian were heading to Wendy's to get something to eat before heading to Brady's house to chill that afternoon. Lillian had already been to choir rehearsal and had just come in the house from hanging clothes on the line in the back yard before deciding that instead of making lunch; she would take Jay to *Wendy's*. While heading to the car, Jay got a very unsettling feeling and began to ask Lillian to let her drive. Now at age eleven, Jay had already been taught how to drive by her grandfather, James. Though everyone else in the family would allow her to drive, Lillian and Brady were frightened. Yet that Saturday afternoon, Lillian allowed her to drive for the first time since *Wendy's* wasn't that far away.

Jay backed out of the driveway and headed up the street. They made it about one block and Lillian tells her to turn the car around and go back home. "I have to use the restroom, turn the car around," she says anxiously to Jay. Jay does as she was told but as she heads back down the street she looks over to see her grandmother having a seizure; eyes rolled to the back of her head, tongue out, body shaking sporadically and head beating hardly against the headrest. Jay calls out scared as this is the first time she'd ever experienced anyone having a seizure, "Grandma, Grandma, answer me!" Instinctively, Jay now four houses down from her house puts the car in park on the side of the street and ran around to her grandmother's side of the car. She unfastened her seat belt and called 911 on the cell phone that Brady had just bought her several months prior. She requested an ambulance and then did as the operator instructed. "Lean your grandmother facing you, hold her head out of the door, make sure that you grip her head firmly so that she doesn't continue to hit her head against the headrest. If there is anything with a long stem that is hard like a metal spoon anywhere near you, place that on her tongue and press to ensure that she does not choke on her tongue. Though all of the operator's requests seemed to be odd, Jay continued to follow instructions until the paramedics arrived. James recognizing his wife' car and seeing Jay outside the car on the passenger side pulls up at the same time as the ambulance. The paramedics rushed over to Lillian who was finally regaining her consciousness. James had begun frantically walking in circles in the middle of the street as he was shaken from that being his first sight upon his arrival home from work. Jay ran four houses up to her house to change her vomit-covered shirt and gets in the ambulance with Lillian. James gets back into his truck and follows them to the hospital.

Days later, she too is released from the hospital and Jay is now beginning to realize how much of a gift her grandparents are in her life regardless of their flaws. Lillian was poor and James was cheap, there were some days Lillian would give her nothing but Vienna sausages and crackers but Jay didn't know the difference. She loved Vienna sausages and crackers, so she thought it was a treat. And despite the situation, Jay never went hungry living in that house. Brady was just unreasonably strict. She would often take her frustrations with her daughter Jane out on Jay by comparing her and sometimes belittling her. Later in life, Jay realized that was Brady's method of deterring her from becoming like her mother. Though Brady wasn't wealthy by any means, she provided Jay with the best experiences beginning with her being enrolled in a very expensive private school. She didn't have much, as she lived paycheck to paycheck, but the little that she did have was spent making sure Jay experienced life to the fullest and that she did so fashionably.

Lillian sat on the couch in the living room as Jay stood looking out the front door listening to her grandmother explain to her, "Brady, James and I are old and we're getting older. We won't always be here, but we are trying to instill values in you that will carry you once we're gone. I know it's tough not having your dad around as often as you'd like to play sports with you or run around with you at your school events like some of the young parents can do. I also know the feeling of not having your mom here to teach you what a cycle is or how to do your hair and makeup. You're cursed with us old folks, but you are blessed nonetheless. When you get in certain situations that kids your age won't know how to handle, you'll be alright because you've been there before. Those times where kids your age will need their parents to figure their issues out for them, you'll have already won that race because you've always had to do it on your own; we old folks can't do it for you. You are wise beyond your years my child and that wisdom will carry you, even when I'm long gone. You're gonna make it. You're gonna get through life alright. I don't raise no fools."

From that moment onward, she devoted herself to taking care of her grandmothers as best she could as they had done for her. Jay began to think that God was trying to awaken her senses by allowing two near death situations to occur within days of each other to people whom she couldn't live without. A full week has gone by and she stands at the front door reminiscing on how difficult the past week was for her emotionally. She is so blessed to have her grandmothers; the place she is in at this exact moment exudes peace and thankfulness. She stands there pondering in her own thoughts about what her grandmother had just told her as she prays to God *"Thank you for my grandmothers, I pray that you take me before you take them, I could never imagine losing them."* She appreciates them now more than she ever had and she longed for them to always be with her. She thinks of where her life could have been if she hadn't been blessed with such gracious grandparents.

She goes outside and sits on the front porch to sing the song her grandma taught her years ago as she watches James cut the grass *"If it had not been for the Lord on my side, tell me where would I be,"* where…POW, POW…POW POW POW. Her song is interrupted by gunshots, retorted out of her blissful thoughts about her grandmothers and back into the reality of living in south Memphis.

Battle Ten

Harsh Reality

Shot to death right in front of her. "Jo Jo get in the house" Jay shouts out from the porch as James runs through the front yard as quickly as he could. "You get in the house Jay and shut the door!" he screams back at her. In a state of paralysis by what she just saw, she stands on the porch watching as the young man who was just shot falls out of his vehicle and the three men who just shot at him flee the scene in different directions. The car going so slowly now stops on its own. Knowing that she could not just go inside and shut the door leaving this man out there by himself to die, Jay never went inside. Jay hears her grandfather calling 911 and neighbors who had just heard gun shots began to trickle out of their homes and into the streets to get a better view of the scene. Jay was already outside, right in front of him. She and her grandfather had experienced firsthand what had ensued because it took place steps in front of their front yard, while James was outside and Jay sitting on the front porch.

Jay and her grandfather are now right by the young man's side as he is pugnaciously trying to breathe. James was talking to him and trying to keep him alert. Moments later, Jay looks him directly in the eyes as he takes his last breath. "Damn it, he's gone," James whispered. Being an army veteran had prepared James to see death right before his eyes, but Jay was traumatized. Police sirens are heard from a distance and James says to Jay firmly "Go in the house and keep your mouth shut." Jay partially does as she is told as she goes back in the house, standing in the front door with the door wide opened. Lillian joins her at the door as they stand there together watching the police close off the scene and James is now talking to one of the neighbors across the street.

Police and detectives began to canvass the neighborhood in search for this young man's killer(s). They are asking people in the neighborhood if they had seen or heard anything. Jay had a lot of respect for her grandfather James until he looked the detectives in the face and told them he didn't know much of anything. "I was outside cutting the grass when the boy was shot, but my back was turned to the scene, all I saw is him taking his last breath," James said unbothered. "He knew everything, he was closer to the scene than I was" Jay thought to herself.

The young man's family had arrived and his mother gets out of the detective's car screaming "my baby, my baby, somebody killed my baby!" Hearing her cries was a sound that would forever haunt Jay as she'd never forget how the boy's mother laid in the middle of the street wallowing in the pool of her son's blood. Just as she was lying there another young man rode by the scene on a green and black motorcycle asking "Yo, who was it, what happened?" Jay looked at the boy cautiously to make sure this man was who she thought he was. She replayed the shooting in her head and began yelling to the detective James was talking to "That's him, that's him, that's one of the guys who was shooting!" She shouted as she pointed to the man on the bike. The young man looked at Jay threateningly and raced off on his motorcycle as he was chased down by police and taken into custody where he later confessed to being one of the shooters.

The police officers stayed at Jay's home for a couple of hours gathering information. At eleven years old, Jay was the key witness to a homicide "I was sitting on the porch, watching my grandfather cut the grass and talking to my grandmother who was right inside the doorway, and I noticed three boys chasing a car. I thought they were playing around and trying to catch up with the car so that they could get in. The driver never sped up though, it seemed like if he wanted to get away he could have, because he was driving like ten miles per hour while they were on foot. When the three guys made it up to the car, each of them began to shoot. Two of them took off running down that back alley way. I couldn't see the faces of all the guys because two of them were on the left side of the car and ran in another direction. The one closest to my side of the street turned in my direction and ran toward the side street closest to my house, which is how I saw his face. He had on black basketball shorts with a red trim going up the side, a red t-shirt and some red and white sneakers. I didn't pay that close of attention to what the other two were wearing other than they both had on white shirts and black bottoms. But the guy that came around on that green motorcycle was the same guy that I had seen shooting at the deceased." After telling that same story to about four different detectives, the police finally left her home. Jay felt proud of herself for the good deed she thought she had done, but James' anger with her was about to be unleashed.

"I told you to go into the house and to keep your damn mouth shut for a reason. You are a hard-headed little brat and your big ass mouth is going to get you killed one day. You live in the hood, do you understand that? You go to this private school and you're so sheltered there, but when you walk out of those school doors and come back home, this is the real-world. They don't care about you here. They don't care about me. They don't care about anybody. You can't be informing the cops about stuff like that, regardless of what you saw. Now, they know who snitched on them and exactly where you stay. You have put our entire family in harm's way. Who is going to protect us? You better pray they catch all three of those guys because if not, they'll definitely retaliate and when they come searching for the snitch, I'm sending you out there first. Learn to shut the hell up before your face is the one on the news."

All the same, James was trying to make a point about the realities of living in that neighborhood, Jay was pissed off about how he'd spoken to her but she was not afraid and she knew that if she were ever placed in that situation again, she'd react in the exact same manner. After seeing the expression on that mother's face and hearing her cries of distress, she knew she had done the right thing. Her conscience would never allow her to witness such a violent act and do absolutely nothing when she had the potential answers that could possibly bring someone to justice and prevent the same act from happening to someone else.

Later that night, Brady called and told them all to turn on the ten o' clock news channel and that their house was on the news. Of course Jay's face never appeared but Jay sat there with satisfaction as the news reporter informed "Today shortly after two p.m. a twenty year old man by the name of Mr. Twan Hoover was killed on the block of Glencoe Rd. in south Memphis. Two of the three suspects have been taken into custody and charged with first degree murder thanks to some tips from a neighbor who witnessed the assault and confessions from two of the three suspects. The public is asked to please report any known information to the authorities regarding the third suspect." To Jay's delight, by that time the next night the third suspect had also been located and taken into custody in which all three men were later found guilty of first degree murder. Although Jay was pleased to have been of assistance in bringing Mr. Hoover's killers to justice, she was saddened by the fact that none of the young men (including the deceased) were over twenty-one years of age. All of their lives were over and for what? Because they lived in the hood, and with that comes unescapable truths.

Jay's life was altered forever. It was like another layer of her innocence had been peeled back. She had witnessed a cold-blooded murder for the very first time and (against her grandfather's wishes) bravely faced a fear that even adults were afraid of confronting. Growing up in her neighborhood presented a number of ferocious situations: murder, domestic violence, robbery, burglary, prostitution, drug busts and gang wars all of which she was exposed to well before reaching adulthood. Sadly, this was only Jay's first of many encounters with the harsh realities of south Memphis. Never would she be able to watch a movie where someone witnesses a murder or holds them as they take their last breath without reliving that reality. Never again could she see a corpse on television (whether it is on the news or in a movie) without remembering the real sight and smell of a bloodied carcass lying in front of her on a blazing hot summer day. Regardless of the many ordeals she was assured to witness in the future, nothing would ever compare to the hopeless feeling she had as she looked that boy in the face and watched him die on the afternoon of June 11th, 2004.

Sadly, by the time she was sixteen she had become numb to the murders, drug busts, high school dropouts and illegitimate children floating about. It was just another veracity of living in the hood. By the time she graduated high school, she had witnessed the bloody aftermath of a robbery gone wrong as she drove home from school to see her neighbor across the street lying face down, shot to death in the front doorway for all the passersby's to see. Both he and his wife were killed in the gunfire leaving five children in the house alone without parents and scarred forever from witnessing both of their parents killed right in front of them. The oldest of the children was six and the youngest had just been born and brought home from the hospital two days prior. Jay had just gone over there the day before, to meet their new baby girl. In her neighborhood, it was inevitable that by the time a child reached adolescence, their views of the world were already taunted. To wake up and face another day wasn't counted as a gift but another curse to be lived out.

Battle Eleven

Step-Mother from Hell

"Jay, how would you feel about me marrying Angie, we've been dating for some time now and you've met her and her daughter's, Carmen and Castel, on several occasions. Carmen is actually your exact age and will be going to the same high school with you. So as my child, I want your opinion. As you know, I am now on my third marriage and if it doesn't work this time around then, I'm not meant to be in love." At age twelve, Jay could care less about whom her father married, after all, she did not have to live with them. She was more concerned with being in high school within the next year. "I don't care dad, as long as you like her, it doesn't matter what I or anyone else thinks," Jay says. However, if she knew then the detriment this woman and her two daughters were capable of, she would have warned her father of the mistake he was making.

December 17, 2006, a day Jay would never forget and would soon learn to regret, Curtis and Angie got married. Jay was extremely excited because it was the first time she had seen or been in her father's wedding. Though he had wed two times prior to his union with Angie, Jay had never been there to witness it. When Curtis married Jane, Jay's existence was not even being thought of. No one was made aware of his second wedding with Jill when Jay was seven years old; he went to New Orleans (Jill's hometown) for an *Alcoholics Anonymous* retreat and came back to Memphis with a wife. It was becoming apparent that Curtis had a void within himself in which he was searching to fulfill with women. Still, none of the women he chose could fill that empty space, only adding havoc to his life and to Jay's life as well. He continued searching for love in all the wrong places. He'd met Jane in the projects that his buddy delivered to and he'd met both Jill and Angie in his *Alcoholics Anonymous* meetings. Each of his partners (other than Jane, who got on drugs after him) faced the same issues of prior drug addiction and alcoholism that he did, which were obviously disaster-prone relationships from the start.

Nonetheless, he is in love (so he thinks). Now Angie, Jay, Carmel and Castel are all in the ladies holding area waiting for the ceremony to begin. Jay had been a flower girl in a number of weddings including her uncle Leon's when she was two and her aunt Grace's when she was five. But nothing topped being the flower girl in her dad's wedding (despite how age inappropriate being a flower girl was at the age of twelve). Jay marches down the aisle, handing flowers to the person sitting closet to the edge of the pew and starring at her father as he beams with joy. The next few hours passed and the wedding and reception had come and gone. Curtis and Angie's life together had just begun and the separation between Jay and her father was slowly about to unravel as well.

A couple of months after Curtis' union with Angie, Angie began to overstep her bounds as a stepmother. The signs were always there, they just went unnoticed for a period of time before becoming blatantly disrespectful. Until this point, Jay was indifferent about Angie (and most people), but after this day, Angie would remain on Jay's bad side. One Saturday afternoon, Jay was supposed to be spending time with her father as they would usually do on weekends after attending choir rehearsal with her grandmother, Lillian. However, this Saturday would be the day where Jay's unreserved detestation for Angie would begin.

To Jay's surprise, her father was not outside to pick her up, rather her stepmother Angie. Angie pulled up in the driveway, blew her horn and waived her hand out the car window. Thinking that maybe she was just there to bring her to her house where her father was, Jay shouted to Lillian, "I'm gone, Angie's here to take me to daddy." She got in the car with her, excited that she would be spending the next couple of hours with her dad. Little did she know Angie's plan was to get her alone so that she could begin her torment on young Jay's mind.

The conversation between them started off casually and within an instant turned sour. Angie begins her rant "Jay, there are going to be a few changes now that your father and I are married. Changes are good and will benefit everyone in the situation, so you have to be opened to change. First of all, it's not normal that a child lives with her grandparents rather than her parents and that has to change. So your father and I have had several conversations and upon our move into the new house, you will move in with us. And, to answer your questions before you ask, no you don't have a choice in the matter and yes you may visit your grandmothers but only when I say that you can.

I do know that you currently take dance classes and swimming lessons, sing in your youth choir, play basketball and volleyball at your school and are about to try out for the Memphis volleyball club team. You have no free time to do what you want to do; you are participating in all of these activities because your grandmother Brady is forcing you to do so. Therefore, you can choose one extra-curricular activity that you enjoy the most and we'll stick to that. Thirdly, I need to tell you how spoiled you are. You're grandmother Lillian cooks whatever you request to eat and Brady constantly buys you clothes and all this unnecessary junk that you clearly don't need. You have so much stuff you don't know what to do with it and giving a child that many options is overwhelming. So when you move in with us, you will no longer have that luxury. You will eat whatever I decide to cook because you are way too skinny, you look sickly, and we need to put some meat on those bones of yours. So, carbs are going to be your best friend. You will be bought the essentials for survival because no child should have as many options as you have been provided; it only leads to unrealistic ideals of the world. You will now go to the hair stylist that myself, Carmen and Castel go to because you need healthy and long hair, it is obvious that your hair is damaged and you need it to be revived. Lastly, I am going to have a conversation with both of your grandmothers because they need to understand that there are three of you now, not just one. You, Carmen and Castel are sisters now. You will act as sisters."

Jay was sitting there completely distraught at the conversation that was taking place, but she was always taught not to talk back to adults regardless of her disagreement with what was said and she abided by that rule (other than when she was talking to Brady or James). Therefore, she sat there silently with a look of disapproval and thoughts of lashing out on her mind. "Who does she think she is? I have lived with my grandparents Lillian and James for as long as I can remember, and I see Brady literally every day, sometimes a few times a day. There is no way that I would even consider living anywhere else.

My dad has been married before and he would never force me to even spend the night with them but especially not to live with him. Yes, my grandmother Brady has forced me to participate in all of the extra-curricular activities that I am involved in but I have actually learned to love all of them (with the exception of swimming; I hate water) and I don't want to give any of them up right now; I have become a pretty decent ballerina, I can swim like a fish (despite my hatred of it), I love to sing in the choir with my

99

grandma, Lillian, I enjoy playing basketball and my favorite sport to play is volleyball. In terms of me being spoiled; I know that is true, but what other choices are there. I am my dad's youngest and my mother's only child, I am also the youngest grandchild on both sides of my family in which I am being raised by my grandparents as an only child.

Grandma Lillian always told me that I didn't have to eat what I didn't want to eat; and rightfully so since I was allergic to a number of spices and seasonings. Even at school, if they were serving something I didn't like for lunch, I would just wait until I got home to eat. Angie must have been blind because being small was noticeably hereditary. My father was six feet four inches and weighed two hundred pounds, whereas my mother was five feet one inch and weighed one hundred and ten pounds. The heaviest Jane had been her entire life was when she was carrying me where she then weighted one hundred and twenty-one pounds. Curtis Jr. never weighed over two hundred pounds and he's taller than my dad and my sister Lea who just had her seventh child only weighs one hundred and fifty two pounds. Clearly, regardless of what I was fed, I wasn't going to be a very large girl, even well into my adulthood and I wasn't "sickly", just slim, she wants me to be a whopping three-hundred ponder like her I guess.

I have been going to the same hair stylist since I was five and I thought my hair was fine the way it was. And as far as I am concerned I have two sister, Lea (my biological sister) and Kenya (my second cousin who was the closest sisterhood I had), that's it. And regardless, if she just took a look around the neighborhood I lived in; it would be evident that a child growing up under these circumstances needs options. They need to be kept busy in order to stay out of trouble," Jay thought; conversing with herself.

After the twenty minute car ride to their house that would usually only take seven minutes, she finally saw her dad. He greeted Jay at the door and told her that he was heading to a friend's house to drop some maintenance equipment off and that he would be right back. Knowing that she didn't want to be around Angie or her two brats, she asked "Dad can I please go with you?" After agreeing to let her come along she asked her father to take her back home. "You just got over here, why do you want to go back home so soon," Curtis inquired. "I just want to go home please, or I can call grandma to come for me; either way, I don't want to be here" Jay responded irritably. Confused as to why Jay didn't want to spend the day with him and with slightly hurt feelings, he dropped his irritated daughter back off at her home.

She kissed her dad goodbye and rushed into the house heatedly. Lillian surprised that she was back after only being away for about thirty-five minutes asked her, "Why are you back so early?" Tears of anger spilled down her face as she began explaining all that Angie had just said to her. Lillian now infuriated asked, "Well, did you tell your father?" "No, I didn't want him to get upset, you know he has anger issues and he'd probably bash her face in with his fist if I told him that. He has to live with her and I don't want to be the cause of breaking up his home like I was with him and Jill's marriage. If he's happy, so am I. But my life shouldn't have to change. And if all these changes need to be implemented, it wasn't her place to have that conversation with me, that should have been left up to my father," Jay said to Lillian. "I agree with you child, and she deserves to have her face bashed in just like Jill deserved it, and one day you're going to have to have that conversation with your father," Lillian explained. Jay now imagining how upset her father would be with Angie if she told him the true reason why she wanted to come home, she then had a flashback of how her father's previous marriage to Jill had ended because of what she had told him about her.

Approximately five years prior to the conversation with Angie, a very similar situation arose and landed Jill (Curtis' ex-wife) in the hospital, and Curtis in jail. Jay remembers it was a warm spring Saturday morning and she and her stepmother at the time (Jill) were having a disagreement. Her father was gone and would be returning shortly to pick Jay up and get her ready for a birthday party that he was taking her to. Curtis had asked Jill to get Jay ready so that all he'd have to do is pick her up and take her to the party. However, she never went to the party. Jay had finally spent the night over her dad and Jill's house but she hadn't packed an overnight bag. Her father had pajamas, underwear, soap and a toothbrush for her so she didn't really have to bring anything over when she chose to spend the night. Yet, the night prior, Curtis washed her jeans and shirt so that she could wear that to the party the next day but to Jill (the diva), wearing the same clothes two days in a row was unacceptable.

That morning before he left to run errands, Curtis had washed and ironed Jay's outfit and hung it neatly in the closet for her to put on the next day. However, after putting the outfit on and going downstairs to the kitchen to wait for her dad to come back home, Jill caught a glimpse of her clothes and noticed that she had on the exact same outfit that she was wearing when she had arrived the previous night. Jill yelled out "Jay come here! What is wrong with you, I bought you an outfit months ago that you have never worn and it has been hanging in your closet for a while now. Take those filthy clothes off and go put on the outfit I bought. Ladies don't wear the same outfit within the same week," she demanded. "But Ms. Jill I don't like the outfit that you bought me, it doesn't fit right and my dad washed this outfit last night so it's not dirty," Jay responded. The quarrelling went back and forth until Jay was given a whipping and sat there until her father arrived. Once Curtis came through the door, he found Jay sitting at the bottom of the stairs in tears. He told her to come upstairs to his room and he locked the door to keep from being disturbed by Jill or Jill's kids.

After explaining what had transpired between her and her stepmother, Jill, Curtis simply said, "It's not that big of a deal and you can wear whatever you want as long as it is clean. And I'll kill her if she puts her hands on you again, especially if you've done nothing wrong." In that moment Jill barges into the room breaking the lock on the door screaming at Curtis about how he is undermining her authority as a mother figure and that Jay has to change clothes because she said so. Thirty minutes later, Jill was still following Curtis around the house yelling at him regarding her issues with Jay. He remained silent and attempted to distance himself from her in effort to deescalate the situation. Finally he tells Jay to go to the car as they are now preparing to leave. As Jay and Curtis are walking to the car, Jill follows them outside still shouting out words of profanity and name calling. She grabs her purse and throws it at him, followed by a branch that was lying at her feet when she walked outside; both items hitting him in the back of the head. Without saying a word, he picks her purse up from the ground and calmly walks back over to her. He reaches the purse out to her and as soon as she snatched it from his grip, he balled up his fist and hit her square in the face.

Completely knocked out, she falls to the ground with her eyes rolled to the back of her head and lying there unresponsive. Jay had never seen anyone get hit that hard before nor had she seen anyone fall to the ground so bluntly. Jill's teenage daughter ran out of the house as she seen her mother lying unconscious on the pavement. She then grabbed the phone and called the police. Curtis demanded that Jay get in the car and the two of them sped off into the distance. Jay began to sob as she knew her dad was going to jail. "It's all my fault dad, if I had just put on the other clothes, you wouldn't have hit her and now you're going to jail" she cried out. "Nope, this is not your fault at all, she's a drama queen and she hit me first so she got what she deserved. Listen to me Jay; I want you to always remember this. You never put your hands on a man or throw objects at him if you can't take his retaliation, because man or not, he is a human being. When you get upset, you remove yourself from the situation because not every man believes that a man should never hit a woman. I don't believe that. If you hit me, regardless of if you're a man or a woman, I am going to hit your ass back with all my strength guaranteed. If you want to face a man and act like you're stronger than him, irritating him and pushing his buttons, then you get what's coming to you," Curtis explained to Jay.

Though that was a lesson Jay would always take with her, she was still very distressed because she knew that her dad was going to jail all over the fact that she didn't want to wear a different outfit. Curtis explained to Jay upon their arrival at Lillian's house that he was going to turn himself in to the police. "I made a decision to retaliate and I must face the consequence of my action, I just wanted to make sure that I got you back home first. I'll be out in a couple of days and I'll talk to you later, and don't tell my mama, just go in there and act normal." Of course she did just the opposite of what she was told; she walked in and screamed for Lillian "Grandma, my daddy's going to jail." She simply responded "Ughh, my damn child" as she nodded her head and continued frying her chicken and asked Jay to spare the details.

Curtis was released that same night because Jill had not pressed any charges against him but shortly afterwards, he filed for a divorce. Later in life, Jay would come to realize that she was not the cause of their divorce and that situation was simply the last straw for her father, but she still blamed herself. Nevertheless, as that altercation replayed in her head, she knew that the same situation was likely to occur if she told her dad about the inappropriate conversation Angie had just had with her. So, she decided to keep it to herself and asked her grandmother to do the same. That conversation with Angie was only the beginning of the torment she caused with Jay and is also where the hatred of her surfaced.

Jay's self-esteem had already been discolored from the lack of a relationship with her mother. She felt dejected and worthless because she always thought that those were the feelings of her mother towards her. "It had to be for your own mother to give you away like a raggedy piece of fabric left behind in a thrift store," she thought. There was no way that she would choose to be further suppressed by the slander of a woman that she could care less about. She felt badly enough about herself without adding the debasing comments about her hair, body image and personality to her thoughts. Enough was enough.

Battle Twelve

Forced Rebellion

A few weekends following the dreadful conversation with her step-mother, Jay was forced to go to the final *Destiny's Child* concert with Angie, her step-sisters and her step-sister's best friends. It was obvious at this point that Angie was trying to force Jay and her two daughters to have a relationship. Jay sat there with them completely uninterested and hoping that the concert would soon end (though it had just began). As she sits in the nosebleed seats in the Memphis convention center right between Angie and Carmen, she becomes a bit uneasy by what she is hearing. "She is so lame; why is she so skinny and her teeth are so big? Her teeth are larger than her body. Does she ever eat? With those teeth, she could chew through a brick? But how does it feel to have a new sister?" Carmen's friend asks as Carmen responds snipingly, that's not my sister. Maybe they thought that they couldn't be heard over the music, or maybe they were trying to elicit a response. Either way, Jay was extremely uncomfortable and wanted nothing to do with any of them other than taking them both by the hair and smashing their faces together repeatedly until her arms got tired. Angie simply said to the girls, "Ya'll be nice." Jay sat there in total annoyance trying her best not to lash out at her father's stepchildren and wife because knowing how violent she could get; her new longing was to punch each of them in the face hard enough for them to fall over the nosebleed balcony rail.

Jay was never a Beyoncé or Destiny's Child fan; she didn't enjoy concerts because of the large number of people invading her personal space and hearing people scream like the world is ending over other people. "They're just people." Jay thought. Also, she was not fond of any of the people she was with, and she was forced to be there listening to people make fun of her for the entirety of the concert. Moments like this were additive components to the trust issues she already had. From her infancy up to this point people in general but especially the adults, continued to prove to her that they were not deserving of her trust. She had very few friends because she stayed to herself even in the midst of a social environment and the three friends she did have (one from church and two from school) were very similar to her. She only interacted with people if she had to and even those who knew her well, thought that she was either a mean girl or all about her business; no fun. In actuality, she was simply reserved, because her situation had taught her to be that way. First, she had inherited her father's temper and it didn't take much for that beast to be unleashed. Secondly, she didn't want people becoming close enough to her to hurt her and instances such as this demonstrated to Jay that people were not trustworthy. Though this concert situation could be written off as not that large of a problem, it was an act that stuck with Jay. Her trust for Angie and both of her daughters were non-existent but surprisingly, her trust for her father for allowing it was beginning to dwindle as well.

At first, she didn't quite understand why the relationship between she and her father was becoming so distant, but she knew that parts of him were changing. Jay had always had a very open and close relationship with her father, but his union with Angie was definitely creating a rift. Angie's demise had begun as she had started to implement the changes she'd spoken of toward Jay in the car that Saturday afternoon. Shortly thereafter, Jay was forced to do everything with Angie and her daughters. Every two weeks she was made to go the same hairstylist as Carmen and Castel, she went to their parties, family gatherings and was even forced to spend Christmas day with them that year, and it was the worst.

That Christmas, instead of waking up to her family and many presents, she woke up to a Christmas card from Angie and her dad with fifty bucks stuffed into it. She was very grateful because she knew that there were so many other children that would not be receiving anything for Christmas. However, she wanted to be with her own family, especially her Aunt Grace who only had long visits at Christmas. Instead, she spent the entire day with them. They went from house to house, and she was sitting in the farthest corner away from everyone and watching as Carmen and Castel were showered with gifts and money. She knew at that point that Angie's conversation had with her grandmothers about how "there were now three children instead of one" was not had with her own side of the family. Surely, if Angie had requested that her family treat Jay the way that they had been used to treating Carmen and Castel, Jay wouldn't be sitting there awkwardly wandering if anyone even noticed she was there.

Jay was just sedentary, quietly taking notes of it all. She was not surprised that she was being treated like the step-child because to Angie and her daughter's she was. What was so astonishing was that she was being treated like that by her father too. "Does he not see what's going on here? Look at all the stuff Carmen and Castel received and all I got was a bunch of damn cards. And, instead of him taking up for me, he sits there cuddled up with Angie smiling and grinning like a chest cat; not even noticing that I am over here in a corner alone and wanting to be with my real family. I just want to go home, I have family that loves me too," Jay thinks to herself. The final straw was soon to be pulled and from that moment forth, Angie and her daughters were just a set of people that meant nothing more to her than a stranger on the street. Actually, Jay thought more of a stranger than her own step-mother and step-sisters, at least strangers get the benefit of the doubt of being decent people. But Jay would've bought Angie and her daughters three first class one-way tickets to hell if she could have.

Following the Christmas incident Jay was again forced to go to Angie's family reunion that was being hosted in Birmingham, Alabama despite her numerous attempts to tell her father she did not want to attend. Though initially, Jay was downright dismayed by being forced to go, there were some aspects that turned out to be quite enjoyable (though none of them included being with her dad, Angie or her step-sisters). While on the family bus to Birmingham, she was sitting with another girl that she instantly connected with. Neither of them wanted to be there and they were both loners. So for the entirety of the trip, they were loners together. They played *knock knock* on the hotel room doors of Angie's family members, went swimming together and spent every bit of leisure time away from the family and talking about the things that interested young girls. Another pleasant event was the day the family saw the historical sites of Birmingham. Jay's personal favorite was being on the grounds of the Birmingham bombing of the 16th Street Baptist Church where the four little girls were killed in 1963. She remembered being taught about this incident primarily by her grandmother Lillian and then again during black history month at her church. Notwithstanding the fact that she couldn't go into the historical site with the rest of the family because of the severe cramps she was experiencing because of her "aunt flow" and walking for long distances was out of the question, it was an educational experience. So, she sat on the bus in admiration of even being able to view and stand on the grounds of the historical cite.

The family reunion was coming to an end and surprisingly everything had gone well up until the final night because she was spending as little time as possible with the people she had come with. Angie was in charge of picking everyone's outfits for the formal night ball and no one had seen their dresses for the evening but as expected, Jay was completely embarrassed. The theme of the evening was red, white and blue, assimilating the American flag.

Carmen was given a pretty bright red cocktail dress that flowed loosely over her developing curves with a sheer lace covering the bottom half of the dress and lengthened right at her knee. Castel wore a sleeveless fitted royal blue dress with ruffles gathering from the waist down and came right above the knee. Jay's dress was a grey back-out with sparkles that came to the middle of her thigh and a few sizes too large. The dress was meant for someone with a "B" or "C" cup sized breast of which Jay's breast were the size of mosquito bites at the time. After Jay put the dress on, Angie gathered the back of the dress and pinned it with a grey flowered pin to keep from exposing Jay's smooth chest. As they entered the ballroom for the final event, everyone complimented Angie, Carmen and Castel's attire. Even Curtis was getting complimented on his grey suite. Jay however, was being acknowledged with "Oh hey, how are you tonight?" or "Have you enjoyed yourself on the trip?" Once again, she sat at the table for the rest of the night, not wanting to show the awful dress she was wearing. She was humiliated. She decided that upon their return to Memphis, she would have to have a blunt conversation with her father.

Father's day of that year, she bought a card for Curtis, but instead of filling it with sweet words boasting about how good of a father he was to her like she did every year, she did just the opposite. She knew that having a verbal conversation with her father was not going to be successful as she had already tried that on several occasions. After the family reunion, she decided that she would be persistent as she would call him every night until he listened to her issues with him. She never wanted to say anything negative directly aimed at his wife or her daughters; she just wanted her life and their relationship to go back to how it once was. The last phone call she attempted ended with her father Curtis telling her to stop calling him about the same issues and hung up in her face. So this time around, she decided to communicate with him the best way she knew how; through writing. The father's day letter said the following:

Dear Dad,

>*We have become very distant over the past couple of years, and though I try to act as if I don't know the cause, I do understand why. I am not the kind of daughter that would sabotage your relationship nor am I the type that gets jealous of the fact that it didn't work out with my mom. No one has a relationship with my mom, so I'm definitely not upset about that. When you asked me years ago whether or not I cared if you and Angie got married, I told you that I didn't as long as you were happy. That is still true today. I do not care about your relationships or marriage because you're the person that has to deal with them. I just want to be left alone. I was happy before they came in the picture and I am still happy whenever I am not forced to be around them. They treat me horribly*

111

and at this point you have realized it and chosen to turn a blind eye to it.

I've always felt like I wasn't good enough to my mom but it sucks that I'm starting to feel like I'm not good enough to you either. I feel inadequate every time I am forced to go to her hairstylist; you have even told me that I am going there so that my hair can be healthy; my hair was fine before she started sticking her hands in it. And if you really know me, you'd know that I could care less about having long European looking hair flowing down my back. I am black and I like my black hair just the way it is. I have edges, I have no bald spots, I have no split ends and the growth of my hair has not been stunted, I just keep it cut at a certain length. Too much hair is too much responsibility that I don't care to have.

Her girls can get whatever style they like whereas I'm forced to get Shirley Temple curls that make me look like a ridiculous three year old. That is the reason I comb it out after every visit and put it back into a ponytail or head wrap. Every aspect of my life is being compared to Carmen and Castel. I am not them and they are not me. We have different tastes in everything from hairstyles to music, Carmen and I have been going to the same middle school for two years now and no one even knows we're step-sisters (which is completely fine with me). You have never cared about things like my hair, clothes or my sets of friends and up until now, you have never interfered with or undermined grandma's parenting; because she, James and

Brady are raising me with assistance from you and Aunt Grace. Why does it now matter to you? And why is Angie so obsessed with my life, she has two girls already whose lives she can control? I understand that you want us to be one big happy family, but we're not. I hate being around them and Angie will not make me into another Carmen or Castel; I promise I will rebel with all my strength.

Dad, I am the only one of your children that has a relationship with you and now even our relationship is compromised. You told me to stop calling and so I have. This is my final attempt to express to you how I feel and I hope that you are receptive. As always, I love you and Happy Father's Day since I'm sure neither of my siblings Curtis Jr. or Lea has told you that today.

Love,
Jay

He'd finally gotten the message that Jay had been trying her hardest to convey. After being made aware of his daughter's frustrations for the last time, that conversation didn't have to be had again until Jay's adulthood, where Angie crossed her yet again and they faced each other woman to woman in a driveway with no one else around. Angie at that point made it clear that she did not care for Jay, and Jay being a woman then made it a point to let her know that she didn't give a damn.

Close to eight years later, Curtis had finally gotten enough of Angie majorly due to how she treated his children. He began to see Angie for the bitch that she truly was. Though Carmen and

113

Castell had a great relationship with their biological father, Curtis had a hand in raising them as well. After all, they lived under his roof; he bought their necessities, which in many cases was more than he had done for his own children as he had raised none of his children. Nonetheless, Curtis Jr. wasn't informed about his father's marriage to Angie until five or so years after their union. Lea had only visited their home once out of the ten years they were married, and anytime Jay went over there, it was because she was forced to do so.

Angie was the type of woman who became jealous about anything and anyone, including Curtis' children. If it didn't involve her or her two girls, she forbade it. Though Curtis had never had a close relationship with his son, they definitely couldn't build a relationship with Angie's jealous spirit contaminating their home. Curtis had become fed up with never being able to go out with his friends without his wife, and if he did go, she went as well and the entire time she would be there she acted miserably (despite her begging to come with or giving Curtis an ultimatum if he told her "no, she could not come"). Lea had expressed to Jay how she wanted her children to have a relationship with their grandfather but he never has the time. Upon that conversation, that was the first time Jay had ever seen her big sister cry. Jay didn't think her sister Lea knew how to cry, she was so tough all the time. Nonetheless, while he was raising Angie's children and serving as a second father to them, he wasn't even being a father or grandfather to his own and none of his own children (other than Curtis Jr. who had never met her) liked or pretended to like Angie.

The final straw for him occurred upon him being informed of the conversation Angie had decided to have with Jay without him being present that left Jay giving her father an ultimatum too.

114

The ultimatum was not that he leave Angie or he loses her as a daughter, but it was to inform him that as an adult now, she had made a decision not to ever step foot in that house again as long as Angie was alive. Angie had crossed the line for the last time and she would forever regret what she said to Jay that ultimately got Curtis to file for divorce and leave her and her brats behind.

One August afternoon, Angie called Jay to come over to her father's house as she had a gift for her. This was already extremely awkward as Jay didn't want anything Angie had to offer, she still did as she was asked and came by her father's home. Upon arriving, Angie was waiting in the driveway for Jay with a gift bag. Inside the bag was *Love* by Toni Morrison; a book that she had previously asked to borrow but Angie had refused. Jay accepted the book and thanked Angie. Angie then began to expel the true reason why she wanted Jay to come over. Jay quickly realized what Angie was doing as she didn't invite her inside the house, but instead met her at the driveway so that her father (who didn't even know Jay was there) couldn't overhear what she was about to say to Jay.

Angie began "Jay, first things first. You don't take a married man anywhere without first informing his wife about your plans (as she was referring to Jay taking Curtis out to dinner for Father's day earlier that year). There are a few things that you need to understand. Secondly, I am his wife. In our union, there is God, there is me and then there is you and his other kids. I could care less if you, your grandmother Brady, your grandmother Lillian, your aunt Grace or anyone else dislike me because Curtis comes home to me every night, not ya'll. He sleeps with me not you. He chose me, that's right, I am his choice (which everyone knew wasn't true as she had had her eyes on Curtis while he was still married to Jill, once he and Jill got divorced, she pushed and pushed until Curtis accepted her advances). You are his child and obviously you need to be made aware of your place. I am not into the ass-kissing business, so let's just be real. You are an adult now and its okay for you not to like me, I don't really care because as you can see, I'm not going anywhere." Jay's response was simply "Go straight to hell bitch" before getting in her car and leaving Angie looking stupid in the driveway. In that moment, all the manners and respect for elders she was brought up with was thrown out of the window. Jay had to remove herself quickly because there wasn't too much more talking Jay was going to do before she went to her car, got her blade and sliced Angie's fat ass face into as many pieces as she could or just ran her over with her car, right there in the driveway (even though her car would've been too low to the ground to completely run her over as big as Angie was).

Jay eventually decided to tell her father about the incident, not to cause confusion in his relationship, but because she thought that she at least owed him an explanation to his inquires as to why she had completely stopped visiting him at his home. She told him in detail what was said (of which he was very surprised because he didn't even know that Angie had called Jay nor was he made aware that she had come over to his house that day because she didn't go inside, she left). Jay told him that if he wanted to see her, they'd either have to meet somewhere or he could come to where she was. But as a then twenty-one year old with her own means of transportation, she wasn't going anywhere she felt unwelcomed or didn't want to be. Curtis told Jay that he would discuss it with Angie because he wanted answers, Jay didn't really care because she was through with Angie, and Jay didn't need answers or an apology from her. All she needed was to be left the hell alone, for good.

Curtis had a conversation with Angie a few days later of which she denied everything, including giving Jay that book (which was her excuse to get Jay over to their house in the first place). However, Jay had given the book to Curtis and had asked him to return it to her. On the very first page, Angie wrote the same little phrase she wrote on every birthday card reading: *With Peace & Love, Angie.* When Curtis showed her her own signature in the book that she had denied ever giving to Jay, she realized how badly she had screwed up as she was caught dead in the center of a lie. That along with her not paying any of the bills other than her cell phone bill and taking money from Curtis' account for her two daughters to be in a cotillion without even discussing it with him, landed her signing that pretty signature on the lines of her and Curtis' divorce papers. Though that was not Jay's goal, she was finally rid of Angie and those two little pigs of hers too. Unfortunately, that didn't happen until later in life, but for now back to the present; Jay is headed off to high school.

Battle Thirteen

High School - Love at Third Sight

It was the first day of high school and Jay had been well prepared for this moment. For the second time in her life, she walked into school by herself. Thrilled to finally be in high school (though the high school and middle school were connected; the middle school was downstairs and all of the high school classes were upstairs) she is greeted in the freshman hall by her two best friends of several years, Mitch and Morgan. "How does it feel to be in high school?" Morgan screams. Jay responds agitatedly, "Ugh why are you so loud? Other than my grandmother not walking me to class, and finally being upstairs it doesn't feel much different. I'm surrounded by the same faces I was with all through elementary and middle school. But I am excited because I'm one step closer to being an adult then I can get the hell out of Memphis." The two girls stood at their lockers talking and rolling up their "catholic school girl skirts" as Mitch watched in amusement until the bell rang. He and Morgan jetted off to class leaving Jay in the hall still trying to organize her first period books and materials. "This is probably why Brady didn't trust me to walk to class alone all these years, had she been here I know I wouldn't have been late to first period, nor would my skirt be rolled up, but hey I look cute," Jay thinks.

All of a sudden, every book that she had placed in the locker began tumbling down at her feet. Now knowing that she is going to be even later, she sighs loudly and begins cussing the books as if they could hear what she was saying. She was so upset by her disorganization that she didn't even notice a young man was kneeling and picking up her books for her. After seeing the kind act that he was doing, she stands there and watches him as he struggles to put each book back into her locker. Finally being able to close her locker, she says, "Thank you, I appreciate that." Then, Jay turns to walk away trying to avoid conversation. She hears him call her back, "Wait, what's your name?" he asks as she continues walking away and without stopping or turning around responds sharply, "Why?" "Well, my name is Xavier, I'm new here, and I am really not sure about where I am going. May I walk with you?" Wanting him to stop talking she says hurriedly, "Sure" as she continues to walk away. He catches up with her and they walk together down the freshmen hallway. After looking over each other's class schedules, they realize that they have all of the same classes except for first period. And even though they weren't in first period together, that one class was still right next door to hers. Xavier enthusiastically says "Looks like we'll be together all day," Jay responds mordantly, "Oh, joy." She then walks off dramatically to her class as he shouts out to her "See you in fifty minutes."

She walks into her first period class and sits in the front row next to Mitch and Morgan and begins to curse them both for leaving her in the hallway alone. After venting about how upset they'd made her, she begins to tell them about the new guy she'd just met in the hall and how he had helped her out without her asking or wanting him to. Morgan instantly gets defensive, "Well do you like him?" she questions angrily. As best friends, Morgan and Jay were very territorial about each other because allowing a prospect in the other one's life would lessen the time they had together as best friends. Mitch wasn't fond of either of them having prospects as it was his lifelong dream to marry either one or both of them if polygamy were legal by the time they would be old enough to marry. However, Jay was uninterested, at that time as she explains, "Guys don't worry; I don't even know if he likes me, he was just being a gentlemen. Actually, Mitch could use a few pointers. You should have been walking both of us to class, but instead you left me in the hallway as I struggled to get my life together. But, he may even have a girlfriend; he was just talking to me guys. I didn't even get a good look at him; I just wanted to be left unbothered." Morgan then spats out jokingly, "Yeah right, since when do guys with girlfriends pick up another girl's books and chase her down just to walk her to class? Are you really that naïve that you can't even tell when a guy likes you?" Jay responds, "Um yes, no guy has ever liked me before, other than Mitch. He doesn't count: hell, he likes every girl he sees." Mitch then refuting the claims and sparks up a conversation about why supposedly no one liked Jay before of which would be a conversation that she'd rewind often in her head even later in life as an adult.

"It's not that guys dislike you or are not attracted to you Jay; you're just hard to connect with. You only associate with certain people and even those people are often masked from your truth most of the time. People who don't know you simply write you off as mean or stuck up and you've accepted those connotations because you want to be alone anyways. But "alone" is a lonely life Jay. Besides, Morgan and me here at school and Amber at your church, you have no friends; choosing not to let anyone completely in, not even us. And sure, you're okay with that now but as you become older, you're going to need someone. Your independence is very attractive but very offsetting at the same time. When your name comes up in conversation with other guys, they constantly overlook you because of your attitude. In their eyes, you don't care about anyone but yourself, and you're definitely not the most approachable person. Your true friends know that you can be difficult at times, but you have the purist heart of anyone I've ever met. For example, when I met you in fifth grade, I was being bullied by some guy, and you defended me. Later when I showed my gratitude for your actions, you simply said "I don't care about you. I didn't do it for you. I just don't like the guy that was bothering you. So any excuse I get to punch him in the face or push him down a flight of stairs, I'll do it." That wasn't the nicest thing to say but regardless of why you did it, I felt safe around you and have clung closely to you ever since. When Morgan introduced herself to us in middle school, your response was "I don't care what your name is. Why are you talking to me?" "Now, two years later she is your best friend." Morgan chimed in and changed the subject back to Xavier. "Well, I'll find out whether he has a girlfriend or not" as Jay then says "I'd rather you not, because I really don't care."

They had been dialoging in the front row for the entirety of the class as no one was paying attention to the Spanish teacher, Ms. Hopkins. She had finally given up because all the conversations floating around the classroom seemed to be far more important to the students than this introductory Spanish class. Hell, she could barely speak Spanish herself so that class was simply a fellowship hall for the students and time for the teacher to browse the internet. Finally, the bell rings and everyone hurries out of the classroom to gather for the daily convocation in the auditorium. Luckily, Jay doesn't see Xavier in the hallway as she heads to the auditorium with Mitch and Morgan in her ear, "Where is he, I don't see any new guys." They ask. They get to the full auditorium and find three empty seats that they rush to occupy before anyone else does. Just as they sit, Jay realizes that she has sat directly behind Xavier. She tries not to bring attention to him as she doesn't want Morgan to say anything embarrassing. However, Morgan had already detected that this was a guy that she didn't know; there were only a few new students so this had to be him.

There were only three hundred students in the entire school and thirty-seven in their class of which majority of them had gone to the same elementary and middle school. Hence, everyone knew each other pretty well. "Excuse me, hey you, is your name Xavier?" Morgan asked as he responded, "Yes." Jay puts her chin to her chest with awkwardness. "Well, I'm Morgan and this is Mitch, we're Jay's best friends and clearly you two have already met. But, inquiring minds want to know if you have a girlfriend?" Xavier blushingly answers "No, I do not. Does she have a boyfriend, since you're her mouthpiece?" They are then shushed by Sister Agnes as convocation had begun.

Following the assembly, Jay rushed out before everyone trying to avoid Mitch, Morgan and especially Xavier. The bell had rung for everyone to be dismissed to second period. Jay was purposefully late to this class in hopes that class would already be in session leaving no time to chat. To her surprise, when she walked in the gymnasium for her physical education class, everyone (other than Xavier) was in his/her clique and talking amongst themselves on the bleachers. "Well look who disappeared for all of twenty minutes and finally decided to show up to class"! Mitch hollers out across the gym. Ignoring him and not wanting to be bothered with anyone, Jay sits on the opposite side of the gym away from everyone. Xavier waits awhile before mustering up the nerves to approach her again. Jay sees him walking toward her and begins laughing to herself thinking, "The last time someone bothered me when I was intentionally distancing myself from him was kicked in the face. I hope he doesn't say anything stupid, I don't mind kicking him in the face too."

"Hi Jay, how was your first period?" he asked. "It was fine. How was yours?" she responds as she has decided to actually entertain his conversation. Xavier goes on to expound on how excited he was to be in his Spanish class and how engulfed he was in the language. As he was rambling on and on, Jay began to notice how attractive he actually was. He was tall, muscularly built, and had light caramel skin with hazel brown eyes. He was obviously quite intelligent because new enrollees attending the private institution had to have maintained a 3.2 grade point average as well and had to pass the school's board entry exams. Though it was the third time she had seen him that day, it was the first time that she had ever been enticed by anyone through physical attractiveness. She was oblivious to the feelings of romantic love, but with him she learned quickly and deeply the impact of the four letter word.

Battle Fourteen

Softer Sides to Rough Edges

Everyone Jay encountered was beginning to notice the changes happening with her including her classmates, teachers, friends and definitely her grandmothers, Brady and Lillian. Her entire demeanor was shifting. She was not as reserved; she laughed often and was much more pleasant to be around. Though Morgan and Mitch were primarily against Xavier entering into their friend group, the change he was affecting in Jay was irrefutable. Having him around made everyone involved with Jay much happier, except for one person, her grandmother Brady. Brady had always been extremely hard on Jay and all of her grandchildren. To Jay, Brady was like an insect repellent attempting to kill anything that had to do with boys or bliss.

Nonetheless, Jay was more excited to go to school than she had ever been before. To have someone (other than her friends and family that had no choice but to deal with her) admire her and take a liking to her was unbeknownst up until that point. She and Xavier sat next to each other in every class, during lunch and quickly became an item in the eyes of their peers. Though the time seemed to disappear when they were around each other, Jay's affection for Xavier was still a long process. Sure, she liked him profoundly and imagined a future with him as she would day dream, but her past trust issues ran deeply into the cusps of her unconsciousness. Xavier wanted so badly for her to trust him wholeheartedly and to be present in her times of distress. But Jay didn't know how to dissemble the brick wall that had guarded her heart since her early childhood. However, the change remained evident as he was the only person thus far that she was willing to try for.

Jay and Xavier had a connection where very little needed to be verbalized with their feelings toward each other. They knew that they enjoyed each other and they had a number of things in common, which sparked even more of an attraction. Xavier was originally from Chicago but had relocated to Holly Springs, Mississippi with his grandmother, mother, step-father and two younger siblings. Though his younger siblings lived with their mother, Xavier stayed with his grandmother because he and his mother's relationship was extremely tainted. He also did not get along with his step-father or younger siblings. Like so many African-American males; he had no recollection of ever meeting his biological father. His mother had always favored his younger siblings over him because of who their father was as she would explicitly express her favoritism to each of her children. However, Xavier's constant mission was to prove himself worthy of her approval and love. His and Jay's lives mirrored each other. They faced the same battle of insecurities daily which would eventually be their downfall. But the love they grew for each other was very much worth the journey they traveled.

One Thursday night well into their rapport of friendship, Xavier confided in Jay some of his deepest insecurities and finally conjured up the courage to officially ask her to be his companion over the phone. "Hey, Jay I hope I'm not calling too late but I just needed to talk to you and couldn't wait to see you at school tomorrow," Xavier explained. Jay responded worriedly, "Is everything okay?" She immediately knew something was bothering him because they never talked via phone. Because of their academic and athletics consisting of football practice, weight lifting, volleyball and basketball practice, there was usually only time to shower, eat, do homework and sleep after all of their activities. Xavier then takes the necessary steps to opening Jay's

125

heart for the first time. He professes, "We've been friends for a year or so now and I know that in the grander scheme of things, that is not a long time but you are the only person I have ever met that understands me completely. I know it's probably very cowardly to ask over the phone but every time I think of approaching you at school, I get tangled in a net of nervousness. I would like to ask you to be my girlfriend." Jay amused by the anxiety in his voice replies, "Yes." So it became official, Thursday, September 6th 2007, Jay was unleashed from her shell of seclusion and entered into a relationship that would guide her into womanhood.

Shortly thereafter, they became the most lovable yet hated couple in the high school. Where one was spotted, the other would be two steps behind. They won cutest couple of the year that year and every year for two years to follow; being featured in the school yearbook. Xavier was a star football player, and Jay went on to pursue volleyball full time with her high school as well as a traveling team for the city of Memphis. This all occurred after getting kicked off of the basketball team for a gruesome technical foul. While in the company of one another, their softer sides were unveiled. However, they both still struggled with being a little rough around the edges in terms of their temperaments. Xavier was feared by many of his classmates because of his large physique and short fused temper, whereas Jay was dreaded because of her blasé attitude but vengeful nature when pushed too far.

One day, in between one of their classes, Jay's overprotective boyfriend stood guard from afar as Jay entered the ladies restroom. The bell had just rang and the hallway was clear but upon her exiting the restroom, there was a guy (Billy) there greeting her. "Hi Jay, how are you? You look so good today baby," he probed. Billy was one of the guys she had known for years and used to always make fun of her and Mitch. She was not flattered by the compliment and ignored it because she looked the same every day because they wore uniforms; she continued walking pass him. "I know you hear me talking to you, you think that because you have a boyfriend now that you're not a skinny, bucktoothed bitch anymore." She turned back around to kick him in his groin as she would do to any guy that offended her, but he had already taken off in a full sprint down the hallway knowing exactly what her retaliation would be.

Xavier saw her coming and ran to his seat before she noticed him. She entered her fourth period art class angrily and sat in her normal spot as Xavier asked her why she was so upset. Not knowing that Xavier was standing outside the classroom the entire time and had witnessed the full encounter, she answers "Nothing, just drop it." He did as she requested for the time being but was thinking of the appropriate retaliation for the boy that had disrespected and upset his girlfriend. Later that day, after school Xavier walked Jay to the gym where her basketball game was being held and where her grandmother Brady was waiting for the game to begin. "Good afternoon, Ms. Brady," Xavier said as Brady gave him the stare of death howling out, "Let her hand go, and get to where you're supposed to be boy!" Jay ignoring how rude her grandmother was being, simply walks pass her to the locker room to change into her basketball gear.

Xavier and Mitch meet up outside of the boys football locker room as Xavier slightly explains to Mitch what was about to unfold. "Now that Jay is not with me, I have some business to handle. Football practice starts in thirty minutes, and I need a favor. After everyone gets changed and heads out to the yard, I am going to have a very private conversation with Billy about an issue I have with him. All I need from you is to stand at the locker room door and watch out for me. If you see coach coming just knock on the door. Can you do that for me man?" Xavier asked. Mitch replies, "Sure, but tell me the full story. What did he do and if you just want to talk with him then why do you need me to guard the door?" Xavier spats back irately, "Just do it. Mitch, you ask way too many damn questions. Just know that something happened earlier today that I do not approve of and I am not one to put on a show. I handle my business in private. Billy is known as this hyper-arrogant guy that feels like he can say and do whatever he wants. Well, I think it's time for him to be brought back down to earth. Just have my back on this. Thanks man."

The boys go in to the locker room and change which is their usual routine while Xavier begins to enact his plan. He walks over to Billy and says, "Hey man, stick around for a minute, I need a little advice about something and it's kind of private." "Sure man," Billy responds, completely unaware of how badly he was about to regret what he had said to Jay earlier that day. As everyone leaves the locker room and heads out to the field leaving the two of them alone, Mitch goes and stands on the outside of the door and does his best to hear what was being said. Xavier then looks Billy in the eyes and asked, "What did you say to Jay earlier today in the hallway?" The moment that he noticed Billy was about to lie, without warning, Xavier punched him in the mouth knocking several of his teeth out and continued hitting him until he was bloodied on the floor. Mitch now hearing screams from inside the locker room enters to see Xavier shoving Billy into one of the full length lockers. Mitch grabs him frantically asking "Man, what are you doing? I can't believe you got me involved in this mess. We're all going to get expelled." Xavier responds dispassionately,

"No, we're not. Nobody's going to find out." Mitch then shouting out, "How are you going to hide this? He's missing three teeth and covered in blood!" Xavier still unbothered says, "As far as I'm concerned I tackled him and knocked his teeth out." He looks to Billy and warns him that if he said anything, there would be a lot more beatings lined up for him in the future. Mitch then pulls Billy from the locker; Billy changed his shirt and they all three walked out on the field with their helmets on and began to practice. Shortly into practice, Xavier tackles Billy, knocking the guarder out of his mouth and the wind from his body. Billy was known by his peers as the school bully and a pretty boy. Billy was the guy that Jay kicked down the stairs after she witnessed him push Mitch onto the floor for about the fourth time that day in elementary school. However, that day, his evilness was matched by Xavier's prowess. Billy was no longer the school bully, nor the pretty boy.

Inside the gymnasium, Jay was fighting another battle. She was the point guard of the junior varsity basketball team at the time and throughout the entire game, the injustices she was experiencing as a player began to take a toll on her temper. Here they were, all black girls team heading to the championships, and this all white team is losing badly. If Jay's team won this game and the following two games, they'd be headed to Nashville to compete in the Tennessee National High school Championship. The referee had been ignoring all of the jabs to the stomach, trip and falls, and racial slurs that had been shouted out to her as she had done her best to not retaliate while on the court. During half-time, her coach and the parents instructed her to just keep a cool head. Though the other player's actions were clearly visual, Jay was told to just keep playing. However, Jay didn't take too kindly to being called out of her name and definitely not thrusted in the

129

torso every time she was on defense. The last straw was pulled in the fourth quarter.

Jay's team was leading by at least seven points and there was only two minutes left in the game. Jay now on offense and with the ball in her hand was blatantly elbowed in the face, to the point that blood began to trickle off of her lip. She stops dribbling, looks to the referee as he says absolutely nothing. In that moment, she chose to beat this girl's face into her skull until she was covered in blood. She passed the ball to her teammate and launched at the girl. All within two milliseconds Jay had grabbed her blonde ponytail and swiftly wrapped it around her left wrist to get a sturdy grip on the girls head; she then began bashing her face in with quick and hard jabs with her right fist as the referee stood over them screaming and waving his hands, "Technical foul, tech, tech, tech!" Jay's coach rushes out to the floor to grab Jay but it took the coach and two teammates to halt the grip that Jay had on the girl's head. Brady just shook her head from the bleachers and gathered their belongings as she knew that they would need to leave now.

She and the coach gathered in the locker room to discuss the altercation that had taken place. The coach began to lecture her about how appalled he was at her behavior and how she'd allowed her anger to cloud her judgment. However her body language depicted her true feelings toward her coach and his opinion of her behavior. He told her that due to the circumstances leading up to her action, that she would not be suspended or expelled from school though that was the regular procedure for students who are involved in physical altercations while at a school function and on the institution's premises. However, she would not be able to finish out the season with her team.

He was able to make all of the decisions because of the number of titles he held. Coach Green was the female basketball coach, one of the three football coaches, religion and advanced placement English teacher and most substantially, the dean of students. He asked her to wash her jersey and return it the following day. Nonchalantly, Jay took her jersey off right in front of him, standing in her camisole and compression shorts that she wore underneath her jersey. She handed it to him. "You can wash it yourself," she stated as she put on her favorite sweat pants and walked out of the locker room.

She walked calmly out of the locker room as the security guard escorted her and Brady to their car in fear that the opposing team would retaliate or that she would again lounge after the opposing team's point guard. Either way, Jay was carefree. The only thing she was exultant about was that she had not been suspended or expelled from school. Subconsciously, she was relieved to have been kicked off the team because Brady was the one that forced her to try out for basketball anyways. The only sport that she thoroughly enjoyed and she performed her best at, was volleyball though it was also introduced to her forcefully. She liked the fact that at all times there was a net between her and her opponent. Jay never willingly tried out for high contact sports because she knew that with her temper and huge discomfort of being touched by people she didn't know, she would end up kicked off the team or worse.

Though Jay's temper had almost gotten her suspended from school, Brady was more concerned about what she had seen prior to the game. Brady's relationship with Jay was very similar to her relationship with her own daughter, Jane. Brady was known and prided on being the disciplinarian but her tactics were rather irrational at times (most of the time). Just as Xavier was doing with his own mother, Jay was looking for approval and acceptance from Brady and Jane. She never felt good enough, because even in her best efforts, the negative was the highlight of Brady's conversation. Though there was no positive outlook to have on the encounters of that day, Brady still chose to speak on the one with the least relevance.

"I saw you and that boy holding hands today. You were so busy following up behind him that you didn't even acknowledge my presence. You are a nuisance; you are a fast ass heifer and you've gone boy crazy. I talked to one of the nuns here in passing today and Sister Agnes tells me that you are always hugged up under that boy during school. I am not paying all this money to send you to a private school so that you can end up like your dad's side of the family." When Jay asked what she meant by that statement, Brady responds "Your dad's side is ignorant and ghetto. All they do is sit up and have a bunch of babies and you are being heavily influenced by them." Jay reverted the attention back to her, "Brady, the only one of your children that has a degree is Aunt Grace. My mom and uncle Tray went to college but didn't finish because of their drug addictions and alcoholism. And I am the youngest grandchild on both sides of the family in which none of my cousins (including your two grandchildren, Nicole and Paige) finished high school without having a child first. So I am not really sure how you're placing all the blame on my dad's side." Brady then becoming offended asks, "So, are you calling me a liar?" Jay responds by stating, "Well, it's definitely not the truth." Before the sentence could get completely out of her mouth, Brady had adjusted her rings to fit like brass knuckles and had begun punching Jay in the lip and face as she told her that she talked too much and was disrespectful to adults. Though Jay later in life

132

comprehended that she was hit because of calling her grandmother a liar, what was never understood was why there was a constant comparison between the sides of her family. Both sides had their flaws and were both loved equally but her father's side was transparent about their faults, whereas her mother's side upheld a façade of perfection.

After being hit sporadically over the course of the ride home and continuously being told how much of a whore she was and how she would end up just like her mother, she was finally happy to have reached Lillian. She got out of the car and sprinted into the house in tears as Brady came in behind her to inform Lillian and James what she had already been declaring to Jay. Lillian listened patiently to Brady before becoming exasperated by how harshly she was speaking of Jay. "Ok Brady, I get the point. I'll handle it. Can you please leave now?" Lillian said to Brady as she escorted her to the door.

James was very similar to Brady in terms of having no filter and reminding people how much he does for them. So, as expected, he jumped on Brady's bandwagon of slandering Jay. He retorts, "She should have punched you in the face, you have a nasty attitude and a smart mouth. Trust me your days are numbered child, you won't live a long life disrespecting your elders the way that you do. That boy that you've been hanging out with at school must not know you very well. No man is ever going to want to put up with the attitude or the mouth that you have. So, I suggest you get an education and learn to take care of yourself because the route you're heading; you'll be alone for the rest of your life. Besides, I am helping Brady out with your tuition and if that's all you're going to school for, I can be making a better investment." Lillian then interrupting him and an argument between the two of them infused from there. Jay just went to her room and closed the door and stared in the mirror of her dresser at her bloody, scratched up face from her grandmother's blows.

Still no one had mentioned the more relevant topic of the basketball game, and Jay lay on the floor of her room confused and hurt. Despite all that was being said about her, she was a straight "A" student. She played on the basketball and volleyball teams, was on the board of the student government association, was the Sunday school primary teacher, and was a candidate of becoming the Sunday school superintendent (which was receiving notable attention, as she would be the youngest appointed superintendent within the history of the Christian Methodist Episcopal church). No matter her accomplishments, the downfalls were emphasized.

Above all the commentary, Jay hated being compared to her mother for two reasons: obviously because Jane was a less than adequate role model and because Jay attempted to maneuver in her own path, not following the footsteps of anyone. When asked who her role model was she'd always respond, "Visions of the future woman I will become." Of course, Jay was guided by inspiration but never attempting to model the behavior or lifestyle of anyone else. That's why she never cared what people thought of her as long as there were no hands laid, no name-calling or outright disrespect. Not sure of who or what she would become, she was more than certain on who she did not want to become; her mother.

Overcome by feelings of depression, Jay begins to envisage life. She didn't want to be alive nor did she want to die. Though she knew she could always turn to one of her three best friends, Mitch, Morgan, Amber or her boyfriend, Xavier, she chose to suffer alone. There was no need in bothering them with her disarray. "They have their own shit to deal with," she thinks. As she sat there attempting to drown out the argument taking place between Lillian and James, she began to write out her feelings and sang softly. Writing and music were her only escapes.

Searching For Answers:

I often ask myself, where to find the answers?

I've searched through the books of philosophy, journal articles and magazines.

I've rifled through intellectual conversations, prayer and meditation, anti-depressant, anxiety medication and wholesome remedies.

I've explored therapies and answered a plethora of someone else's questions for them to familiarize themselves with me.

Yet, still no answers to the questions I so desperately seek.

I am at a loss for words; mental stability is beneath me I am overawed with frustration and unimaginable hatred of myself. I hate anyone who dares to ask me a question.

You enquire about my past as I desire to discern my future.

For my past is not my present and my present is not presentable enough to anticipate restitution.

They say the answers are within and my external search is in vain.

I've looked internally, turning to insanity, and insinuating the fabrications made up in my brain.

If you cannot provide the answers to my questions, don't dare attempt to put yourself in my situation; it will kill you.

No one else can bear the load I transport, and along with carrying this weight, my search for answers continues.

135

Future conversations with her older cousins and even Brady's own children shed a lot of light on why Brady was more about hashing out the negatives than embracing the positives. A dialogue with her Aunt Grace enlightened her on Brady's attitude. Grace explained that Brady was the third oldest of nine children of which she and her older sister, Brenda, dreaded seeing their mother pregnant because they knew they would have more responsibilities. They never enjoyed their childhood or adolescence because whenever another sibling was born they were given to one of them to raise and care after. Brady and Brenda wouldn't see their mother again until she was dropping another baby off for them to care for. Brady dropped out of school between the sixth and eighth grade to help take care of her siblings. Therefore, when she had children of her own, she raised them in bitterness because she still had not had a chance to be a child herself or to explore life without being a caretaker. Now all the generations (Brady's children and grandchildren) birthed from that attitude had a different method of escape. Of Brady's children, Jane turned to drugs, Tray turned to alcohol and Grace turned to dancing/cheerleading. Of her grandchildren, Nicole turned to men, Paige turned to depression; which both led them to drugs. Jay was the last of that generation as her Aunt Grace asked, "So, what will be your escape?" Already being diagnosed with severe depression, Jay knew that soon, she'd be faced with making that same choice.

Upon Jay's return to school the next day, she was greeted by Mitch in the hallway. "What's up Jay?" he asked uneasily. It seemed that word had gotten around about the game last night. As she and Mitch stood there, she heard her classmates jokingly saying things like "There goes the heavy weight champ." To her peers at school she was the little girl with the big attitude and temper. Apparently, her companion was in the same category, though his temper matched his appearance. Despite Xavier specifically telling Mitch not to tell anyone (including Jay) about the locker room incident, he couldn't resist. After all, Jay was his friend first and his primary loyalty and allegiance was with her, Mitch thought.

She didn't know whether to be upset or delighted by his behavior but she was becoming aware that the two of them together made a very dangerous couple. It wasn't until years later when their tempers began to gear toward each other that she realized the perilousness of their connection. But for now, they loved every part of each other, including each other's tempers.

Battle Fifteen

Fight for Your Life

Blow by blow, she is once again fighting for her life. She is not living in reality but camouflaged with shades of red. Underneath her, lies an unconscious body as she is being forced by her rage to continue to strike. Witnesses watching and people screaming, police calls being made and ambulances in route, still not relinquishing the fight that someone else had started; Jay combats. Covered in the blood shed by the aggressor, she snaps back into veracity. "What have I done," Jay asks as she backs away from the scene. Running home she meets her grandmother Lillian on the front porch. She runs to her crying, "Grandma, Grandma." Clearly seeing that she has been involved in a fight Lillian asks, "Jay, tell me what happened? I sent you to the corner store and you return with blood all over you and no groceries."

Jay begins to explain, "I never made it to the store. I was walking to the store and all of a sudden, I could hear two girls screaming, 'Does anyone know that bitch, Jay? Where is she, we're going to beat her face in.' Not saying a word, I continued walking and minding my own business. Eventually, we met up at the corner and they blocked me asking, 'Are you Jay?' I simply responded, 'Why?' They had to be several years older than me because they towered over me as they began to push me back and forward between the two of them before I landed on the concrete slitting my hand on the broken glass. As they stood over me threatening me and telling me to get up so that they could knock me back down, they were stomping my chest and ribs. I looked over and beside me laid a shattered beer bottle. I knew that I'd be ok if I could just get back up on my feet. 'Damn it, number one rule is not to fall and now I've fallen all the way down,' Jay thought. I grasped the bottle, got up swiftly, grabbed the girl closest to me by her hair and began to swing as fast and as hard as I could with that bottle. When she fell to the ground, I saddled on top of her and continued to hit her with those broken glass edges. The girl she was with backed away in awe of all the blood her friend was shedding all over the pavement. She ran away and called the police. Suddenly, I looked up and realized all the people who were watching, then I took a glance down at the girl lying beneath me. I didn't even remember how the entire situation had escalated so quickly but there was so much blood, I could no longer see her face. So I ran home and now, here I am," Jay cried out, "Grandma, I didn't mean it; I don't even know that girl's name, I have no idea who she or the other girl is. Oh, my gosh! I'm going to jail."

Lillian calming Jay, "You are not going to jail, but the police are on their way. Clearly, you were defending yourself so when they get here, you tell them exactly what you told me and please stop crying." It was then that she and Lillian heard a group of people coming and looking for Jay. Here was an even older woman, "Where is she, she thinks she can just hurt my child and there be no revenge. Now, in plain sight, there was no doubt about who had just attacked her daughter, because there Jay was on the front porch covered in blood. The lady and the group that was with her begins walking swiftly towards their house as Lillian tells Jay "wait right here." "Grandma, don't leave me out here!" Jay screams out. Lillian returning hastily now standing on the porch with her double barrel shotgun pointed in the direction of the group that was quickly approaching. When they got up close to the house Lillian warns, "If any of you step onto my property, I am within my rights to blow your asses off and I plan on exercising that right." The group of women now idly threatening Lillian, continue to talk about what they were going to do but are extremely careful not to place one foot on the premises of Lillian's property. Jay stood behind Lillian crying, scared and shocked because she had no idea that her grandmother even owned a gun. Hearing the sirens toppling the hill, everyone backs down and Lillian puts her weapon inside the door of her house. "Jay, just tell the truth," Lillian whispered to her.

The ambulance had already taken the wounded girl to the hospital and the police stood talking to Jay, the other girl involved in the fight and neighbors who were sitting outside and witnessed. The story began to unfold in Jay's favor as one of the elderly couples that had witnessed the altercation corrected the lies that had been told on Jay by the other girl. After they spoke up, another group of people began to tell the truth of what had occurred. When asked by police why the two girls had attacked her in the first place, she was confused as she had no idea. "My grandmother normally doesn't let me go further than the porch so no one in this neighborhood should even know my name," she explained to the officer as she is handcuffed in the backseat.

Upon further investigation of what led up to the altercation, the girl finally confessed. She and her cousin were looking for Jay because of the way Jay had treated their younger brother. There was a young boy named Clint who was about ten years old. He had a major crush on Jay and would always come around and either sees her sitting on the porch alone or with her grandmother. Lately, he had been approaching her whenever he would see her. He would ask, "Hey Jay, can I come play with you?" She'd always respond with, "No, I'm not even playing, I'm just sitting." Jay would then go in the house closing the door behind her. If he didn't see her outside, he'd go up to her door and ask Lillian, "Is Jay

140

home, can she come out and play?" When asked, Jay would scream out, "Tell him NO I'm not home" or "I don't want to play with him." I guess she had deeply hurt his feelings and he went back and told his older sister, who then grabbed her cousin and went on a search for Jay. Jay just so happened to be at the right place at the right time when they were making their inquiries about who she was.

Now that the full truth had been revealed, the cousin who was also involved in the fight was handcuffed and taken to jail as she and her cousin were ages nineteen and twenty-one. Jay was only fifteen. Jay was then un-cuffed and released from the backseat of the car as the police sat with her and Lillian on the porch and had a heart to heart with her. "Young lady, you are very lucky. Had you been over eighteen, you'd be on your way to jail with them. This is a rough neighborhood. Hopefully now, you see why your grandmother doesn't allow you any further than the front porch. It could have been you on the other end of that beer bottle or headed to 201 Poplar with an aggravated assault charge; so watch yourself. It's obvious that you were defending yourself, but you now realize how easy it is for you to fall victim to violent crimes whether being the aggressor or not. I was standing here conversing with your grandmother about you as you and the other young lady were being questioned. I am very pleased to know that you attend a private school (thanks to a scholarship and your hard working grandparents) are a straight "A" student, involved in extra-curricular activities, never been arrested and have no children. As an officer, it breaks my heart to see children your age laid out on the pavement; dead or to be driving them to jail. All I ask is that you be careful; respect your grandmothers because they (above anyone else) have your back. Though it has been a pleasure meeting such a bright and talented young lady from this side of town, I never want to see you like this again" the officer said as she shook Jay's hand and hugged Lillian before getting into her squad car and driving away.

Lillian and Jay went into the house and after Jay cleaned up and disposed of the blood stained shirt, Lillian decided to have a heart to heart of her own. "Jay, as I have always told you before, you will never get in trouble for defending yourself. I have always taught you that if you must go down, you don't go down without a fight. Fear no man, regardless of age, height, weight or any other intimidating factor. You are small in structure and because of that, there will be many times where you will be underestimated and have to prove that you can hold your own. But always remember, you were born equipped with everything you'll ever need for survival. Now, I am not telling you that every battle you'll ever face is worth fighting, you'll have to choose those wisely. But, I am telling you that if you do find yourself in an inescapable predicament (such as the one you faced today), you fight for your life because where we're from; your life depends on it. They could have killed you, stomping on your chest and ribs like they did, but you got up, you didn't stay down, you fought back. I am proud of you, not because of you winning a fight, but because you fear no man, and that is how I have raised you to be. Now, that we've had this little discussion lets agree to keep today's events between us. I don't need your grandfather or Brady telling me how bad of a parent I am for not punishing you for this. So, I won't tell anyone if you don't," Lillian said light heartedly. Jay responded, "Agreed."

Although Lillian's conversation was geared around the physicality of fighting, Jay interpreted her words in a metaphorical sense. "You were born equipped with everything you'll ever need

142

for survival," she repeats her grandmother's words in her head. She was well aware of the many dangers associated with her neighborhood which gave her even more of a yearning to reach beyond what was readily available to her. She knew better than to lounge around outside and associate with the elements of the neighborhood. For once, Jay understood one of Brady's parenting tactics. Brady forced her to participate in every extra-curricular activity imaginable: singing, basketball, volleyball, dance, soccer, softball, cheerleading and swimming. She realized that through her grandmother forcefully involving her in these activities, not only was she well versed (as she could do it all), but she was always busy. Brady would always say "Idle hands are the devil's playground." For the first time ever, she understood. To be so indulged in constructive deeds minimizes the chances of trouble finding its way, leading to the ledge of calamity.

Jay then took both the officer and her grandmother's advice as she decided that she would fight her hardest for her life. She would fight to keep her grades well above average, go on to receive a collegiate education and fulfill her desire of becoming successful in a career which the career path she wanted to take was beginning to be informed by her own personal experiences and the elements of her surroundings. She knew by the age of eight that she wanted to attend Spelman College and despite being discouraged from attending such a prestigious institution, being accepted became her mission. However, now she was beginning to discover what she wanted to do post collegiate education. She resurfaced a conversation with Lillian. "Grandma, I think I want to be a criminal defense attorney." Lillian was appalled and asked, "Why criminal?" "Because of where we come from. I was just sitting here thinking of what the police officer said earlier about how easy it is to fall into the traps of the criminal system.

Everyone that I can think of on both sides of my family has been incarcerated (other than me, you, Brady and Aunt Grace). Knowing all of these people, I have realized that all criminals aren't bad people. In an instant, I could have been carrying that label of *criminal*, too. Regardless of the labels that people may carry, they are still people with unalienable rights. I am not saying that criminal behavior is inexcusable nor am I protecting people who blatantly cause trouble and deserve to be in jail (like the two girls who jumped me). However, people who were at the wrong place at the wrong time or who are misguided into the path of recidivism, those are the souls I want to help and defend. Maybe even start a rehabilitation program for convicted felons to become readjusted to society. Everyone doesn't have the opportunity to attend private schools or have grandmothers that care enough not to allow them outside of the house while living in such a neighborhood, but that doesn't mean that they don't deserve a chance," Jay explained. Lillian pleased by what she was hearing simply responded, "You are destined for greatness and I expect nothing less."

Jay was aware that in order for this dream to be accomplished, she would have to put forth substantial effort. It's not every day that a child raised in the Westwood/Walker Homes area of south Memphis makes it out with no children, a high school diploma, college degree or a successful career. Hell, you're lucky to be alive at twenty-one. Nonetheless, Jay was determined. She knew what fighting for her life would entail, and it would be a far greater task than putting up her fist to strike another being. Though physically fighting people came with the territory, she had to build a mindset of fighting her circumstances, her thoughts and her family. Little did she know that soon after, she would be battling the biggest fight of her life.

Battle Sixteen

Cries of Survival

Class is now in session and despite Jay telling her grandmother that she wouldn't tell anyone about the incident that occurred over the weekend, she couldn't help but to spill the tea to her significant other, Xavier. The expression on his face from hearing the story and seeing the scars on her ribs indicated infatuation as he asked questions regarding the juicy details. In spite of the ordeal being rather gruesome, Xavier was mentally stimulated by how well Jay could handle herself. It was as if having a *Bonnie and Clyde* type of relationship gave him an extreme euphoria; elated by the thought that his never before matched temperament had finally found its solace. The broken bottle had left permanent marks on the girl's face and chest; her left eye completely severed. Jay asked Xavier to keep the news to himself though she was neither proud nor ashamed of her actions; she had faced the harsh reality of what must be done to survive where she's from.

The two of them together were definitely trouble but coated in bliss by the presence of each other. She was the calmer of the two. Sadly, even on her calmest day if crossed, she was the engulfment of a gasoline fire. Nonetheless, they brought out a love they had never perceived before in one another. Neither of them knew what a healthy relationship embodied as they had both come from broken homes. The marriages Jay had witnessed either never lasted or were a painful passing of years. Her father was on his third marriage to the most odious woman imaginable and her Aunt Grace was married only for two years before divorcing. Every husband Brady ever had perished far too soon. Thus, James and Lillian were the only example of a lasting union in which, their relationship was one that should have ended far before Jay was even born. They'd argued around Jay so much that hearing them screaming over the television, shattering glass, Lillian crying and him leaving not to return until one or two in the morning and then another argument stemming from him being gone all night, was normal to her. There were even times where Jay would intervene due to how recklessly James would be speaking to Lillian until all three of them were in a brawl; Lillian and Jay against James. It seemed like Lillian only stood up for her children, but far too often would she just put up with the drama from James.

Jay never fully understood why her grandmother had stayed with James for so long if they both seemed to be so miserable. Everyone on the outside would have never believed Jay if she told them the truth of their marriage behind closed doors that she witnessed on a daily basis. Her uncle even told Jay of how he had ran into James at a local Wal-Mart with another woman. But in denial he never said anything about it. And even Lillian had disclosed James' infidelity to Jay once out of anger. However, she saw a pattern with a number of the older adults she had come in contact with. It seemed to be so taboo for a woman to divorce her husband back in the day unless there was an extreme case of physical abuse. But (in Jay's mind) to live such an unpleasant life for the majority of your life, is indeed abuse; killing your soul and any chance of true love finding its way into the heart. Regardless of the tainted picture she had on love, she was beginning to feel it for herself, and she knew that it could be a beautiful thing if the two involved were willing to make it work.

She and Xavier enjoyed adoration for each other that extended far beyond the "puppy love" phase as they grew in love together. They were each other's comedians, confidants, tutors (as they remained in the same advanced placement classes throughout high school), personal trainers (because they were both athletes), psychologists, spiritual partners, protectors and friends for years now. She had fallen in love with his fearlessness, enamored by how he wanted the world to know about how in love he was and how quickly he'd come to her defense if anyone were to offend her. He showered her with unexpected love notes expressing his gratitude for her being his peace when everything else around him was a war zone. She would be caught off guard with a bouquet of flowers or a simple silver bracelet with a pearly pink trim (knowing that pink was her favorite color). Instances like this would show his attention to detail. Everything he did for her materialistically only added to the countless efforts of being there for her physically and emotionally. Years into the relationship, he was still just as charming as he was the day she first noticed his beauty.

Her most favorite aspect of their relationship was how easy it was to depend on him. He always seemed to be there in her times of grief and though she wouldn't always share every detail of her anguish with him, the mere thought of him being there to accept her would ease her worries. Jay's life was becoming a brew of entities that were about to blossom into a whirlwind of uncertainty. She had been carrying around so many emotions up until that point until having to face the head on collision of danger.

One cold winter evening she receives a call; a call that should have never been answered, a call that would leave her in the biggest fight for her life. "Jay, I need you darling. Please, I really need a favor. Go to Brady's and pick up my heart medication. I left it there during my last visit home. Bring it to me please, I cannot live without it. I promise I wouldn't call you if I didn't need it, here's the address to where I am." It was her mother. She had just received her license though she had completely learned how to drive before the age of eleven. Without questioning her mother, she did as she was requested. Lillian and Brady would normally only allow her to drive to and from school and sometimes to her volleyball games. However, that night she told Lillian the situation and without James there to say "no" and Brady out of town at a bowling tournament, Lillian allowed her to go help her mother out.

She had picked the heart medication up from the exact spot in Brady's house that her mother had said it was. She then travels across town to north Memphis. She pulls up to the address her mother had given her to see her mother in the front yard stumbling around and looking out for Jay's arrival. It's clear that she's high. Jay says a short prayer to herself and gathered her feelings before getting out the car to greet her mother because there was never an instance where she wanted her mother to see her cry. Crying (in Jay's mind at the time) is for the weak and she never wanted to be that vulnerable with the person who was the elicitor of most of her weaknesses. Around her mother she had to be strong. In the presence of her mother, she could not be broken.

"There she is, look at my pretty little girl. Isn't she pretty?" She shouts out into the distance. "Walk with me for a minute; I want to introduce you to my friends." Knowing that it was far too late in the night to be walking around in north Memphis, Jay decided that was a bad idea saying, "I don't want to walk with you." "Well, can I at least have a hug?" her mother asks with much frustration. Now hugging her mother, she notices forcefulness. Her mother seemed to be pushing her in the direction of the dim porch as she looks up and notices about six men. "Whoo, Jane, who is that? Is that your daughter you've been telling us about? She looks just like you." They shouted out sexual slurs to her as her mother continues to gravitate toward them. "Yep, this is my baby. Come on here girl and meet them; they ain't gon hurt you." Jane says to Jay. "Well, how old is she?" the drugged up men ask as her mother responds, "She's a teenager" not even sure that she knew how old Jay was.

Fogged by what seemed to be a dream, she looks toward the porch and all of a sudden she was bombarded by all six men, as her mother watches from the bottom step. "Don't fight them Jay, you weren't raised to be rude." Jay disregarding everything her mother was saying, she stood on that front porch fighting for her life. With each blow, she punched as hard as her small but sharp fists would permit. Car key between her knuckles, she grazed the skin of the man in front of her as she tried to use dead weight on the men that had her within their grasp from behind. Knowing that this was a battle she was about to lose, she wasn't going down without a fight.

Her mother stands in tears and pleading for them to just let her go before lounging out at the man closet to her. Her mother is now thrown off of the porch and she screams out to loosen her child from their subversion. He places his hands around Jay's neck, choking her until the imprints of his thumbs press deeply into her throat, and she struggles to breathe. Another man grabs her left leg tugging on her as if she were his possession as Jay raises her right leg and plunges it upward into his nose as if she were playing soccer. Jabs to the eyes, elbow blows to the torso, kicks to the face and head all led to their submission. Jay still fighting and screaming for her mother as her young body was being disgraced. One man grazed his hand over her small chest and down her side until finding his hand over her pureness, places that not even her boyfriend had touched, she pushes him away. Fighting until they had given up. Not only were they all over the age of forty but they were all drunk, high or both. Clothes ripped to pieces and bruises covering her neck, legs and arms, with tears running down her face she runs to the car and takes off. She had escaped the grip of six men all with lessons she had learned from previous encounters that began at age five when she kicked the little boy in the head and out of a tree. She whimpers and thinks to herself, "This cannot be real."

Her words resonated to the nadirs of her subconscious reverie. Snapping back into the reality of the present moment as she stood there hugging her drugged up mother who was thanking her for coming. "Thank God, that wasn't real" she thinks before she looks toward the porch as the six men she had just had a phantasm about began to trickle off the steps continuing their inquiry to Jane about Jay. Two of them now standing near Jay, are looking at her with fanciful eyes, undressing her in their minds with thoughts of unraveling her purity. Jay stands there uneasily as her mother tries to introduce her to them. They each take her small wrist and kiss her hand. One guy's grip beginning to tighten around her, she snatches away as he forcefully pulls her back to him. He hugs her closely and allows his hands to drift over her small behind before quickly grabbing at her crotch. Snatching away from him for a second time and now prepared to throw the hardest punch she could spring, her mother (as expected) begins to gear her toward the other men waiting on the porch as she breaks her mother's embrace. The two men struggle to retain grip over Jay again, and she realizes this is about to be a nightmare come true; she begins to fight them off and is released. The other men rushing over to her and circle her in, she fights. Finally having enough leeway to find an escape she turns her back to her mother and the elements that surrounded her as she says goodbye while sprinting to the car in tears as the guys jokingly say, "You're so bougie, we just wanted to meet you and give you a hug, pretty woman." "I am not a woman, I am a child, which should not be touched, thought of or looked at in that way by middle aged men." Jay thinks. Though they all stood there laughing, this was not a game to be played. Choosing not to see her mother for years to come, she travels back to south Memphis.

With rattled nerves, a broken spirit and a forever blotted heart, she walks into her house to find Lillian and James arguing about allowing Jay to take the car. This time though, James was right. If he'd been home, he never would've allowed her to drive his car without him being present. Brady's car was the only car Jay was allowed to drive alone; and that was only a privilege to be enjoyed for school or school related activities. Still with dried up tears on her cheeks, Jay goes straight to her room. They were so engaged in their bickering that they didn't even acknowledge that Jay had come in the house. Again in this same spot on the floor of her room, she lies there in fetal position wondering whether or not to end it all.

Fighting for her life she picks up the phone and dials Xavier. Without having to utter a word to him, he knew something was wrong. He sat on the phone and just listened to her cry for minutes as he consoled her with words of love. "Whatever it is, know that I love you and I am here for you. If you need me to I will come to you." Like he had done so many times before, he was willing to sneak out of his grandmother's house, steal her car and come to Jay's rescue. Knowing that if she didn't tell him what was going on, he would be at her front doorstep in less than an hour, traveling forty-five minutes from Holly Springs to be with her.

"I can't believe what happened tonight. I am so muddled and hurt. Firstly, I have known my mother has been on drugs for the entirety of my life, up until tonight she shielded me from seeing her in the extremity of that state. She could barely stand up; as I was hugging her she was using me like a crutch. Her eyes were bloodshot red, face and nostrils swollen, hands shaking like a Parkinson's inflicted person and her speech slurred. When asked how old I was, she didn't even remember. I am her only child. Then, her guy friends shout out vulgar slurs about my body and what they'd do to me as she stands there laughing like they are joking. In the midst of me hugging/holding her up, I was carried off into a cosmic space of precognition.

I stood there thinking of these six men that I saw attacking me until being retorted back to the reality that two of these men were actually about to attempt and followed by the other four. Had I not broken free of the two guy's grasp, what would have happened to me? I questioned, was this set up? Was the one person that I am supposed to trust the most, which is supposed to be my protector willing to offer the pureness of her only daughter for a temporary high? How low can a mother stoop or was it really just a joke? She's a fighter, too. Would she really let someone hurt me? I'd hate to believe that she would do that to me. I'm always hearing through the grapevine that my mother speaks so highly of me and that she tells everyone she knows about me and how proud she is of me. I heard that she spoke so well of me that people would think my existence is a fabrication. She always wanted to show me off to her friends and to prove that in the midst of her 'fuck ups', she had done something right. Maybe, this was her chance to prove to her friends and to those that never believed I was real; she had a beautiful and intelligent daughter. Maybe, she was so high that she didn't even notice the predicament she put me in. I don't know, but as if I didn't already doubt her, I don't think I can trust her again," Jay explained to Xavier.

Not knowing how to further console Jay, Xavier reaffirmed his love for her and stayed on the phone with her until she fell asleep. Jay cried until she couldn't breathe and eyes were bulging out of her face. She thought about the countless amounts of tears she had cried because of her mother over the course of her young life.

She cried whenever her mother didn't show up to a school event because she had promised to come. She cried whenever her mother did show up to a school event as she would get a plate of food and leave without even speaking to Jay (like she had done at her kindergarten graduation). She cried whenever she would come around high. She cried whenever she would come around sober as it was obvious she was anxious for her next high. She cried whenever Brady would tell her that her mother had been locked up again. She cried every time her mother would go to rehab only to relapse. She cried every time she thought that she should be getting her mother's advice, she cried whenever she would witness a daughter being scolded by their mother. She cried whenever she talked about her mother and definitely when anyone else talked about her mother (like Brady did often). She began to think that her mother had never had an informative conversation with her. She was never present at any extra-curricular activity. She had never showed her how to dress appropriately or how to put on make-up. She had never told her about boys or what to look out for. She had never once curled her hair or placed a bow in it. She had never posed for a picture with her. She didn't even know Jay's favorite color and for all those reasons and more, Jay cried.

That night, Jay cried because she knew that what her mother allowed to happen indicated that her mother was to the point of no return. However, she made a vow to herself that when she got up off the floor that night and the tears in her eyes dried, she would never shed another tear over her mother again; and she didn't.

Upon going back to school it was just another day to her peers around her. She walked the hallways laughing and joking as she always did with Mitch, Morgan and Xavier. They noticed no difference in Jay's behavior or attitude. Not because there was no difference, but because Jay had become good at guising her emotions for the betterment of those around her. The only person that was somewhat cognizant of the life altering event that had taken place was Xavier, but even he was misinformed by her now usual behavior. He thought that seeing Jay act normal around their friend group meant that the situation that occurred was momentarily painful but she was over it. Little did he know that everything to the core of her being was incessantly changed. She was already more reserved than the average person when pertaining to her true friendships and interactions, but trusting others became an even more challenging task than before in which she faced that inner battle alone.

A few Sundays following that incident, the pastor at her church made a shocking announcement. "I would like to announce our new superintendent over our Sunday school program here at the church." He announced that Jay would be the new superintendent. She had made history for being the youngest superintendent overseeing a Sunday school program in the C.M.E. church. She was called to the pulpit and formally introduced as superintendent and newest member of officers in the church. She received a standing ovation and words of encouragement as she processed up the isle to receive recognition from her pastor. She stood at the podium nervously and thanked everyone who had voted for her and for their belief in her abilities at such a young age.

This title provided her the opportunity to go on out of state youth and missionary conferences, be the speaker of nationally recognized events and network with a number of pastors, ministers, clergy members, secretaries and officers from all over the world. She was receiving accolades from people in the adult class that she taught in which she didn't know how to respond. The most memorable statement one of her adult students said to her was, "Jay, you are such an amazing model for our youth to be looking up to. Even I want to be like you when I grow up." She pondered on that phrase for years to come as she thought about how the woman that said that was well into her sixties, and she was only sixteen at the time. Another comment made by one of her mentees was, "Jay, you can't be my role model anymore. You're too perfect, and I could never be like you," Jay was perplexed.

Though she knew that it was an honor to be held in such high regard, it was also one of the most difficult challenges she'd ever faced. Jay would often deliver speeches, taught the adult and children's Sunday school class while still being a teenager, student and athlete. People would always rave to her grandparents about how well they had raised her, saying things like "Jay is proof of the scripture *raise a child in the way that they should go and when they are older they would not depart from it*" or they'd say *"out of the mouth of babes."* "But what is it that they see in me?" she would think to herself. She quickly learned how hard it was to be ministering to the masses and having to profess a love for life and others when she had not yet learned to love herself. Every day she was facing the cruelest demon ever: self-hatred, depression. She questioned herself; she questioned God about how it was possible to prophesize and minster when she had become the epitome of brokenness. Her mind and spirit were broken, and her heart was filled with hatred and bitterness. No one around her was aware of the pain she transported daily and not trusting anyone enough to disclose her fear; she carried that pain in solidarity. She was becoming an extroverted introvert. The world around her knew only the mask that she wore in public. Behind closed doors she was in a constant fight for her life. She was crying out silently; loud enough to disturb her own inner peace, but too inaudible to alarm those around her. Yet, she carried on, suffering in silence and pretending to be okay.

She wrote:

"I am a false profession of God's love and light, his devout affection has gone unused I have been used and abused, above all I don't love myself.

I am the blasphemous raven spreading messages through the sky to God's people of which I teach love, I preach forgiveness but am numbed to the words, "I love you." I know that they are not true. Forgive me father though I know what I do yet I cannot forgive her for what she has done to me.

It is my mother of whom I am speaking, why am I here fighting for a life I didn't ask for. Take me away God to that place of strong mental health, of heartfelt genuine love of self. Take me off the podium and put me back on the shelf.

I am broken, the quintessence of brokenness. I choke on the words of truth I speak. I eat lies told about who I am supposed to be and expel into the spirits of others all the hell, that I've felt and all the things broken about me."

Innocence Traded for Piece of Mind

Jay's public speaking was becoming impeccable and with each event attended, she gained more experience and more confidence. She was blossoming into a young woman with superb presentation skills and keen on professionalism. Jay was enrolled in interview training by her church member who was also her mentor. It appeared that she was becoming a renowned public figure to those who knew her, but she was faking very well. Every adult who surrounded her idolized her; from the pastor at her church to the principal at her school. All of her supporters did not know the secret battle she was facing. She was being pushed forward in every direction of her life; yet, she was pulled back by her own insecurities.

Sister Agnes approached her at school one afternoon expecting two things from her. "Jay, I want you to be a part of the *Saint's Day* celebration here at school. You will be required to open the ceremony with a prayer and our school anthem. You will have to be a part of the *Waltz All*." Not knowing what the *Waltz All* even was, she hesitantly agreed. "Sister Agnes, I can definitely do the opening prayer and sing the school anthem (as she did at all of the school events), but I don't know how to Waltz." "Oh, Jay don't you worry about that, the school has hired professional dancers to come out in the afternoons and teach you and your partner how to waltz. I will choose your partner, and you will be chaperoned during the rehearsals. You will need to get a long, flowing evening gown that will have to be approved by me a week prior to the ceremony. The event is exactly one month and two weeks from today. The program is being held during school hours as a day to honor our saints. There will be no classes that day but school is

157

still in session. The entire school will be indulging in age appropriate activities that are designed to help discover themselves and God. So, in the *Waltz All* there will be eight couples and your rehearsals will begin next Monday. I've already spoken with your grandmother Brady. Thank you for agreeing." As if she had a choice Jay just shook her head and said, "You're welcome."

Just as Sister Agnes had stated, waltz practice began promptly at 3:30 p.m. that following Monday and it continued every Monday and Friday until the day of the event. Though Sister Agnes had assigned the couples and organized everything according to her standards, Xavier was not happy about that arrangement as he was not selected as Jay's partner. Every day he warned Jay, "You cannot have another dance partner. No other boy needs to be that close to you or to put his hands on you, I will break his hands." Although Sister Agnes made it very clear that the practices were closed, Xavier attended practice every day, refused to leave and even threatened the gentleman that Sister Agnes had assigned to Jay. As a result, Jay's partner resigned from participating in the event.

Though Sister Agnes' disapproval of Xavier and Jay's relationship was evident, she knew that Xavier would not stop pestering her until he was assigned to be Jay's dance partner. So, she allowed him to join the ceremony under strict guidelines. "Xavier, I am a nun, but I am not naïve. If you are not waltzing, I do not want your hands on Jay's body, EVER! And even when you are dancing, your hands shall not be above or beneath her waistline. If I catch you touching her inappropriately, I will do my best to have you suspended from this school," she screamed at Xavier as Jay stood behind her mocking her and trying not to laugh aloud. Xavier could care less because he knew that Sister Agnes was an extremist and that he was going to do what he wanted regardless of what she said. He didn't fear her or her idle threats of suspension. However, just to be close to Jay, he obliged by her rules.

A week before the ceremony, Brady brought Jay's evening gown up to the school to have it approved by Sister Agnes. It was a long pastel pink dress with rhinestones at the top and sheer lace covering the bottom. Compared to the other girl's dresses, Jay's gown looked like a wedding dress, and Jay hated it. It was so over the top, but that was expected whenever Brady was in charge. When it came to dressing Jay, Brady was having growing pains. Brady could not handle the fact that Jay was not a little girl anymore and she controlled that aspect of her life. Jay was not allowed to wear heels taller than an inch, her earrings could not be larger than the size of a quarter and make-up (other than lip gloss) was a definite "no." Nonetheless, Sister Agnes was so impressed by the dress that she placed Brady in charge of wardrobe and decorations for the event; the gymnasium, where the *Waltz All* ceremony was being held, looked like an evening Gala.

Even so, the dancers had gotten the waltz down perfectly and the day of the event had come. An hour before the actual ceremony, Sister Agnes directed Jay to her changing area and of the other seven girls she could be attending to, she decided to stand guard outside of Jay's fitting room. A few moments later, Jay had gotten her hair pinned up and her evening gown on. Suddenly, she hears someone coming in from the back entrance. Not knowing who it was, she quickly tried to cover herself as her gown had not yet been zipped up. In walks Xavier with his tuxedo and bow tie to greet Jay. Never before had they seen each other dressed like this, and they both were pleasantly surprised. Xavier motions for Jay to stay quiet as they would be in major trouble if he was caught in that room with her.

Innocently, she asked if he would zip her dress as he responded to her question by smoothly sliding the dress off of her shoulders. From behind he grabbed her by her waist and gently ran his fingers down her spine. Nervously, she trembled and clinching her dress tightly, Xavier could sense her uneasiness. He kissed her collar bone and assured her that he wouldn't harm her, "Just relax; I will never hurt you, Jay." Turning around to face him, she kissed him and told him that he should probably leave now before they got caught, and he agreed. Though Xavier walked out embarrassed as he thought he had done something wrong, Jay had begun smiling from ear to ear. Feelings that she had never experienced before were overcoming her body as she could still feel the trace of his touch down her spine lingering on her skin. Knowing that pretty soon she would have to face Sister Agnes and her grandmother who are now both waiting outside the door of the front entrance conversing, she temporarily ignores those feelings only to revisit them the moment she touches Xavier again on the dance floor.

Now, with the entire school watching, she and the other participants process into the ceremony. Normally, feelings of anxiety would overwhelm her prior to a public speaking event but of all the times that she had spoken and sang in public, she had never been so relaxed. As she sang the school anthem she kept her eyes on Xavier and his presence ceased all tension that she would have had if he were not there. None of the students cared about the ceremony and were always bored to hear Jay sing because she sang at every event and everyone knew of her talent, they sat there as Xavier stood up clapping so loudly that it was almost

160

embarrassing. But all she could do was blush. He escorted her off the stage and their waltz began. First he bowed, then she curtsied, everything else was a vague memory because for the entire dance they giggled jokingly and enjoyed each other's closeness.

After that day, they began to see each other differently but in the most enticing way. Physical attractiveness had already been there, but their innocent eyes were beginning to notice each other's nature; developing breasts, widened hips on her, broad shoulders and mustache hairs on him. Being completely transparent with each other, they decided to have a conversation about their feelings. Although Xavier and Jay were both usually not considered shy at all, the first conversation was full of awkward pauses and uncomfortable glares off into the distance. With time, they became more comfortable talking about their sexual feelings toward each other and the appropriate time within their relationship to explore each other in that way. They contemplated for some time and enjoyed the foreplay that would one day lead up to that special moment.

It seems like the two people that could see Jay's contemplation the most was Sister Agnes and Jay's grandmother, Brady. Sister Agnes was Brady's eyes when Jay was not in her sight and neither Brady nor Sister Agnes cared for Xavier. When at school, Sister Agnes made sure to keep them separated as best she could. For example, she knew that Jay and Xavier were in all of the same advanced classes together. So every class that she taught, she would force them to sit on opposite sides of the class. While at home, Brady would only allow Jay to go out with Mitch and Morgan but Xavier was rarely invited as Brady chaperoned. In the next few months, Sister Agnes again approached Jay with another activity that she wanted her to partake in, also with hopes that she could keep her busy and unfocused on Xavier. Little did she know that what she was about to expose Jay to, only led to more of a connection for the young lovers.

There was a pro-life oratory contest with a cash prize and scholarship funds for rising seniors and Jay's experience with public speaking made her stand out as the perfect candidate. After assembling her speech, making revisions and practicing for hours throughout the day, the competition had finally come. She won the contest for her school, the local competition against students in Shelby County and went on to nationals which gained local and national attention. Though she did not win the national competition, Jay was listed in the newspaper and all over social media for being the local and regional winner out of south Memphis.

Along with other accolades, her oratory speech garnered so much attention that she was invited to speak at numerous pro-life events and even went to Washington, D.C. where she was afforded the opportunity of meeting the forty fourth president, Barack Obama. That following year, she and a few of her classmates also went to her first *March for Life* in Washington, D.C. in front of the Supreme Court building. Here Jay was again being placed on the pedestal of infallibility as she makes a choice that could have ultimately proven that she is no role model, but a regular person struggling to survive just like everybody else.

Xavier had also been a chosen delegate for the D.C. trip (which came as no surprise because there is no way Jay would be going out of town without his presence) and together they were having the time of lives; their lives as they knew it was about to change. On the last night of the trip when everything had calmed down and none of the chaperones cared anymore, it happened. Jay and Xavier went upstairs to her hotel room because they were tired of hanging out in the lobby with all of their peers. They wanted to be alone and be in a space of quietness within the presence of each other only. They talked for a few hours, laughed goofily at each other's playfulness and pillow fought until white feathers covered the bed and floor. Finally, they lay.

She placed her head on his chest and listened to his heart beat. She wanted to experience him like she had never experienced another and as if he were reading her mind, he kissed her head softly. Repositioning himself to face her and looking her directly in the eyes, he told her, "I want you to be my first." Responding with body language she clinched him tightly as their arousal for each other grew; he whispered in her ear, "Jay, I love you." With a heart of admiration and a mind of exploration, he asked, "Do you love me the way that I love you?" She simply responded "Yes," as she couldn't find any other words to say. Then ensuring that neither of them was making a mistake, again he asked, "Jay, are you sure? I don't want you to do anything you're not comfortable with. I've waited for years, and I will wait for you until you're ready. I have dreamt about this moment since I first laid eyes on you, certain from the beginning you would be my first, but are you sure?" With reciprocal feelings, she loved him and wanted more than anything to share the purist of herself with him, again she said, "Yes." On January 21st, together, for the first time, and completely unknowledgeable about how it was supposed to work, they dove head first in the sea of carnal bliss. They had both placed their innocence in the hand of the other and in that moment, she knew that regardless of their fate, she would never love another the way that she loved him, and she didn't.

Jay was confident in her decision and was pleased by the fact that she had for once, given herself willingly. For once, she had made a choice for herself and by herself. She was no longer dragged by the hair and forcefully punished for her resistance. She had taken a bite from the forbidden fruit and indulged in the most painful pleasure she could have imagined and against everything that she was taught, she liked it. She was thrilled by the thought of giving her innocence away. In her young but twisted mind, she felt emotions and thoughts of peace. She was at peace because over the course of her life, there had been so many attempts by grown men, little boys both of whom were undeserving. Jay had even been approached by a woman before. They all wanted the same thing, to take her most prized possession. At least at this point she had given herself to the one of her choice. She had peace of mind, knowing that it hadn't been taken from her, like every other part of her childhood. Maybe now that it was no longer in her possession, it wouldn't be such a hot commodity that her life could be jeopardized to obtain.

Though her breath was short and her palms were clammy, she was not afraid, but relieved that it was over. She was in love with the strength of her lover and though strength had never done anything but hurt her before, his strength eased her, his strength protected her. After they had ridden that wave for hours, they both went to an empty ballroom where Xavier carried her into the room on his back, sat her on the piano stool and told her to listen. Amazed, she sat on top of the piano as he began to play soft tunes. She never knew of this talent. He told her that he had taken piano lessons from toddler age up until he came to high school (which was obvious because he was very good at it). He explained how he used to be teased about it so he never shared that talent with anyone. He disclosed to Jay that the reason he had built such a tough exterior was because of him always being bullied as a child by other students and even by his own mother and step-father. Xavier exposed to her how his mother would watch as his step-father would beat him until he was bruised and bloodied and sometimes join in on the abuse. He had gotten one too many beatings and had been bullied for far too long. He began eating twice as much, weight lifting, boxing and playing sports until his mere appearance would make anyone rethink stepping to him with ill intent. He prided himself on being thought of as mean, crazy or intimidating because being that puny little kid that was constantly at the tail end of someone's fist was a part of his history that was never to be repeated. Tears began to welt up in his eyes as he had never shared that part of his life with anyone before; including playing the piano because that too reminded him of his endured abuse.

With respect and complete understanding of his feelings, Jay just placed her arms around him and clinched him tightly as he continued to play a few more songs for her. Never before had she grasped the concept of why Xavier was so off-putting to other people and never had she imagined the trauma he had experienced in his past. Later that week he went even further to show her some of the life-long scars he had obtained from the parental abuse that she had never questioned before; like the mark on the center of his forehead from his mother ramming his head into the corner of her dresser. Jay's and Xavier's connection stemmed further than physically, there was a spiritual connection. Now that they had become intimate, it seemed perfect. Jay thought that the pain suffered in their pasts and the insecurities that stemmed from it would yield a better future. Unaware of the fact that the person she had loved the most would soon turn into her worst enemy. Her once abused lover would soon turn to be the abuser and before too long, his strikes would be additions to the scars she had already suffered from everyone else who was supposed to love her. She had traded her innocence for yet another false hope, blurred visions of love and high-temporal flaring of pain; she was no role model.

Battle Eighteen

Tit For Tat

Everything was a sphere of confusion. "I thought he'd
never hurt me" Jay thought often. Their conversations were
revolving into arguments, their giddiness was turning into
frustration and their insecurities were weighing heavy, especially
Xavier's. Jay was being chastised for having male friends other
than Mitch of whom Xavier was becoming jealous of that
relationship too. She couldn't even be seen talking to a person of
the opposite sex as Xavier would begin to publically shame her;
saying things like, "Stop being such a whore." To Xavier's
discomfort, Jay had become more social with her peers as she was
seriously involved in the Student Government Association and had
been voted president for two years in a row now.

Upon months of dealing with his jealous tendencies and
domineering behavior, things got physical. It went on for some
time, and she still didn't stop regarding him as her boyfriend. The
things that he would say to her she had been used to hearing.
Though the level of discipline never matched the abuse that Xavier
had endured, Jay's face had been at the tail end of belt buckles and
diamond rings that hugged the fingers like brass knuckles. Jay's
inner voice was already filled with Brady's comments about her
likelihood of becoming her mother. Jay's face had already been
scarred from being punched so many times because she had said or
acted in a way that supposedly disrespected her elders. Though
Lillian had only given Jay two whippings her entire life, Brady
made up for the physical disciplinary shortcoming with words,
fists, belts, switches, shoes, extension cords; whatever she thought
would get across to Jay or to release her own anger. So when
Xavier started with the first stage of name calling (which escalated

into public shaming and then to physical abuse) Jay was used to it. She knew that it wasn't right and though she was a fighter in every other situation, he had garnered a respect that was of the status of her guardians of which, regardless of what they had done, she'd never fight them. Those people included Lillian, Brady, James, Curtis, aunt Grace and now, Xavier. If upset, the most she would do was leave, knowing that she'd have to face them again once she or they had calmed down. So when he got in one of his moods and started on his rant, she'd sit and take it for as long as she could before either making a scene in the hallway (which she knew she'd later regret) or walking away from him. Sometimes the things he would say to her would be true and other times (though she wouldn't let him know it), she slightly agreed with the things he said. He called her stupid often, and despite being on the principal's list all through high school that was a word Jay had been called by Brady since childhood. It was her first word of self-criticism. When she talked to herself, it was negative self-talk that sounded like the voices of Brady and Xavier. But she loved them both.

Xavier had always been overprotective and got a little uneasy when seeing Jay interact with other guys, but never had he acted and spoke in this manner to Jay, he had become obsessed. Trying not to focus too much on the red flags, Jay distracted herself from the relationship just as she did from her family by writing and further delving into her academics and athletics in hopes of getting a scholarship. Knowing that it was now time for her to be thinking about college, she began ignoring her relationship altogether. Not only was Xavier no longer getting the responses he sought after from calling her out of her name, screaming at her and discouraging every guy around her not to talk to her; she now acted like they weren't in a relationship. He pushed further. If she walked away he grabbed her, if she pulled away he restrained her. Now, many phone calls were being ignored, no affection given whatsoever and countless tears being shed because though she was trying to ignore his behavior, she was being deeply hurt by it.

However, it all ended one day after lunch and in the middle of the hallway. The night prior, they had gotten into a dispute as Jay had gotten off the phone with Xavier to speak to a male associate who had just lost his mom in a car accident. The guy that called her to confide in her was no more than a friend of a friend who literally had no one else to talk to. Rather than sitting on the phone and listening to Xavier bash her about how she's not supporting him, how she chooses her friends over him and how stupid he thinks she is, she chose to speak to her associate Daryl. Daryl had lost his mom a few hours prior to calling her in a four car accident, and he just needed someone to be there for him and pray with him. Though Jay was just trying to help him get through that difficult situation, all Xavier could see was that she was getting off the phone with him to talk to another guy. Therefore, the next day when she was in Xavier's presence, he made his feelings toward her very clear.

The bell had just rung dismissing all of the students from lunch. Xavier and Jay were walking together. Normally, he would open all doors for her and allow her to walk in first (as a gentleman should). However that day, he actually hit her in the face with the door, hard enough for her lips to become swollen from the force of the glass door. As the second bell rings and the hallways cleared out she approached him angrily about what he had just done. A few minutes go by and they had completely forgotten about class as they stood in the hallway in a full-fledged argument.

169

Unexpectedly, Xavier grabbed her by her waist and pushed her so hard into the lockers that the two lockers beside the one she was slammed into opened and a dent from her head was engraved in the locker. The blunt force to the back of her head caused her nose to bleed for the majority of that day. The slam into the locker was so loud that the principal, secretary and teachers in the classrooms closest to the lockers began trickling into the hallway to inquire about the noise. Finding them in the hallway when they were supposed to be in class and tears running down Jay's face, the principal asked, "What are the two of you doing in the hallway?" Jay turned quickly to wipe the blood from her nose without anyone seeing but when neither of them answered him, the principal demanded Xavier to go to class and called her into his office.

"What did he do to you Jay? Did he put his hands on you, where did that loud noise come from?" Not bulging, she refused to answer his question as she responded, "Am I in trouble or can I just go to class now, it was nothing?" Released from the principal's office and headed to class, she went to the restroom instead and continued to cry as she knew her relationship with Xavier had to end because she had reached her limit. Knowing how badly her temper could get and mixing that temper with his would be deadly for one or both of them. And she refused for her relationship to mirror the relationship of her parents; fighting one minute and with a bruised body making love hours later. That was insane to Jay and when she looked in the mirror at her own scars and saw the reflection of her mother's bruised face starring back at her, she knew that this relationship was over. He had lost her respect.

They went for the entirety of that day without speaking before she approached him again that next morning and told him,

"Xavier, I love you and I always will but I'll never trust you again. You said you'd never hurt me, and I believed you. Not only did you speak to me like a savage for months but you put your hands on me, too. I know that it will only get worse if I stay. It's over," she said painfully. With tears in both of their eyes, they walked away never to be joined in that way again. He supposed his regret for his actions and took full responsibility for the suffering he had caused over the months prior. He declared his sorrow and pleaded for clemency. But it was too late. Jay was beginning to see her relationship with Xavier echoing the relationships of everyone around her; Lillian and James' relationship, and Angie and Curtis' relationship. Every intolerable action being projected in those relationships was spilling into her own and she refused to be miserable for any man. Never did she want to become so passive as to allow a man to demean her in the way that James did her grandmother. Jay was beginning to mimic that passiveness too. So, it had to end immediately. She could no longer ignore the abuse nor could she continue tormenting herself with thoughts of unworthiness.

Thinking that she is going through this problem alone, her grandmother, Lillian was noticing a difference in Jay's behavior. Jay was subtly becoming more and more reserved and as each day passed, Lillian tried even harder to connect the dots to the problem. Her Grandmother knew that when she became more reserved than usual (especially towards her), that her depression was being affected by something that had happened to her that was worse than the normal toils of daily living. One evening, Lillian opened the door to Jay's bedroom to find her balled up on the floor crying hysterically. Jay quickly repositioned herself in an attempt to hide her face from her grandmother as she pleaded for Lillian to leave her alone. Suddenly it came to Lillian. "Jay, I want you to always remember this, it's not your first that matters, it's your last. I know that look in your eyes, I've felt that pain, but at least you're not pregnant." Jay looked up at her very confused as to why she would say that. Lillian explained; "Jay, I lost my innocence at sixteen to someone who I thought loved me too, I thought we'd be together forever and after only one time of getting to know each other in that way, I became pregnant with your uncle Leon. Nothing hurt worse than the day I told Leon's father that I was expecting only for him to flee to St. Louis that same day never to return again. Every day, I looked my child in the face and carried the weight of raising a child that I didn't create alone, on my own at seventeen and with no job or education. But, I survived and brighter days came. You will survive Jay. It hurts right now, but you will always survive."

Even with those comforting words, the break up was the beginning of a downward emotional spiral. She began having severe feelings of depression and her own insecurities began to shade her life once again. As the beginning of senior year was in full force, nothing was seemingly going as planned. Firstly, she had to get a job to help her Grandmother Lillian pay for some much needed blood pressure medication and make some of her senior year purchases that she didn't want Brady to have to fund. Luckily, there was a tutoring job that she was offered at her school; tutoring younger students in the subjects of English and History. Her responsibilities ranged from helping her grandmother out when she needed it to buying her own prom dress and accessories (because she did not want to look like she was getting married on her prom night; which is exactly what would've happened if Brady had anything to do with her prom attire).

Senior year began with Jay losing the senior class presidency to the school's popular queen, Diana Taylor. Though she and Diana had known each other since kindergarten (as did mostly everyone in that school), they weren't very fond of each other. Diana was the most popular girl in the school along with Jay's step-sister, Castel and a girl named Winter, who were all three best friends. The upsetting thing about this particular election was not that she had lost, but the fact that the loss was so unfair. Diana had won for all the wrong reasons as everyone knew that she slept her way to the top; top of the class as valedictorian, top of the popularity poll and now as the class president.

Leading up to the Election Day, Jay invested much of her time into her campaign. She had won presidency two years in a row, once by default and once against a very poorly organized classmate. This year, she loses because the vote on class president was turned into a popularity contest. Proof of the unfair judgement was confirmed as everyone running in the campaign had to present a speech in front of the entire school. Months in advance, Jay had posted flyers around school, gave insight on the plans for senior week as well as the senior class trip; all of which was a waste of time as "Ms. Slutty" had already slept her way to presidency. On the day of the election, Jay had introductory music as she took the stage, a well-organized power point and a detailed ten minute speech about the connections she had already made with a travel agent to go on a *Disney Cruise* for their senior trip. Not to mention Jay's aunt Grace worked for *Disney*. Not surprisingly, Diana got on the stage with no prepared speech or presentation. Her speech was literally verbatim, "Hi everyone, as you all know my name is Diana Taylor, and I'm running for senior class president. Soooooo, yeah vote for me. Thanks guys, I know you will!" As the expression on Jay's face and many others in the audience showed a "wtf" look, she laughed goofily and took her seat. She was like the popular "dumb blond" only she was black and book smart; no common sense whatsoever. Her hair was dyed blond though.

Following the speech that Friday evening, Jay, Mitch and Morgan stayed behind to take down all of Jay's posters and flyers. To her disbelief as she was cleaning the confetti from the senior hallway, she could hear the conversation being held around the corner. It sounded like Diana and Coach Green (who was also the dean of students). Not knowledgeable of Jay's presence, he asked Diana, "Well baby girl, how did you think the election went? You know we'll announce the winners on Monday." "I don't know Coach Green, Jay was really good with her speech and her overall campaign" Diana said as he responded, "Don't worry about it, all of the votes come through me, and I'll make sure you win" before they both went into his dimly lit office.

Just as promised, Coach Green announced Diana as the senior class president the following Monday. Along with that announcement, he went on to say that there would be an election celebration for the newly voted class presidents. The new arrangement was clearly favoritism as Jay had been class president twice before that year with no accolades or celebrations attached to that title. Nonetheless, Jay had been warned which made it bearable but was still very unfair. As Jay could have foreseen to her peers, the senior class quickly became agitated with the structure of senior year events and activities because Diana was not a leader. She was a slightly intelligent young girl learning how to use her womanhood to get what she wanted. There was no senior class trip or any other memorable event. Diana even asked Jay if she could still make the *Disney Cruise* happen and of course Jay's response was, "Hell no, that's your job!" Ironically, a few weeks following the senior class presidential election, Jay was appointed by the principal and administration staff as the president of the school's chapter of Future Business Leaders of America (FBLA). The principal and staff members wanted to refurbish their student involvement in national clubs and associations and thought that there would be no better way than to bring some of those organizations back to the high school. Therefore, he wasn't going to leave it up to the student body to select a president. He chose Jay because he knew that she was a true leader rather than a popular face. Though Jay came out on top with being appointed to a much more prestigious organization than class president, she was still in a tit for tat situation for the remainder of her senior year.

Jay knew from an early age that she wanted to attend a historical black college or university (HBCU) but more particularly; Spelman College. Therefore, she was doing everything possible to be admitted. She applied early decision signing a contract that if accepted she would turn down any other offer. Although she had done her part; completing and paying for her application, taken the admissions tests and worked rigorously in extra-curricular activities, she was still facing adversity. Spelman's admissions office contacted her months after she had sent her application with a bit of disconcerting news. "Jay, we have received your application and all of your personal information, but we're still missing your entire high school write offs. None of your transcripts and high school information has been received by your guidance counselor or school dean. And because we don't have any of those things, you probably won't be admitted this fall with our incoming freshman class. However, we will keep you posted. " Furiously, Jay went to her guidance counselor and asked for an explanation as to why those things had not yet been sent to the school, because she had paid for her transcripts to be mailed. The guidance counselor responded, "Oh, Jay, I apologize; I thought I had already sent that but in my honest opinion, you don't need to go to that school anyways. Why do you want to attend an HBCU? Maybe, you should consider staying in state or attending a junior college first." Completely offended, Jay spat out, "With all due respect Mrs. Simmons, I didn't ask for your opinion and if I have paid the fee to have my transcripts and write offs sent, the only job you have is to ensure that they are received by the school of MY choice." Again, the ironic thing was that Diana had applied to Spelman and already received her letter of denial (of which Diana was very close to both the guidance counselor and Dean/Coach Green).

Not bothering to ask either of them again, Jay went to the one person she knew had access to all of the student records; the school secretary, Ms. Champ. With great desperation Jay explained the dilemma to her. "Jay, you know I don't have the authority to send any of your records so if I do this, you have to promise not to tell anyone (especially Mrs. Simmons and Dean Green) because this puts my job on the line." Jay complied and within the next few days all of Jay's school information had been signed and received by Spelman. Every day from that day Jay called the admissions office, waited anxiously and was distressed by having to listen to school announcements during each convocation. During convocation, Dean Green announced every school that the seniors had gotten accepted into. Jay had been accepted to several other schools, but Spelman had not yet made their decision. So in her mind, having an announcement made about any of the other institutions was pointless.

Along with dealing with the anxiety of waiting to receive a response, the favoritism from the dean, aftermath of a break up and her own family's jealousy, Jay was struggling to retain her sanity. Dean Green who was also her AP English and Theological Theories teacher was beginning to tamper with grades and ultimately, Jay's future. Jay's high school had just recently began using this online grading system that was connected to the student's/parent's email. However, being that neither Brady nor Lillian was computer savvy, Jay was the only one checking her grades and updates. One day she logged into her account to find all grades of "D." She had been a straight "A" student since the beginning of high school so she was rather baffled by this discovery. She consulted with each of her teachers who all told her that she had an "A" in their classes. It then became obvious who the common denominator was, Dean Green who was in charge of all the grades before they were posted onto the student's accounts. She called her dad and Brady on three-way and told them about the issue and informed them that she would be talking with Dean Green at lunch. Curtis told her to speak with him and if she didn't get the answers she needed that he would come up to the school and speak with him on her behalf.

"Dean Green, I am here to speak with you regarding my grades online. I am not sure why I have the grade of "D" for my classes. I have the hard copies of all of my assignments with the grades on them if you need to see them, but there is no reason why I should have a "D" in any of my classes sir," she inquired politely. "Come in and close the door, Jay," he said creepily to her. "Um I'd prefer to keep the door opened, thank you," she responded. He snapped, "Well, I don't have to tell you anything regarding your grades, and I will not speak with you about this again. Your grades are reflective of your work ethic. So, if you have an issue with your grades maybe you should improve your studying, now get out of my office and go to lunch." Jay walked out and began to cry as she knew she did not deserve anything less than an "A." Also, her transcript could not take any "D's" if she was to be accepted into Spelman. She called her dad and Brady again, upset and extremely panicked as he told her to calm down and that he would handle it. Brady was at the nail parlor, so she was too busy cussing at the nail technician to be fully engaged in what Jay was saying. However, she commented to Jay, "You cry way too much, everything doesn't deserve tears. Actually, very few things deserve tears Jay, toughen up little girl, it will be fine now go to class and don't use your phone at school unless it is an emergency, goodbye my child and bye Curtis." Brady said before hanging up.

She went through the rest of the day in hopes that her dad could talk some sense into the dean and within an hour's time span, her grades had been corrected. Curtis had come up to the school very irritated and prepared for the worst. Everyone knew that Jay's father was there as you could hear him screaming down the hall and if anyone walked pass the dean's office, Curtis was seen tossing papers from Dean Green's desk. Everyone other than Jay was quite amused. Calling her father to solve discrepancies was always the last (and most crucial) resort because his temper would always get the best of him. Calling on Brady was the next best option to resolve dilemmas. Though Brady herself could be quite ruthless toward Jay, no one else could say or do anything to Jay without Brady injecting her poisonous venom into them for messing with her child. However, in this case, Curtis was the only person to get the job done.

Though that issue had been resolved, there was something stirring within her that hurt even more than seeing those "D's" online. Later that night, Brady asked her about her plans as her graduation was a couple months out. After telling Brady of her

178

dream of attending Spelman College, her grandmother became very short tempered as she began to snap. "Absolutely not, I forbid it. You don't need to go to an out of state school and definitely not to that school. You'll never make it there. I doubt you can even get into that school. Besides, you're far too boy crazy, all that's going to happen is you get down there and get pregnant and come home with another baby for me to foot the bill on, which I hope you know from seeing your older cousins, I will not do. Hell, you can stay in Memphis for that. You don't need to go that far away from home to be worthless." Though hearing such doubtful words come from her grandmother was extremely painful, it was all the motivation she needed to do just the opposite of the destruction being claimed over her life. In a way, she felt that Brady knew this because she'd been doing the opposite of what Brady had been telling her to do for most of her life out of rebellion. She made it a point to get back at everyone who doubted her with success. Starting with Xavier and ending with her grandmother.

Since Jay and Xavier's break up, they hadn't verbally spoken but he was doing his best to get her attention. He dated three different girls in their high school (two cheerleaders and one random girl) which he later admitted that he had done it all to make her jealous. It worked, but vengeance was hers as she also involved herself with one guy at the school that Xavier hated; Carrington Brent. She hung out a few times with him because he had a big mouth and she knew that it would get back to Xavier (which it did). A few months later, she encountered a more serious prospective than Carrington (as she had never taken Carrington seriously, he was like a toy to her). His name was Nigel Law; a freshman at Northwest Community College in Mississippi and the man who introduced her to even more than her first did. This was her second relationship of which began as retaliation to heartbreak

179

but turned out to be her most adventurous relationship and slowly, but surely, she was getting over Xavier.

She met Nigel one Sunday afternoon after church at *Logan's* restaurant. Brady had started letting Jay take her car on Sundays, especially if she had her twelve year old mentee Tiffany with her. Tiffany's grandmother and Brady were very good friends. Like Jay, Tiffany had been raised by her grandmother and she looked up to Jay like a big sister. Thus, Jay took every opportunity to take her shopping, out to eat or just simply to hang out; trying to be as much of a positive influence as she could be. Jay was enjoying a meal with her mentee, Tiffany, from her Church organization and Sade a high school classmate that also happened to attend her church. She sat there laughing and joking with Tiffany as Sade rambled about how good looking the busboy at the next table was to her. "I wish he'd come over here with his fine self," Sade whispered to the girls as Jay rolled her eyes with annoyance. Jay not amused, kept eating her food and talking to Tiffany. All of a sudden there he stood.

"Excuse me ladies, I only have a few minutes on my break but I was hoping that you beauties would let me join you." Sade being the attention whore that she was responds for the table, "Yes boo, you may sit with us. What is your name?" she inquired. He responded by telling her his name and allowed Sade to continue rambling about how cute she thought he was. She had no shame. "Damn, this bitch is trying so hard, the boy hasn't had the chance to get two words out." Jay thought to herself as she sat there with her head down and hand covering her forehead, embarrassed by Sade's thirstiness. Jay hated going anywhere with Sade. She hated being seen with Sade, because she wanted no one associating the two of them together and every youth in Memphis knew Sade, as

180

she dedicated her social media to twerking videos and a few sex videos too. Jay believed in the well-known saying, "You are the company that you keep." For that reason, Jay wanted nothing to do with someone who carried themselves in the manner that Sade did. The only time they were around each other was after Church on Sundays because of their parents' close relationship. At school Sade didn't acknowledge Jay or vice versa. Regardless of where she was at school, a church event or walking in the park, Sade's mind was always on a boy. Brady was always calling Jay boy crazy but obviously she didn't really know Sade despite Sade's mother being Brady's goddaughter.

Nigel responded to Sade's comments as only he could, "Not wanting to offend you sweetheart, but I actually came over here to speak to her, he says as he points to Jay." Sade had once again made an ass out of herself and Jay wasn't paying enough attention to even know that she was the girl Nigel was speaking about. Jay was still sitting there with her head down, stuffing her face out of embarrassment and cussing Sade out silently in her head. After an awkward silent pause, Tiffany kicked Jay underneath the table to signal that Nigel was talking to her. With a mouth full of food, she looks up and spats, "What?" before realizing why Tiffany had kicked her. "He's speaking to you, rudeness," Tiffany said. Gulping her food down as quickly as possible, she simply asks him, "What did you say?"

Nigel smiles and says "I don't have long, because I have to get back to these tables, but I noticed you when you walked in and I was just waiting for the moment to get close enough to you to speak to you. Would it be too forward of me to ask you for your name and number?" She was flattered one because of his smoothness and also because for once a guy dismissed the advances made by Sade, which was rare. Guys (especially attractive guys) never approached Jay when she was out with Sade because Sade was always in active pursuit of attention, and she was rarely ever denied.

Jay and Nigel went on their first movie/dinner date that following Saturday evening after a week of talking for hours each night on the phone. It was Jay's first unchaperoned date. Though she had dated Xavier for years and briefly talked to Carrington, their alone time was at school events and the only way Brady allowed Jay to go out on weekends with Xavier was if Mitch, Morgan or Amber went too. The only reason Jay was attending unchaperoned was because Brady had no idea about Nigel. Lillian knew where she was going but said nothing as she was not the strict type. Lillian responded to Jay's inquiry of whether or not she could go out with Nigel with "As long as you can find a ride there and back, the gas tank is on "E" and James ain't giving me no more money." Jay thought to ask James herself as he would be more inclined to give her money than to give his wife Lillian money. James spoiled Jay more than Curtis did and between Brady and James, she could have whatever their pockets could afford if used for what they approved of. However, she reneged on that thought because James was basically the male version of Brady when it came to boys. When they'd be out, the second James noticed a boy even looking at Jay, he would curse them as if they were the spawn of Satan and then blame Jay for attracting rats (as he called all boys).

Jay called her sister. Jay's older sister, Lea, picked Jay up from Lillian's house and took Jay to her date. The restaurant where they ate was directly across from the movie theatre so they walked across following the movie. Lea told Jay to call her when she was ready to come home and she would pick her up. However, that was an instruction that went unwarranted as Nigel's father had to take Jay home because Lea went home, overslept and forgot to return to pick up her little sister.

Regardless, Jay was happy because for the first time she knew the feeling of going to the movies on a date alone. Something that seemed so normal for an older teenager was so foreign to Jay. There was no one there to monitor how close the two teens were becoming to each other, how curiously their hands danced about each other's anatomy or how excited the two overprotected teens both were to be in the sole presence of the other. Following the movie, they walked across the street to *Chili's* restaurant where they shared more laughs and made fun of their overbearing parents. He shared stories about his childhood and how he had ended up living in Southaven, Mississippi with his father. Though he was the exact definition of a "mama's boy," he had to leave Oxford, Mississippi (his hometown) to attend community college in Southaven. They chatted for a few more hours and agreed that they would be going out again the very next Saturday. From there they had a standing date night every Saturday to follow.

Within a few weeks' time they both entered their second relationship with each other and Nigel was already head over hills in love, while she was in full, satisfying infatuation. He was a country boy, and she was a city girl. She exposed him to the confines of city life that he hadn't experienced before, while he awakened erotic sides of her that she didn't even know laid dormant. Eventually they couldn't stay away from each other. Waiting until Saturdays to go out (because of his class and work schedule, and her class and athletics) became so unbearable that they had begun going to extreme lengths to get their doses of the other person. They saw each other at least three times a week plus on Saturdays on their usual date night.

Even as a freshman in college, Nigel was just as sheltered as she was by his father. His father was a pastor who took every opportunity to control his son's life through religion. He was constantly reciting scripture, comparing their lives to the lives of characters in biblical parables. Although Jay was well versed in the Bible, Reverend Law was simply annoying. Nigel didn't live the life of a college student because of his father's overbearing rules, despite him being eighteen and paying his portion of the mortgage. No parties, no friends that are not approved of; nothing other than work and school. Likewise, Jay had never attended a sweet sixteen, homecoming dance or anything a normal high school senior would be allowed to attend. Reverend Law and Brady had very similar parenting styles and the more they pushed their children the more Nigel and Jay pulled away.

Nigel was far braver than Jay however, because he introduced her to his father before she introduced him to Brady and the rest of her family. Reverend Law couldn't stand Jay from the very beginning, she found out as she had once overheard Rev. Law refer to her as a "bitch" when talking to Nigel. He told Nigel that Jay was too opinionated and that she needed to be taught a woman's place; speak when spoken to, cater to her man, never undermine the male's authority. What was most baffling was not the things that he said but the fact that he would then want to have conversations about religion, spirituality and holiness. Jay's interaction with him was the beginning of her distorted view of clergy members. However, Jay's dominance was unwavering as the idea of changing herself to fit the mold of any man was repulsing. Luckily for her, Nigel had been raised by his mother his entire life before coming to live with Rev. Law for college, thus his father's corrupted mindset on the place of women had not contaminated Nigel's perception of them.

Reverend Law's dislike for Jay grew as his lectures about a woman's place in relevance to her husband slowly turned into advising the two sex-crazed teens of how their fornication would lead them both to the pits of hell. Neither of them took him seriously. After all, if he wasn't casted to hell by the way that he spoke to and treated people (especially women), then the two of them shouldn't be casted to hell when their actions have no effect on anyone else. Not to mention that he had three children by three different women and had been divorced from Nigel's mother for quite some time. "I wonder why." Jay thought to herself.

It seemed that for Rev. Law to be so educated, he would know that his constant defiance, rejection, imperious attitude, and overprotective ways of parenting only made Nigel pull further away from him and was probably the reason he was miserably divorced. Jay understood because, those were her exact sentiments for Brady. Though Jay is fully responsible for her actions and decisions, most of her sexual exploration wouldn't have begun if Brady weren't already accusing her of it or if Brady weren't so domineering; trying to manipulate and control every little aspect of Jay' life. Though many of the things Jay had done were done out of spite of Brady, there was also a profound satisfaction unbeknownst to her up until that point; it was a certain thrill in doing what she was told not to do. Nonetheless, Jay wasn't stupid and she didn't start enjoying life as a teenager until she was a senior in high school, because it wasn't until then that she stopped fearing Brady. Still, she was not naïve.

Nigel knew that as a senior in high school his girlfriend would soon be going away to college. He had done his best to encourage her to stay in Memphis for school so that they wouldn't have to deal with a long distance relationship. However, despite his best attempt even contemplating purposefully impregnating her against her will to keep her in his life (which he admitted to doing upon them breaking up), she refused to stay in Memphis. Even if she was denied admissions to Spelman, all of her other choices were at least four hours away from Memphis. It was evident that Nigel felt strongly about her but her life goals weren't going to change for anyone, especially him. She loved how he made her feel. She experienced ecstasy with him and though Xavier was her first love, Nigel was her first lust. Jay now understood the struggle of her mother's addiction through what she had with Nigel. He was like a drug that Jay couldn't get enough of, until he gave her an ultimatum that promptly ended everything. His ultimatum was either "you stay in Memphis and attend school or we break it off now." Without ever shedding a tear over him that was their last conversation as partners, though she rekindled her lust for him every chance they got to be alone for years to come.

Back at her high school, Xavier had gotten enough of the back and forth with Jay and he made it clear that he still loved her despite her completely ignoring his presence for nearly a year now, since she'd been dating Nigel. After all, Jay was Xavier's first love too. Finally, after four failed relationships on his part and two on hers, he had a heart to heart with her. "Jay, I am sorry for the way we ended and the way I have been behaving. I know that you know about the three girls I have dated over the past year, all of which I did to get your attention. I've done some things I am not very proud of with those three girls but I was trying to fill the void that you left when you walked out. I didn't care about any of them; I just wanted a reaction from you. But did you really have to talk to Carrington? You know how much he and I dislike each other, he's one of my biggest enemies, that was way below the belt but I do understand. Anyways, I'm over it now and though we will probably never date again, I do love you and I'll always be here for you if you need me, even as our lives lead us in different directions," he said. Though it took a few months, they became great friends and Xavier even ended up asking her to their senior prom. Though the soreness of losing each other and experiencing heartbreak for the first time is something that would forever cloud their minds and future relationships, they ended on great terms and promised to remain friends as adults.

Prom was a success as they danced the night away in their metallic blue and didn't return home until the sun came up the next morning. For a brief moment, Jay had fallen in love with him all over again. But even as a past lover, he couldn't compete with what Nigel had offered her. A few weeks went by and graduation was a couple days away. She comes home to find a huge packet from Spelman College lying on the dining room table. With so much anticipation she could hardly open the envelope. Lillian sat there prayerfully watching Jay dance around nearly having an asthma attack out of nervousness. Finally, she opens the package. "Congratulations! We are pleased to inform you that you have been admitted into the 131st class of Spelman College." Not even reading pass the first line, she fell to her knees overwhelmed and in tears.

She had gotten admitted to the number one HBCU in the country and only two days before her high school graduation and no one; not Xavier, not Nigel or anyone else mattered now. Knowing without a doubt that she was going to attend and graduate from the Illustrious Spelman College, she turned down all other offers as promised. She had gotten a full ride to Murray State University, partial academic and partial athletic scholarship (which constituted a full ride) to attend University of Tennessee in Knoxville to play volleyball. Still with ease she made the decision to go to the most expensive of the options as she thought to herself that she wasn't going to put a price tag on her education, especially when she knew in her heart that's where she wanted to be.

Lillian sat there sharing in on the joy as she cried and told her, "You're the first to do this. It lets everyone coming up behind you know that it can be done." She hadn't seen her grandmother this happy since Obama won presidency in which Lillian didn't believe she'd live to see that day. Jay called her dad, her grandmother Brady and her aunt Grace to inform them. Though Brady wasn't the happiest, no one was going to damper the light glistening from her spirit. "It's game time," she thought to herself. At age seventeen, not only was she the first of her generation to graduate from high school a year early with no children and straight "A's," but she was also the first in her generation to move out of state to attend college and build a life somewhere outside of south Memphis.

Battle Nineteen

Doubt Me Not

Age seventeen was the age of damnation in Jay's family. Her Grandmother Lillian gave birth to her firstborn, Leon, her senior year of high school at seventeen without yet earning a high school diploma. Her father had his first child as a senior in high school at seventeen without yet earning a high school diploma. Each of her cousins on both sides of her family mirrored this same fate, having a child by the time they had graduated from high school. And her sister and brother both had two children by high school graduation age. She thought about Lillian's words; she really was the first. Although being the first held a heavy weight over her head, she was ready to carry the torch and bring a sense of pride to her family. She wanted more than to be a continuance of the revolving cycle that kept deeming nihility. There were little girls looking up to her, especially her younger cousin and mentee Kenya. Kenya was her second cousin (of whom was born to her first cousin at age seventeen) who was raised more like a younger sister to her though she was Lillian's great-granddaughter. She was with Kenya every weekend, and they eventually became so close as to get matching tattoos symbolizing their unbreakable bond. Kenya was only a few years younger than Jay but she still admired and cherished her so much as though Jay was much older and wiser. Because of this, Jay couldn't let her down. Kenya would be the first of the next generation of which Jay was determined to guide and to uplift.

Although high school graduation didn't go as planned, Jay had conquered a minuscule portion of her life. Of course, Diana was the class valedictorian and her friend group came in under her. Still, Jay was unbothered. Castel was ranked third followed by

Winter who was ranked fourth and Jay fifth in their graduating class of twenty-seven. Though Jay had topped the 4.0 scale, graduating with a 4.33 grade point average, Jay didn't even make a fuss over her having the higher GPA than the valedictorian. At that point she could care less because she had already done what she needed to do. Jay was the only person in her class whose college was not mentioned during the graduation ceremony because Mrs. Simmons was officiating and making the announcements but everybody knew she was Spelman bound. Even though the dean and guidance counselor gave their best attempt at making the entire graduation ceremony about Diana and her two friends, Jay's accomplishments did not go entirely unnoticed.

Jay walked away with thirteen awards from the *Dioses of Memphis* (the organization sphere heading all of the Catholic schools in Memphis; acknowledgements that reached far above Mrs. Simmons' and Dean Green's authority). She was awarded *Female Student Athlete of the Year* and *Most Valuable Player of the Year (volleyball)* along with many other accolades. The highest and most treasured honor which was announced last was the *Obama Optimist Award*. This award was only given to one student within the Dioses per year. The decision was made by the dioses based on grades, class attendance, student involvement and votes by faculty and staff. Once the name had been selected, the certificate was sent off to be signed by President Barack Obama and presented by the principal during the school's graduation ceremony. Jay had come out on top.

Within two years following the memorable graduation ceremony, the high school was closed permanently by the Dioses. Dean Green had been reported to the authorities for having relations with students (which was evident for years as he'd choose one senior from each graduating class; Diana just happened to be this year's choice). There was absolutely no love lost for the administration or that school on Jay's behalf but she thanked the institution for the people it brought her such as Morgan and Mitch who were her lifetime best friends.

Several of her family members showed up to her graduation to witness her accomplish this major milestone in her life. Several more didn't show their faces until the end of her graduation party where they grabbed a plate of food and left. Even so, Jay was ecstatic as she announced that she would be attending Spelman College in the fall of that year. A round of applause sounded throughout the room, but the question on everyone's mind was "How is she going to afford that?" Many people decided not to keep their curiosity to themselves and asked Jay's grandparents and aunt about their financial plans for sending her to such a prestigious institution. Though many of their inquiries were highly inappropriate and frankly none of their business, most of their inquiries were met with the saying "Where there is a will, there is a way." It was really baffling to Jay that so many people doubted her; people whom she'd never expect to doubt her. Of course, there was the guaranteed reluctance from some of her family members and friends. One of her church members asked her why she hadn't decided to go to the local university or community college as Jay simply responded to her with a momentous stare. Her older cousin, Nicole, even saying before leaving out with a plate full of food, "Girl, ain't nothing wrong with staying in your hometown to go to school. You gonna get down there and find that it ain't what you thought it would be." The people who had the most to say were the ones who were not or had not contributed to her well-being. So, their distasteful opinions didn't matter at all.

Brady still wasn't happy that her granddaughter would be going that far away from home (which had been the real issue all along). But, she was eating her words that she had spoken regarding Jay's not getting into Spelman. However, Brady was Jay's mouthpiece by telling everyone she came in contact with that her youngest grandbaby was going off to Spelman. Jay didn't quite understand Brady's initial disapproval of her school of choice. However, Brady's constant bragging was enough for Jay to know that secretly, Brady was excited and very proud of her, just nervous because no parent wants their child going too far away from home for that long of a period. Jay's mother was also very excited to see her only child graduating and heading off to college despite the number of barriers Jay had faced in her life. She looked at Jay in amazement saying, "Whoever would have imagined that after everything I put you through and what you've gone through in your life that you'd be heading off to the number one HBCU in the nation." She knew that the conversation with her mother had to occur prior to departing for college. The night of her graduation following the graduation party, the truth was finally revealed.

Her mother finally opened up to her about everything. Jane began the conversation with apologies. She apologized for never being there for Jay, she apologized for the strain her drug addiction had on Jay's life, and she apologized for the bad decisions leaving permanent scars on her daughter's body and heart. She admitted to Jay for the first time that when she was born, she was indeed born with crack cocaine in her system. Aunt Grace began trying to silence Jane as she felt that the information that Jane was sharing with Jay just before going away to college was irrelevant. However, Jane's disclosures were significant to Jay because no one had ever told what had happened to her when she was born or given any information revealing why Jay was born sickly. All that

Jay was told was that she was born with a deficiency and that she wasn't released from the hospital immediately.

Nonetheless, Jay was happy to finally be told the truth about her birth and her mother and to actually have that information come from her mother showed effort. Although Jay would never completely trust her mother, nor have a closely knit mother/daughter bond, she forgave her, she had gained Jay's respect. "Jane, I forgive you for all that has happened in the past. I have severe trust issues that will only be manageable if I learn to let the past go. I have lived my entire life with the mentality that if my own mother could hurt me or allow others to do so, there is no hope for anyone becoming close to me and earning my total trust. I have lived with a fear of betrayal, a fear of being hurt. I have driven myself insane thinking about the possibilities of the trauma they could cause. After trying to trust, I have been let down countlessly. I have staggered in between hating you for brining me into the world and hating myself for not being able to take myself out a long time ago. But, I now accept that it was not you that allowed those things to happen to me. Rather, it was your illness.

I don't want to live afraid anymore, afraid of people, afraid of love, or afraid of myself. Grandma Lillian always told me that I'll only get one mother. Although you haven't been much of a mother for my entire life, I do love you wholeheartedly, and I forgive you. Now, you have to forgive yourself. I am your only child and as long as there is breath in both of our bodies, there is a chance." Jay had reached a level of peace she never knew possible and one major hurtle in her life had been overcome. She had finally untied the rope of bitterness that had been choking her for her entire life. She didn't want to venture into this new chapter of her life still holding on to childhood pain and bitter memories. For a while, she doubted that it could be done, but she had finally done it.

Her mother, now in tears and attempting to pour her heart out to her daughter about how it was never her plan to be in this predicament in life, was hurt. Although it may seem hard to believe, Jane really loved her daughter more than anything or anyone in the world. Jay's birth was the only thing that kept Jane from attempting suicide again. Even if Jane wasn't present in her daughter's life to witness the greatness, just hearing through the grapevine about Jay kept her alive. Jay was all she ever had and would ever have. For the first time in her life, Jay empathized with her mother.

Through the number of tears she had cried over her mother, she never wanted to see her mother in tears. Still, the vow that she had made to herself about never shedding another tear over Jane remained intact. She then had to take a few steps in her mother's shoes. "What misery she must feel to have only one daughter of which she has missed every part of my growing up. She missed every phase. As an infant she missed cradling me or laying me on her chest to feel her heartbeat. As a toddler, she missed my first steps, my first words and seeing me off to school for the first time. As a young child, she missed every dance recital and every school performance. She missed every bike fall, as I would have to pick myself up and try again. As an adolescent, she missed the 'birds and the bees' conversation, she missed being there when I got my first 'aunt flow,' and she missed sending me off on my first date. She has only been present for my birth, christening and high school graduation. I can only imagine the way she must feel because she will never have another chance to experience all of those life events. That's enough to drive anyone into further annihilation," Jay thought to herself. After listening to her mother, she laid that conversation to rest with one last collage of thoughts that she wrote as an attempt to put herself in her mother's situation:

LIFE:

Life, why do you come down so harshly onto me?

Searching for answers to your questions in books, writings, scriptures,

paintings.

Yet, nothing but disarray clouds my pathway; I cannot perceive your calling me.

Aware that you are to be lived step by step and day by day, but you have given

no guidance to the number of steps I must take before stepping off the ledge of

detriment, and my days are shortened through your demise.

Experience has taught me that you discriminate not.

My aged eyes have seen the darkness of your face as you've torn through the

place I call home with no warning, plan or plot.

Stop punishing me for the mistakes of my past; I will not last through the night.

You have taken all that I ensure, as I give in to you with no fight.

You bring me down when I am high, and when I am at the lowest of my low you

continue to kick.

I tried giving you the benefit of doubt, but I guess it's true what they say;

Life, you are a bitch.

Two months later, Jay packed up her grandmother's van with all of her school supplies, dorm room equipment, clothes and snacks galore; headed to Atlanta, Georgia. She said her goodbyes to her Grandmother Lillian and Grandfather James and promised to call once she arrived in Atlanta. With tears beginning to swell up in the corner of her eyes, she said goodbye to her neighborhood, her family and life as she had known it up until that point. Jay had never been away from Lillian for more than a week due to her traveling with her club volleyball team throughout high school or visiting her aunt Grace in Florida. She had never lived in an entirely new state nor did she have family in Georgia. Though she was excited to finally be going to school breaking the horrendous cycle of her family, the hardest thing to do was to leave Lillian and Brady. Nonetheless, Lillian was overjoyed in the child she had raised and she waived her goodbye and blew kisses from the doorway. Jay had no idea that that would be the last time she would see her grandmother Lillian in her right state of mind.

Jay, Curtis, Brady and Grace rode through Alabama, bumping music and telling jokes, stopping at shady gas stations and becoming a bit adventurous with the food they chose to eat. It was one of Jay's favorite moments being with her blended family; no drama, no arguing, no competition, just good laughs and eats. Her father jokingly drove off and left Jay at one of the country and clearly racist gas stations (as everyone had stopped pumping their gas to stare with mean glares at everyone in Brady's van). Jay chased the car down the street. "Hey dad, you're leaving me," she screamed. Curtis finally stopped the car to let her inside as he laughs heartedly; Jay was not amused, and she refused to get out of the car for the remainder of their stops because of her dad's playfulness.

"You play too much, do you ever stop playing," she asked her dad as she crossed her arms and gave him the stare of death." He responded, "Ummm, no. The only time I'm serious is if I'm fighting. Hell, you don't play enough. You've been like a stuffy fifty year old lady since you were a toddler. Live a little babygirl, life is a game; play it or it will play you." She spatted back "But you ARE an adult over age fifty that still plays games like a toddler so I guess we just reversed roles dad." Curtis and Grace continued laughing for the next couple of minutes as Jay and Brady both sat there with the exact same facial expression; unamused and wishing that Curtis and Grace would shut up. Jay turned the radio up loud enough to drown the two of them out. "Thank you my little young adult, because these two full grown children are getting on my damn nerves" Brady said to Jay.

Finally after hours of an exploratory ride, they had reached Atlanta. She called her Grandmother Lillian as promised and began unpacking their loaded van. She walked on campus and for the first time in her life, she knew she was exactly where she was supposed to be. Older students greeted her and other entering freshmen at the gate, cheering her on as she takes her first step toward becoming a Spelman woman. They struggled to carry boxes up four flights of stairs as Jay was on the highest floor in her dorm. She was a penthouse princess as the students called it. None of them had ever visited the dorms to know what to expect. Jay had only visited the school once with one of her high school volleyball coaches because Brady refused her going to take a tour of the college (it was her way of exerting her disapproval and attempt to get her to stay in Memphis). However, Jay and her volleyball coach took a trip to come see Spelman's volleyball team and speak with their coach in hopes that she could try out for the team if she were admitted to the college. Even then, Jay didn't participate in a formal tour of the college, only walking around until they were eventually directed to the gymnasium. Despite how exhausted they all were, Jay was the most happy she had ever been.

For a brief moment she had the room to herself but she was awaiting the arrival of Bria, the girl who was supposed to be her roommate. They conversed via email and social media getting to know each other prior to move in day. At the last minute, Bria decided not to attend that semester and in walks the roommate from hell. Annie Sangers. From the moment upon meeting through the end of their freshman year, they hated each other's souls. Annie was one of those people who felt entitled to everything, not having a worry in the world and thinking because of her money that she was so much better than other people. When Curtis tried introducing himself to her parents, her father wouldn't shake his hand and the chambers of hell opened its gates in that dorm room. Mr. Sangers had crossed a path that he wanted no parts of as south Memphis revealed its wrath through Curtis.

Grace, noticing a Floridian accent, diffused the disagreement with the two men by asking, "Where are you guys from?" Mr. Sangers answering snootily, "We're from Winter Park, Florida." Not knowing that Grace actually lived in Winter Park, she then directed her inquiry to Annie, "What high school did you attend?" After Annie stated some low budget high school, Grace said, "Oh, that school district is not in Winter Park, I know this because I actually live in Winter Park." Now embarrassed, Mr. Sanger stutters, "Well, we are actually from the outer-skirts of Winter Park." Curtis then walking out of the room laughing, "Stop trying to be something that you're not, it's okay to be a regular person. I hate uppity bastards like you and your stuck up daughter. You're definitely going to have problems out of that little brat, Jay." Of which Jay agreed publically.

After everything was moved in and Jay had arranged her side of the dorm room the way that she wanted it, she and her family took a final stroll through the small campus until the departing ceremony. The dean and president spoke to the students and their parents. Before giving the final prayer over each of the young women and their families, the dean spoke of the students' significance; "Out of the thousands that apply, only five hundred are chosen. Many were called but few are chosen. Trust that we only choose the best. Each young lady standing here today graduated within the top five percent of her class, won beauty pageants, studied in all advanced classes, stood as presidents in organizations, studied abroad and so much more. Don't take your being here lightly ladies because guaranteed if each of you looks to your left and to your right, one of the women you just looked at won't be here next year and even fewer will walk across that stage in 2015." Following the ceremony, she said her final goodbyes to Brady, Grace and Curtis. It came as no surprise that her aunt/godmother was drowning in tear because, she was always crying. However, Jay was taken by surprise to see Brady crying as well. The only time she had ever seen Brady crying was when she slammed her finger in the car door by accident. She hugged Brady cautiously (not knowing how to handle her never before seen outpouring of emotions). Finally her dad the jokester dapped her up and said jokingly, "Don't come back home," and then told the two crying ladies "Why are y'all crying, this is a joyous occasion, one less child in the house, now let's go. Actually, she's the last one. No more kids wooohooo!" he blurted out as if he had just had an "aha" moment.

Finally left alone to fend for herself, freshman orientation began. Not then knowing the battle she would have to face with her grades, her roommate and her family, she thought about the president's speech. Regardless of what was laid in her pathway, she never doubted that she would be walking across the stage as a graduate of Spelman College in four more years. In her mind, she faced every battle with, "I'm from South Memphis, meaning I'm a fighter and a survivor. I'm prepared for it all." Also remembering what her grandmother had told her long ago, she knew that she was already born equipped with everything she would ever need for survival, and those words kept her grounded as she entered into this next phase of her life.

Battle Twenty

You Left Me

Jay called home at least three times per week and with each phone conversation, something was changing. Lillian didn't speak the way that she once did and the words of advice that would usually flow from her fountain of wisdom were becoming scarce. Who was she speaking to? "Grandma, do you know who this is?" Jay questions with no response. Her grandmother was no longer cognizant. She had her moments where the old Lillian would resurface; she had changed drastically and with little warning. She no longer recognized the people closest to her. She fought often and argued more than she ever had before.

Jay had returned home to Memphis for Christmas break and was caught off guard by Lillian's behavior. One evening, Jay was in her room with Lillian and telling her all about the college life before suddenly Lillian snapped. She said to Jay, "It's getting late; I'm ready to go home where my dad is." Confused, Jay told her, "Grandma, you are at home and your dad (my great-grandfather) died when I was just an infant." Lillian then becoming outraged began walking toward the door and could not be stopped. As Jay tried to keep her from going outside at that time of night, Lillian balled her fist punching Jay in her left jaw with a bruise that ran deeper than the physical touch. James had to go after her in his car as she was escaping down the street stumbling to stand on her own but not allowing anyone to get close enough to help her. He took her to what used to be the house she grew up in just to show her that there was nothing there. Finally embarrassed, she was snapping out of that episode telling Jay "I'm losing my mind" as she began to cry.

Nothing had hurt Jay more than knowing that she would never completely have her grandmother back the way that she once was. Jay was so deeply miffed by the thought that her grandmother had to face this (whatever *this* is) by herself. "It must be a lonely path to travel in a world where you no longer remember anything that you once adored." Never before had either of them had to face anything without the other being there and for once, Jay couldn't be there for her, she didn't know how. She would converse with her friends about relationships; she would talk to Brady about financial insecurity and life expectations, she would discuss with Grace about fashion trends and beauty tips; she would dialogue with Curtis about history and art, but she would admit to Lillian everything from her most disconcerting insecurities to what color she should dye her hair. She had lost everything. Just as Lillian was losing her mind, Jay was losing her dignity and to gain it back was a battle she faced once again; alone.

Upon her return to Atlanta, she received the phone call she knew would eventually come. "Jay, your grandmother has Alzheimer's." Her uncle Leon's words echoed in her ear like sharp screams of torture in an opened valley. She sat there puzzled and wishing for nothing more than to speak to Lillian. She longed for her voice; singing warm tunes of comfort and wise words of astuteness. "She said she would never leave me and within the blink of an eye, she's gone, not physically but mentally. She's no longer here with me." It wasn't until years later that she realized that Lillian would forever be with her, through her words, through her songs, through her spirit. However at that moment that realization was far from her reach and Jay had begun another downward spiral.

She began partying every weekend and occasionally during the week. She met guys that meant nothing but harm to her and showed that in their every encounter. She was numbing the pain of her grandmother's absence with every drink she downed, every guy she tossed away and every class she missed. She unraveled her common sense for temporary pain relief; the thrusts provided climax; the alcohol anesthetized the self-abuse. But she wanted nothing to do with either of them when that moment ended. It was a revolving cycle that resurfaced each time she would speak to her spaced out grandmother and had to face the fact that Lillian won't be here forever. She begun again to hate; she hated herself for leaving her grandmother when she needed her the most. Jay questioned God, and she was tearing her future a part.

As a declared psychology major, she was learning more about herself and her dysfunction than she had ever known. Through those discoveries, even more destruction followed. Through her studies, she knew that the attachment that she had to her grandmothers (and anyone else whom she became close to and trusted) was an unhealthy one. She had definitely fallen victim to having an attachment disorder that stemmed even further back than Lillian, but to her mother.

Self-destruction was in full effect. It had become obvious with her risky behavior, the main person she surrounded herself with and the number of lies she was beginning to tell herself. Her first regretted mistake was befriending a fellow hall mate and freshman in her class. Her name was Heather Spark. She and Heather did everything together in the worst possible way. She had only known Heather since new student orientation but they had become best friends even announcing to others that they were best friends. The irony of the situation is that within months of them doing all of their dirt together they became the worst of enemies. She had two groups of friend who represented two sides of Jay's personality, the good and the bad. Jay allowed the bad to outweigh. Among her good friends were Kelly, Norma and Tonya. However, she chose to stick closely to Heather for the time being.

They played tit for tat with the guys they chose to deal with, even to the point of having encounters with two other best friends (Landen for Jay and Renni for Heather). This double relationship was surely the beginning of Jay seeing Heather for the conniving individual that she was. What was supposed to be a fling (because Jay was not trying to get tied down with any boy while she was in college) was actually blossoming into a lasting friendship without sex between her and Landen. On the other hand, Heather was searching for a relationship and only getting occasional sex from Renni. Both of them unsatisfied with the two men they had chosen, began delving again into the sea of fish hoping for two men. One who could rock the boat for one of them and one who could become a life partner for the other. To their surprise, everything came tumbling down on top of both of them. Heather had become pregnant (for the second time that year) and along with her, she was willing to bring down anyone in her path. Not to judge because Jay was no angel, she did question Heather's irresponsibility and even asked for reasoning behind her poor decision making. Protection was always fundamental and to indulge with no barrier was a game unbeknownst to Jay.

Early one Wednesday morning around two AM, Heather bangs on the door with tears in her eyes nearly falling on the floor. Jay opens the door knowing something must be awfully wrong for Heather to be crying as she had never seen her cry before. "I'm pregnant, again." Heather tells Jay. Not knowing how to console

Heather as she had never been pregnant before, Jay just invited her into her room as she laid there and held her until she cried herself to sleep. Though Jay was shocked at how irresponsible Heather had been with Renni (who was known around campus as a player), she hated to see her friend in this situation. Heather told her that within the next couple of weeks she would be going to the clinic to get her second abortion and asked for Jay to accompany her. After Jay told her that abortion was not something that she supported, their relationship was never the same. Though Jay tried to be supportive of her friend, she would never be supportive of that act. However, she was not one to boast about her beliefs or force them down anyone else's throat, at the end of the day, it wasn't her business and one phrase Jay used often was "that ain't got shit to do with me." But as her friend, Jay told Heather to make her own decision because she was the one having to suffer the consequences, but that she was not going to go with her to the clinic.

A few weeks had gone by and she hadn't really heard from Heather maybe because of the procedure she recently had. Jay receives two phone calls. One phone call telling her that Lillian was back in the hospital and not doing well. The other phone call was from one of her childhood church best friends, Amber. Amber revealed that after the first semester of college, she too was pregnant (which was later a great experience as she was asked to be the god-mother of her one and only god-daughter at the time; little Ms. LA is what Jay called her because "LA" was the baby's initials). After giving the exact same speech that she had given to Heather to Amber, Jay needed to vent. Heather had decided she'd rather go smoke with her new friend, Bransley, than to be there for Jay like Jay had been there for her. Jay didn't smoke as she knew that marijuana was her mother's gateway drug. However, smoking had become Heather's favorite pastime since becoming friends with Bransley. Nonetheless, she turned to Landen to provide the one thing none of her friends could give her; the euphoria of his manhood. Without speaking a word or shedding a tear, she did her best to quiet the voices in her head telling her to prepare herself for more pain. She hadn't known a life without either of her grandmothers and to lose one of them was unfathomable to her. She just needed to breathe, and she needed to rest and engaging with Landen was the only way to keep her mind off of the pain.

After the one encounter with Landen being the absolute worst experience of her life, she began to distance herself from everyone. At this point, nothing could satisfy her. Jay drank herself into psychosis as her grandmother's health continued to fail. Her semester long best friend was nowhere to be found, and one of her childhood best friends was also with child, Jay was imploding. By the end of her freshman year, Lillian had progressed into the final stages of Alzheimer's. Though the progression seemed to have happened rather quickly, Lillian had been battling the illness in silence for some time trying to shield Jay and the rest of her family from the torture of seeing her in that state. Then, it was revealed that Alzheimer's disease and dementia was hereditary on her father's side of the family. Of course, with more study, Jay searched for ways to subside the effects of the disease; she could only prepare herself for how to care for her grandmother. She learned all that she could learn about how to manage Alzheimer's patients through books, documentaries and even lectures in her psychology classes. She learned more about how to calm them when they experience an episode and furthermore how to calm herself. At that point, the caregiver is suffering more than the patient, so learning how to properly handle stress was the most important lesson to learn.

While having to swallow the most painful pill that her grandmothers won't be with her forever, she had earned her first bad grade since elementary school (of which her GPA took a major hit that would remain unredeemable). She was starting to realize the difference between high school and college. Though she had always studied, things seemed to come more naturally to her prior to college. To now be in a situation where she must wear so many hats at once in an independent fashion, she was starting to feel the pressure. Heather had now completely turned her back on her and was doing her best to ruin her reputation. Heather had told everyone they knew of how bad of a friend Jay had been to her and how much of a conniving whore she thought she was. Of course, Heather left out all the facts about her own promiscuous behavior. For Jay wasn't the one who had been to an abortion clinic at least twice. Instead, Jay had never been nor did she ever want to become pregnant.

Amidst the widespread rumors and gossiping from those whom she confided in and seemingly everyone else that had turned their backs to her or in the process of doing so, she made a life altering discovery. Though she had fallen so low into this rut of confusion as an escape to the tragedy occurring to her grandmother, she was the one to blame for her predicament. After crying to her dad about her first bad grade and hearing him rhetorically ask, "But did you pass?" She realized that life wasn't as bad as she had made it out to be. She in fact had passed. It was just the first time in about seven years that she had seen anything less than an "A." She complained that after all of those years of love, reliance, total dependency and attachment, her grandmother had left her mentally. But in actuality she realized that in dealing with that rough patch of life, she had left herself.

This person wallowing in her own pity and drowning in self-destruction was not who her grandmothers raised her to be and if they were to see her like this, they would both have a fit. With each shot downed and each friend unneeded, she was becoming just whom she derided the most; her mother. As pieces of her heart were fading as her grandmother's memory left, her mother had been long gone before this point and she had no one else that understood. She had to get it together because this next phase of her life that she was about to face left little room for self-betrayal or self-pity. While she may have thought she was alone before the upcoming summer, upon her arrival back to Memphis she was about to experience the loneliest point of her life. Being there for herself, knowing her worth and bringing out the resilient woman her grandmother had raised was the only key to stability. Regardless of who in her life had betrayed her before and the number of people who were about to betray her, she had left herself. Above all else, she had to get herself back.

Freshman year was the year of discovery. She had reached a place in her life that brought about a sadness causing her to give up on her surroundings and herself. Jay had been betrayed before in many ways and by many people but this time seemed to be a little different. After letting the hurt go and after completely forgiving the main person who caused the most pain in her life, there was still more pain to come. Why? She had thought that through forgiveness, a world of happiness and peace would fill the spaces around her that had remained chaotic for so long. She didn't realize that forgiving her mother was just the beginning. Sure, she had let go of the suffering of her childhood but she had yet to come to terms with the fact that with each new phase, a new suffering arises.

Losing a semester long friend was the least of her worries as she saw through the path that Heather was taking, she was much better off without her. Loosening those ties to such a dead-end friendship only scratched the surface of her demise. Jay was angry; not solely at the fact that Heather was gone or that Amber was expecting (despite them making a pact not to have kids when they were thirteen years old), but Lillian had left her, too. She had left her state of mind and had drifted off into a world where Jay could not come along. Jay had never entered a phase in her life without both of her grandmothers and though Brady was completely herself, Lillian was not there. She was not there to give advice or to impart her wisdom; she was no longer there to provide comfort and a sense of security. Jay quickly had to learn to live life without attachments, which was one of the hardest battles for her to conquer. She had to trust that everything she needed to be attached to was already within her. Seemingly alone, she entered into the battle of all time.

Battle Twenty-One

Tattooed On My Heart

Clothes being thrown all over the place, school supplies tossed to the ground, shoes having no match to them, people screaming over each other, name calling, tears being shed left one exiled from the family for some time. This house is a war zone, and it's every woman for herself. Everyone had turned against her. Once again, here she is facing the odds of being doubted, degraded and spoken to as if they don't share the same blood. "Why do they hate me so much, it's as if I have done something wrong for choosing my own path." she thinks to herself as she loads her belongings into her father's truck and he takes her off to reside somewhere else. Earlier that summer, the plot for Jay's downfall was stirring amongst her maternal first cousins, while she was in complete bliss from completing her first year of college, and landing her first legal internship a real accomplishment.

Jay was home for the summer and gladly so. Though she was partied out and had gotten enough of the Atlanta night life to last her for the rest of her collegiate career, she was happy to be home for the next couple of months. She hadn't finished her first year as strongly as she would have liked but she had passed all of her classes. Everything began great, Jay had gotten a summer internship with a well-respected criminal defense firm in Memphis where she would be working full-time and attending court daily. She was so enthused for obtaining the position that her mentor had opened the door to, because the interview process for the job was rather strenuous and intimidating with the Memphis Bar Association. The interview entailed roughly three hundred students of all classifications standing in an auditorium with five city judges on the interviewer panel. Once the student's name was called they

211

would step up to the microphone, introduce themselves and answer whichever questions were asked of them. Of the three hundred interviewees, only seventy five would be chosen to be interns with the law firms that were sponsoring that program. A week after being chosen to be an intern and a couple of days before her start date, her family's jealousy toward her bore its true face in the most unpredictable way.

Her oldest cousin Nicole had just recently had her second child but had gotten into some legal trouble for about the sixth time in her life at age thirty. She had freshly been released from prison on drug related charges and ordered by the judge to attend Drug Court upon her release on probation. Early that summer morning, she called Jay's cell phone asking for two favors. With great anticipation, she pleaded for Jay to babysit the newborn and to drop her off and pick her up from court. She convinced Jay with her cries of desperation as she said, "Cousin, please. They'll lock me up again if I don't show up to court but I don't have a way there nor do I have a babysitter." Jay knowing she had nothing else to really do that day agreed to Nicole's requests. Everything had gone as planned until she picked her cousin up from court.

Nicole gets back in the car. "Hey Jay, let's chill for a while. I haven't seen you in forever and we can sit and chat about college life and all that's been going on." Nicole says excitedly. Upon their arrival at Nicole's house, they both made the spur of the moment decision to get tattoos. Curtis had gotten Jay's first tattoo for her eighteenth birthday. Following that tattoo, she had already planned out what her next tattoo would be. Little did Jay know at the time, the lasting effect this new tattoo would have on her family. Jay's first tattoo covered most of her back and was a picture of two angels with her grandmothers' faces, names and birthdates on it.

Of course, Brady was not at all thrilled about the tattoo; she wasn't too upset because it was a huge tattoo of her and Lillian's faces and names. However, Jay's new tattoo caused hell.

Nicole had a talented tattoo artist (who worked in a shop and that had done two of Nicole's previous tattoos) come to her house for them to get their tattoos. Out of gratitude for Jay helping her that day, she agreed to pay for both tattoos and with the artist doing work outside of the shops, the tattoos were majorly discounted. "With God on My Side, Who Could Be Against Me," was Jay's new tattoo located on her right side. She didn't know then, how many times in her near future, those words would get her through. She would definitely need a daily reminder.

Her cousin got a tattoo of her child's father's name on her neck (which showed the difference in mindsets) but Jay just sat there not saying a word because again, her motto resonated "that ain't got shit to with me, I'm minding my business." After getting their tattoos, the two sat and talked about everything that had been happening since Jay had left for school. Of course Nicole had birthed her first girl after years of saying she didn't want any more children. After all, the son that she had when she was in high school was now eleven years old. Everyone was expecting it to be Jay's turn to have a child as Nicole and her sister Paige would say to Jay every time they saw her, "Girl, you ain't pregnant, yet? Well, it's coming." Jay was constantly disputing that claim and questioning to herself if that was really all her cousins thought life was about, having a bunch of babies or were they just wishing for her downfall. Jay was entering her second year at Spelman and was only eighteen; she had so much more living to do before even considering having a child. Nonetheless, Jay asked a question that led to severed ties.

"Brady told me about your baby's condition and that the doctors said there was a chance of her being autistic and a possibility that she wouldn't walk. What's been going on with her, is there anything I can do to help you out while I'm here?" Within an instant, Nicole's fumes had risen from cool to boiling. "How dare she speak that over my child? Our grandmother needs to mind her own damn business." Nicole exclaimed using an array of other curse words towards Brady. About thirty minutes into Nicole's vent, Brady calls Jay. "Jay, you need to bring my car home, now. You do not need to be with Nicole in that house. The house is under watch for drugs and gang activity and if the cops burst in there, everyone inside that house is going to jail. I am telling you to leave now."

Not paying attention to Brady's request, Jay continues listening to Nicole. Jay just thought Brady was being a control freak as she usually is and Jay having her car was the perfect opportunity to keep tabs on Jay's whereabouts and dictate her every move. Moments later Jay receives another call. It's her aunt Grace calling now. Yelling through the phone she says to Jay, "You need to take my mama her car right now. You being over there with Nicole is only going to lead to trouble." Jay made an attempt to leave the room she and Nicole were sitting in as her cousin follows her throughout the house trying to listen to what their aunt was saying (despite Jay having to later defend the fact to her aunt that she had never placed her cell phone on speaker phone). Rather, Nicole just kept following her and catching bits and pieces of what was being said, Jay was in the wrong. The first mistake was getting a tattoo with Nicole, the second mistake she had made was continuing to talk with her cousin after being told to leave and the third mistake was allowing her aunt to continue talking after knowing that Nicole could possibly hear all of the things that were being said. Nevertheless, the damage done could not be reversed.

Jay decided in order to keep the peace she should just take Brady her car and catch up with her cousin another time. She wanted badly to connect with her maternal cousins that she had never before had a true relationship with because Brady forbade it and because they were a lot older than her, but now that she was old enough to choose her company she thought she'd give it a try. "Sure they had made mistakes, got a little wild in high school and ended up with babies but so had everyone else on both sides of her family. She didn't think that was a reason to limit the relationship she could have with them. After all, pregnancy is not contagious, and we're still family" Jay thought.

As she was leaving the house, the second cousin Paige (Nicole's younger sister) was pulling up in the driveway. Jay spoke with her briefly, showed her the newest tattoo that she had just gotten and headed home. She had originally thought that Brady and Grace were being overly dramatic about her cousin's lifestyle, she realized as she was leaving that there were in fact two undercover police officers sitting adjacent to Nicole's house and watching her like a hawk. All along, there was a reason why Brady didn't want Jay hanging with her two older granddaughters.

By the time Jay had gotten home, Nicole, Paige and their mother Roxy had called Brady to express their anger towards her and Jay. Jay arrived to find her clothes thrown all over the place, several boxes containing her school supplies and mismatched shoes in a pile on the steps. She walks in to Brady on the phone yelling at whoever was on the other end of the receiver. She picked up another phone just to eavesdrop on who Brady was spatting with and find out why some of her belongings had been thrown out. She gets on the phone to hear Nicole, Paige and their mother. "That little bitch isn't any better than us. You think just because she goes to Spelman that she's better than us. I made a twenty-eight on the ACT, and Paige made a thirty, we could have gone to any college in the world that we wanted to. What did she make on that test; a twenty at best. We're smarter than her in every capacity. Nonetheless we're all from the same place. She grew up in the hood just like us. Now, all of a sudden Jay can't hang out with us because you and Grace won't allow it. While ya'll think she's such an angel, the little bitch got a tattoo today, and she has several more. Not only that, but we know that she's out there doing just as much as we're doing, if not more. We know she smokes because she was over here getting high with me earlier, she has 'tramp stamps' all over her body and we know that she's been pregnant before, we just can't prove it. Brady then hanging up the line and approaches Jay with a hard slap to the face.

"How dare you lie to me like that? I've been over here defending you only to be made out to be a fool. You're just as much of a whore as they are. You have several tattoos, you indulge in drugs, and you've been pregnant, too. Get your shit and just get out. I will not have another drug addict slut in my house again. You are just like your mother. She got old enough to call herself grown, got out there in the streets and started off with the same thing you're now dabbing into. I won't allow you to break my heart the way your mother and uncle did. Grace is the only child I've raised to actually be successful, and you've all had the same opportunities. You are my youngest granddaughter, and you're going to be just like everyone else in this family, a failure. First, there was your mom who is the ultimate failure. Then there is your uncle, who is another failure. Finally, there was Grace who is my only success. Then, the next generation comes along, Nicole is a failure. Paige is a failure, and again, you are a FAILURE. I give up on all of you; I want nothing to do with you. GET OUT!" Brady shouts out at Jay. As she tries to explain that all of what they were saying about her were lies (other than the tattoos), Brady shuns her away and continues to shout hurtful things in her direction.

Seeing that she could not reason with her grandmother, she calls her dad to come pick her up along with all of her belongings. As Curtis arrived, he had Angie in the car and he asks Jay where she wanted to be taken as he knew that she would not live in the same house with Angie. They drove around for a couple of hours contemplating where she would now stay. All Jay wanted was to go home to where she was raised with Lillian. But due to Lillian's condition, she had been moved to her uncle Leon's house (Lillian's oldest son). Lillian could hardly remember anything and was now being cared for by an in-home nurse at Leon's home. Finally, she told her father to drop her off at Lenzie's house (her cousin on her dad's side of the family). Though the space was small and only had enough room for Kenya, Kenya's mom (Lenzie) and her two siblings, she knew that she would be okay there. Her dad unloaded all her things and placed them in the living room before taking off with Angie. There she was living in a two bedroom apartment with four other people. Though she thought she had hit rock bottom, the worst was still yet to come.

She sat there that night and cried for hours as she could not believe the divisiveness of those in her family. "How could they say such things about me? I would never do or say anything to harm them or their reputations and they have gotten me put out of my home for the summer through lies." Jay was not a seraph, and she never portrayed to be. But the lies that they were telling were very implausible. She had been too afraid to try any drugs including weed out of fear that she'd end up like her mother, and if and when she ever smoked, it definitely would not be with Nicole or anyone on her mother's side of the family. And she certainly had never been pregnant. She was nauseated by the thought of pregnancy and having children, and even more repulsed by the act of abortion. The worst thing that they could say about Jay was that she had tattoos (only two at the time) and that she had gone off to college. They knew nothing else about her, and though Jay had wanted to have a closer relationship with her family on her mother's side, they weren't those types of people. They all judged, so if any of those things were true (which they were not), they would be the last people to know any of Jay's personal business.

She had known so much about Nicole and Paige that she could ruin their entire existence with the truth. For example, she saw Nicole snort cocaine in the backseat of her car and knowing that between Nicole and Paige, they would have seven children had they not aborted so many of them (and Nicole was the person who told Jay about she and her sister's sex life and the decisions they made because of it). Jay had seen Nicole snort cocaine when she thought no one was looking at a family event. The previous summer, Paige had tried every pill in the pharmacy; even being incarcerated for writing "bad" prescriptions and forging a doctor's signatures. Yet, Jay never uttered a word to anyone about it because it wasn't her business to be sharing, but they have the nerve to badger her with lies. Along with them doing their best to destroy her reputation in the family, Brady and Grace believed them. Granted she had lied about having the tattoo until she didn't care to hide it anymore, Brady should have believed her about everything else. As she closed her eyes to finally rest, she realized the people praying the most for her downfall were in her own family.

The next day she woke up to a message from her aunt Grace telling her to go to the bank immediately and withdraw any money from her general checking account because she was taking Jay off of the joint account formerly shared with her aunt and grandmother. However, the majority of her money was in the savings account which she couldn't withdraw without the presence of Brady and/or Grace. She walked several miles to the bank only to leave with forty-eight dollars. She had been saving since she was twelve but had no access to the money she had earned. Over two thousand dollars she walked away from. Grace and Brady had added her onto the account as her custodians when she was twelve, and she never thought to open a separate account when she became of age. Jay called her aunt to ask if the money she had saved could be released to her. As expected her response was, "No, that's our money" she said before hanging up. Though she was caught up in the moment and clouded by frustration, she sucked it up and moved on. Saying to herself "Money comes and goes. Hell, I've been broke my whole life. Just like I earned that money, I'll just have to earn some more." However, she had definitely learned her lesson.

Later that day after hearing through the grapevine about what had occurred earlier, she picked up the phone and called Paige. Apparently, Nicole's home had been raided and the father of her child was shot and injured badly. Nicole was again taken to jail and her children were left in her sister's care. Paige picks up the phone to hear Jay's voice. "Hey, Paige you already know who this is. Why in the fuck did you and Nicole do me like that? I have done absolutely nothing to either of you. Besides, you had nothing to do with the dispute, you weren't even there. So you three imbeciles go and tell lies on me, get me put out and my money taken from me." Paige laughing evilly responds, "They need to know that you ain't better than nobody. Hell, you need to know that you ain't better than nobody. They place you so high on this pedestal and they try to keep you so sheltered. It's time that you're brought back down to your place. Hell, you're an adult now so they shouldn't care so much about what you do. So what if you have tattoos or children, you're grown and that's what adults do. Welcome to the real world bitch!" she screeched before hanging up.

What a way to celebrate this new internship. The night before her first day of work as an intern, she ironed her suit on the floor because there was no ironing board in the house and hung it up on the hinge of the door. Through everything that was going on, this internship was the small motivation she needed to keep going. Either she rode the bus to work or Curtis or James alternated taking her to or from work, depending on who was willing to do it that day. Each day, she went to court and shadowed one of the best criminal defense attorneys in the state of Tennessee. She met every judge on the panel, other council, law school students and many other elites. She was invited to cocktail parties and legal conferences to Nashville with other attorneys and interns. She worked so diligently during the day but faced demons when she got home. However, every check she earned, she secured in her own bank account. After getting enough money, she even opened a custodial account for her younger cousin Kenya depositing just enough for her to begin her own savings. Unlike what was done to her, on Kenya's eighteenth birthday, she released those funds to her and told her to do with it as she pleased.

Every day she faced the challenge of going to work and acting as if she had no cares in the world. While all along, her life as she once knew it was forever altered. The summer was coming to a close and now after two months of working and saving as much as she could, she faced a new challenge. Her father had been denied the Parent-Plus Loan for that next year and the government had put an end to the money she was supposed to be receiving from her mother. Jane had apparently been claiming disability since Jay was thirteen and she was receiving a monthly check to cover her expenses. However, Jay was supposed to be getting up to five-hundred dollars per month of her mother's check. Unfortunately, she wasn't made aware of that until she applied for financial aid to attend college. Her mother had to pay nine-thousand dollars in back disability (though it should have been a far greater amount) which along with Curtis' loan covered the cost of her freshman year in school. When applying again, she received a letter stating that due to the fact that she had turned eighteen, she would no longer receive a percentage of her mother's checks. So, Jay faced having no funds and nowhere to go but to Murray State where the full-ride offer was again extended to her.

She asked everyone that she could for help including financial aid, her church and even Brady. Financial aid was denied and to her surprise, she sat in her pastor's office in tears explaining her situation for him to blatantly say, "No." She pushed even harder by telling the Reverend that she would pay the money back over time if he would just give her enough to be enrolled in her classes, again and more sternly his answer was, "No." She walked out of the office with her chin to her chest and in shock as she could not believe that after all of her time and service to that church since birth, they offered nothing but still found it in their hearts to pay some of the member's rent when they fell short, without being reimbursed.

Finally, the most painful denial came shortly after. She had chucked up her pride and went to the last person she wanted to ask, Brady. Again, the answer was, "No" with even more hateful commentary. "Your Aunt Grace and I aren't giving you a damn dime. You want to go to Atlanta to whore around, then you do it on your own penny. Instead of spending money on tattoos, drugs and such, you should be putting that towards your education. I don't know whether or not you've been pregnant before and honestly could care less but I guess the only good thing is that you don't have a child, because you can't even feed yourself. You're staying your black ass right here in Memphis with the rest of us and become what everyone else has become, nothing. You had to learn the hard way. You love your other grandmother so much but not even she can help you now. She kept you but it was me and Grace who funded and supported you. We are the only reasons you got to Spelman in the first place. You mark my words; you will never graduate from Spelman or achieve anything else in life without us. You'll definitely need us before we need you."

Brady had always been a vindictive person, but those words hit Jay harder than anything she had ever said. She knew what it was like to love someone but to dislike them because those were the feelings she had for Brady. Jay and Brady had never really gotten along, however, without a second thought if she was ever in danger, Jay would guard her with her life. Jay thought of all the lies being uttered. Yes, she had two tattoos, but she hadn't spent any of her money on either. Her first tattoo (of her grandmother's faces) was an eighteenth birthday gift from her father, Curtis. Her second was a trap set up and paid for by her cousin, Nicole. Children were never in her plan, and she had never been pregnant. Drugs were too far-fetched as she had never even smoked a cigarette or taken more than three aspirins at a time. Nonetheless,

222

Jay hugged Brady, kissed her on the cheek and said, "Goodbye." Although she suspected that the awful feelings Brady had toward her was not how she or Grace really felt about her, she knew that Grace would side with Brady. Jay would never ask Grace to choose. All along Grace was misinformed as she was getting all of her information from her mother Brady and older nieces Nicole and Paige (all of which were known to be perpetual liars). Jay was in the wrong for lying as well as she had lied about getting another tattoo, but she had never placed Grace on speaker phone with Nicole and certainly not told Nicole any information about Grace. Nicole overheard it because Grace was literally screaming through the phone. But if Grace was refusing to speak with her, then Jay would let them all think what they wanted because she had bigger issues to manage. She learned then, that she would always love her family, but never would she be family oriented; she lived by herself and for herself (for the most part).

She had a decision to make and she had contemplated to the last minute. The day for departure had arrived. She hadn't told Curtis where to take her, he just knew to gas up the truck and that they were headed out of town either north or south. They sat there together in the front of Kenya's apartment as her dad asked jokingly "where to my lady." She said a quick prayer to herself, "God, just get me through this," before answering, I'm going back to Spelman. He looked up at her jolted by her answer as he was sure she was going to take the Murray State's offer. He said, "You know that if you go back to Atlanta, you're on your own right? No one can help you. My loan got you down there, but I can't keep you there. I have no money to even feed you, just be sure this is what you want to do." Jay responded, "I've wanted to go to Spelman since I was a child, and I swore to myself that if I got accepted that's where I would go, not just to be an attendee but a graduate. I've come too far to stop now. It's time to prove some people wrong but most importantly, it's time to prove myself right." Holding back tears, he had never been so proud in his life; not even at her high school graduation. Rather she would make it or not was unknown but he prided himself on the fact that at least his daughter tried. She was the first in his family to even do that. They stopped by his brother Leon's, house so that Jay could say her goodbyes to Lillian, then back to Atlanta they went.

Though the rough period in her life had just begun, she was learning two of the most valuable lessons, yet. Firstly, she knew that never again regardless of the relationship would she entrust her finances to anyone else or give anyone full access to it. Secondly, she had learned the meaning of stepping out on faith and her looking at the tattoo on her side that was shamed by everyone else meant the world to her. In a world where she was feeling as small as an ant in the grass surrounded by giants wanting nothing but to see her smashed underneath the souls of their shoes, she realized that, "With God on her side, no one could be against her." Her pastor's denial, her cousin's scheme, her grandmother's vindictiveness and her financial situation were scars tattooed on her heart for a lifetime. But those tattoos reminded her that she made the right judgement and that she was going to be okay, that she would succeed. Every tattoo she got for the years to come was symbolically placed and had a significant meaning in her life.

Tattoo one: her grandmothers' faces attached to angels bodies with their birthdays ~symbolized those two women raising her from birth and they were her guardian angels saving her from the fiery pits that her mother would have left her in.

Tattoo two: the words "With God on my side, who could be against me" ~symbolized the battle she had faced her entire life

*against all odds that included the acrimony of those who were
supposed to love her the most. She later added a rosary outlining
the words with the purpose of paying homage to the Catholic
education she had received since she was in kindergarten.*

*Tattoo three: the words "Order my steps" on her right foot
~symbolized that regardless of where she walks in life, her destiny
has been predetermined and is guided with purpose.*

*Tattoo four: half of a heart on her left hip with an unlocked lock
saying "lock of sisterhood" as her younger cousin, Kenya, had the
other half of the heart on her right hip with a key saying "key of
sisterhood" ~symbolized that the two of them were connected at
the hip since childhood. Although they were second cousins, the
bond they shared (especially after Kenya's mother allowed Jay to
stay with them once she was kicked out) was a true sisterhood.*

*Tattoo five: life-line that says "little sister" and her biological
sister got a matching tattoo saying "big sister" on their collar
bones ~symbolized that regardless of their fourteen year age
difference or the distance, they could always lean on the shoulder
of the other.*

Jay's body was adorned with tattoos that told a story of who she
was. They were therapeutic as she looked at them each day
reminding her of how much she had overcome while giving her the
courage to overcome even more. Some scars were caused by
default through pain and confusion. Others were chosen through
enlightenment and realization. All of which were scars tattooed on
her heart.

Battle Twenty-Two

Karma

Only one week back to Atlanta and a few days before class was scheduled to begin, she enters her dorm to find an eviction notice on her door, access to the online registration/class information site, and school email had all been discontinued. She wasn't surprised as she knew it would soon happen because her tuition was not yet paid to cover the cost of that semester. Many thought Jay to have been extremely foolish. As people would ask, "Who turns down a full scholarship to choose to struggle to attend a different school?" Her financial advisor even told her, "Look Jay, an education is an education regardless of what school you attend" and followed that statement with a question that ultimately got her terminated. "Why on earth would you even enroll in a school as prestigious and costly as Spelman if you could not afford it? You knew your financial predicament prior to coming to Spelman. So at this point, this was your decision." Once again, she stared into the face of qualm yet stood resilient. People could think of her however they wanted because none of those people had her dream: A dream to fulfill or the need to be something greater than average. And Spelman is greater than average. Jay felt as though she wouldn't have been given this dream if it was unobtainable and for that reason, she wasn't going to give up.

Through all of the people who had doubted her and wished badly upon her, she was realizing even more why she had chosen Spelman: for the sisterhood, for the morals, and for the resilience. She came in one afternoon from meeting with her advisor and after hearing nothing but bad news and having her parade rained on day after day; the sun began to come out. It was the day before classes began, and she had awakened early that morning to meet with her educational advisor. Dr. Grim who was a psychologist, professor and advisor shared some disconcerting news. Though Jay had declared her major early in her freshman year and already had core credits toward her degree, she was still not on track. The advisor that she was previously assigned to had accidently led her astray as all along she was taking classes she didn't need. They would be counted toward the overall one-hundred twenty hours she would need to graduate but not toward her major. Dr. Grim advised that due to that mishap and the fact that she wasn't registered for the classes she needed to take that current semester, that she would be an entire two semesters behind and that she would not graduate on time. Not even allowing the advisor to finish her thought, she stood up and walked out angrily.

She walked back to her room too hurt to even cry as she was greeted at the door by a final eviction notice. She unlocked her door to find her roommate Kelly moving her belongings around. Jay met Kelly their freshman year, and they became extremely close (she was in the good batch of friends that had come into her life as a freshman). She was a drama major and quite the character. After freshman year, rooms were no longer assigned but chosen and they both hated their freshman roommates so they knew that rooming together was their best bet. For Jay, having Kelly as her roommate was again one of the best decisions she had ever made at that time. Kelly was rearranging the room to make space for Jay's things. Jay asked "What are you doing?" Kelly responded, "Well roomie, I know you see that final eviction notice on our door so I'm making room for your stuff. My tuition is paid in full and if your stuff is on my side of the room, they can't touch it and it won't be thrown out. The room is small but if they end up moving someone else in, you can sleep on my side as well. We're going to be a cramped but we'll make it work. No worries roomie." With no

227

words, Jay could no longer hold back the tears. Only, these were the first happy tears she had shed in a while. "How could someone be so selfless?" Jay thought to herself. Kelly kept Jay's things on her side for months to come and would bring sandwiches from the café for her because Jay didn't have a meal plan. With their cramped lifestyle, she never complained, and Jay knew that regardless of where life took the two of them, there was a purpose for them being in that space together at that time. Kelly taught her the definition of selflessness.

Kelly was not the only person that proved to be a life saver. She had met and absolutely adored Norma. Though she met Norma her freshman year as well, she didn't see their friendship unfold until sophomore year. Norma was always a reminder to Jay of how to be appreciative. She found a certain admiration in Norma that was unbeknownst toward any of her other friends. Norma was attending Spelman on a full-ride scholarship that was awarded to her because of her story. Being that Norma was one of eleven children that had all been in and out of foster care their entire lives, she was a hero to so many people. Every time Jay hung out with Norma, she was always doing someone's hair, or tutoring or anything else to make money for her family.

As Jay was struggling to stay in school, Norma was struggling to provide for her seven younger siblings and keeping them united. Throughout the years to come, she never once complained about her situation and she was always telling Jay how grateful she was because "it could always be a lot worse." All the while, Jay thinks to herself how amazing Norma is to have that mindset, because her situation compared to Jay's was already a lot worse. It was so astounding to Jay that though Norma had a full-ride (covering room, board, meals and transportation); she too was struggling to survive.

Another one of Jay's friendships yielded happiness. Tonya was a new friend that Jay had known of but didn't actually converse with until they had a class together sophomore year. Tonya, like all of Jay's friends, had a story. She was the middle child of five siblings and often suffered because of it. Of the siblings, she was the forgotten one because the attention was often on the oldest or the youngest, she learned to deal with everything alone. She went through an abusive relationship that took years to get out of all because no one knew. However, in the midst of coming home to "Mr. Crazy", she was always the life of the party. After getting to know her, Jay realized that she was the center of attention on the dance floor because the dance floor is where she existed. Despite any argument, controlling behavior or abuse that she would have to deal with at home, when she went out she truly lived and her smile would make anyone around her forget about their problems too. Tonya taught Jay to live in the moment, not worried about what may happen when the party is over, just dance in this moment.

While Jay was facing the most difficult battle of being alone in a world where not even some of the members in her family cared, she made another life-changing detection. This is when she learned that blood doesn't make you family; your actions do. From that moment forward, she knew that her friends were her family. She realized the power of friendship and between Mitch, Morgan, Amber, Kelly, Tonya and Norma; she had the perfect immediate family. So, together they rode this wave and entered into their second year of college; all fighting different battles but trying to reach the same destination.

The first day of classes had begun and even with the news that she could not register for class and that she was not expected to graduate on time, she was determined. She had snuck a copy of her transcript off of her advisor's desk so that she would know in detail which classes she would need to take since she didn't have access to her online account. She sat in on every class that she planned on taking and at the end of each of those classes she spoke with those professors. She introduced herself, explained her situation to them and pleaded that each of them allow her to sit in on the classes, do the work and take the tests. She didn't have money for books but she took pictures on her phone of the relevant chapters from classmates in order to do her work. She asked for her professors to grade her work as they would any other student and plug in those grades once she was registered in the system. All but one professor agreed and even in that class, Jay didn't miss a day. Though the professor didn't grade her work, she still completed it, which came in handy once she was registered.

About three weeks into the start of classes, she still had no idea what her next moves would be other than knowing she had to get a job to stay in school. Yet, she couldn't afford to miss any classes or assignments as the professors were already doing her a favor by allowing her to sit in on their classes without being registered. However, over the course of the first three weeks of school, Jay had applied to over twenty different jobs. Finally, she was called in to interview for two opportunities. One was to be a sales representative in the New York Times bookstore in the Atlanta International Airport and the other was to be sales associate at Marshalls. On her way to the first interview, she sat on the bus very overwhelmed as she noticed this lady staring at her. The unknown woman starred interestedly at her for some time before she came and sat next to her on the bus. With a closer glimpse of this lady, she started to look very familiar. Jay had been in the Spelman College Glee Club since the beginning of her freshman year and to her surprise, the lady that was on the bus was also in the glee club and was a member of the soprano two section just as she was.

They conversed for the entirety of the ride and before Jay got off the bus, the young lady slid her twenty dollars saying, "I'm a senior now and I've been in your situation before. The look you had on your face and the unfallen tears in the corner of your eyes were familiar, I know your struggle and trust me one day soon, you'll be a senior getting ready to graduate too. Hang in there." Again, not being able to hold back the tears Jay hugs her Spelman Sister and gets off the bus heading to her interview. Jay felt bad because they had an entire conversation, exchanged hugs and she was given twenty dollars yet Jay didn't even know her name. However, she knew that she would see her again as both were in the glee club together.

Slowly, but surely, everything began falling into place. She had begun working full-time at the airport and part-time at Marshall's and was still attending all of her classes. Within a few months, she was registered for classes and doing very well in her academics. She had given Spelman every bit of the earnings she had made since she had been working without even taking a penny out of it. Though it wasn't nearly enough to cover the cost of tuition, everyone in the financial aid department was touched by her effort. After months of watching her struggle to get on her feet, her new financial advisor called her into the financial aid office and a few weeks before midterm exams. "Jay, we have watched you work diligently and your efforts to remain at this institution are countless. Therefore, we will be presenting you with the maximum amount of the Need Based Scholarship that will help to cover the cost of this semester and as long as you apply for the scholarship each semester, I will see to it that you are awarded this amount each year. However, you must still make payments towards the balance that will be left over as this scholarship will still leave you with about five-thousand dollars for you to come up with for the academic year."

After being awarded that scholarship along with several other scholarships and with the assistance of two student loans, and much help from an older lady named Ms. Gardner (a lady from her church who shared the same birthday and had loved Jay like a grandchild since she was a small child in that church and helped her out whenever she had the extra funds to spare), she was registered for classes though it was now the middle of the semester. When Jay went to have a conversation with Dr. Banister (the professor that would not grade any of Jay's work because she wasn't registered) about some material that she could not grasp in the lecture, she was once again doubted. Dr. Banister said, "I am not taking up my time to speak with you when you were just registered into my class. Honestly, you should consider withdrawing from my class because there is no way that you will be able to catch up on this semester's work" she said thinking that Jay had not been doing the work all along. The next day, Jay compiled all the work she had completed for Dr. Banister's class throughout the semester, placed it chronologically in a folder with a note attached and slid it under her office door. The note simply stated, "Completed semester assignments - Jay." Needless to say, Jay finished that semester and the rest of that year off strongly.

The next few years brought unforeseen toils in which she was facing one step at a time. Though it seemed to be a never ending battle for success, she reigned undefeated. Between the time of her sophomore year and the year she graduated she had faced a number of encounters that all made her a more irrepressible woman in the end. She had balanced working two jobs while attending school, moved off campus to help lessen the cost of her tuition to one of the most dangerous neighborhoods in Atlanta. She was followed home from work and school twice, was at the tail end of an attempted robbery of which she fought her way out and had entered into the unhealthiest relationship she'd ever been in.

One of the scariest nights of her life, she looked a man in the face with all intention to attack him before he attacked her. If it came down to it, she knew that she would kill if she had to. She would normally work a 3:30pm to 11:30pm shift at the airport during the week and if a flight was delayed, she'd have to stay even longer. Due to the fact that she didn't have a car at the time, she was using the public transit system. After her shift ended, she would get on the train and head home. The buses stopped running at 12pm so unless it was one of those rare occasions where she got off at her exact closing time, she would ride the train to her nearest exit and walk the remainder of the way home in the middle of the night. On a normal night, she would get off from work, ride the train to her side of town and walk fifteen to twenty minutes to her complex. She would then shower, eat a snack, study and do homework until about four in the morning, sleep until about 7:30 and start over at eight the next morning as her first class would begin at 8:50. Well, that night the unusual and unexpected occurred. She walked pass this gentleman and made sure to make eye contact with him as he began spatting out sexual comments and making advances at her. Jay not wanting to aggravate the man spoke to him briefly attempting not to be rude and kept walking. She continued walking five minutes into the distance without any further disturbances before she got the feeling that encouraged her to turn around facing the opposite direction. As she turned, she saw the man that had just spoken to her running towards her with full speed. Knowing that he was either about to try to rob or rape her, her south Memphis instincts kicked in. He was running too fast and at too close of a distance for her to get away on foot and he clearly had something that looked like a gun in his left hand. "He's going to kill me but I'm not going down without a fight," she thought to herself.

Within a few milliseconds she had put her door key between her fingers to serve as a weapon and when he got close enough to her, she began to punch and kick as hard as she could, allowing the tip end of that key to rip into his flesh, puncture him in the eyes and draw blood from his neck as her knee pounded into his groin forcefully and repeatedly. She didn't stop until he was lying on the ground moaning in pain with the fallen gun a few feet away from them. She looked at his mangled body lying there for a second and took off running as fast as she could to her home before he conjured up the strength to grab that gun or get back up.

Upon her arrival home, she called the police with hopes that they'd be able to catch the perpetrator but they didn't show up until forty-seven minutes after she placed the call. By then, she was sure that he was long gone. Though the officers made it apparent through their body language that they were going to be of little assistance in catching this guy as they pulled up in front of Jay's complex joking and having a causal conversation, they pretended to care by asking an array of annoying question. "Ma'am, can you provide a detailed description of the perpetrator? Why were you even out walking the streets at this time of night? Why didn't you confiscate his weapon? What direction was he last seen going in? etc." Jay responded with an attitude to all of their inquiries as she was already uneasy around police and having to call them sickened her. "He was a black male wearing all black with a hoodie that covered most his head, didn't pay much more attention to the details as I was busy fighting for my life. Not that it should matter why I was out and I am clearly still in my airport uniform, I was just returning home from work and this is the route I have to take in order to get home from the transit station. I am not a street-walker if that's your implication. I wouldn't dare put my fingerprints on any weapon that does not belong to me. And I left him lying on the sidewalk so I can't tell you which direction he went after I took off, but I'm sure that after waiting close to an hour for y'all to arrive that he's nowhere to be found now. Any further dumb ass questions officers?" They finished their report and walked away laughing and picking back up with the casual conversation they were having prior to approaching Jay.

Not only was it time for her to move away from that neighborhood, but it was time to invest in a vehicle as well if she was going to continue working graveyard shifts (which was inevitable, as that was the only shift that would allow her to attend her three morning and two afternoon classes). Nonetheless, she gathered her thoughts, thanked God that she had made it out of that situation alive and began her studying for midterm exams. Although working at the airport brought her financial support to help her pay for school, it also brought about her most regretted companionship.

Every day during her lunch she would go to this bakery and sit there until her break was over. She would take her school books; sitting at the exact same table, order the exact same beverage (small coffee with a shot of expresso and added caramel), and look at the same guy that busted tables and served customers at the bakery. His name was Chase Anderson. As Jay sat there studying and trying to keep herself awake with the coffee, her eyes would always find their way back to him. He had never noticed her in the store before but after studying for a while, the rest of her break was spent just admiring how gorgeous he was. She hadn't seen a creature as dazzling as he; golden caramel colored skin, a little over six feet tall, curly dark brown hair, muscular in build with almond colored eyes, perfectly trimmed mustache with a full beard and pearly white teeth. Not expecting anything more than for him to be her daily eye candy, their eyes connected. "Oh shit, put your head down," she thinks. Quickly she turns away in hopes that he had not noticed her. It was too late. Beginning to breathe heavily as she notices him walking over to her, she looks up astonished never before being that close to a fantasy.

He asks, "What is in that pink binder? Every day I see you in here reading and writing in the same pink binder. Every day you order the same small cup of coffee and every day you sit at this exact same table in the exact same chair. So, tell me, what is so important in that pink binder?" He had noticed her, she was charmed. After explaining to him that the pink binder contained all of her notes for her most difficult psychology class, he became impressed. As his boss began yelling at him to get back to work, he shouted out as he walked away. "Meet me by the north side entrance of the airport at the end of your shift." He commanded. He got off an hour before Jay did, and he waited for her at the entrance. They rode the train together and exchanged numbers. From that moment up until he broke her heart for the last time two years and four months later, the two were inseparable.

The highs and lows of life continued to be amongst the everyday encounters. The highs included, purchasing her first vehicle, having her fantasy man come to Memphis to meet her family and asking her father for her hand in marriage, and her gearing up to complete her junior year of college. The lows were traveling back and forth to Memphis due to Lillian being in an induced coma for a few weeks, being placed on six month watch as she was at high risk of developing cervical cancer (being told that there was a large possibility that she would not be able to conceive in the future) and facing her now fiancé's infidelity. Jay was beginning to see that nothing lasts forever, neither happiness nor . anguish.

She and her aunt Grace were finally rekindling their tarnished relationship, and though Jay had never convinced her that she hadn't betrayed her, her aunt forgave her. The money that Brady and Grace had not returned was still there and instead of handing it over to Jay directly, she helped her to purchase her first car with it (which down the line Jay appreciated). Despite, no one completely getting pass the course of dramatic events that took place that summer, her family was beginning to realize the fallacies against Jay. Nicole had since, gotten pregnant again, been incarcerated again for drug possession with an intent to sell and both she and her sister Paige had gone to jail for identity theft as well. Though Brady never apologized or even acknowledged the hell she'd caused with Jay in the past, she finally realized that Jay was not the enemy, her oldest grandchildren were.

Nicole and Paige's scheming didn't begin or end with what they had done to Jay. But they had begun stooping too low for their dissidence to go unnoticed and ignored any longer. One afternoon Nicole and Paige called Brady asking if she could give them a ride to the grocery store for pampers and milk for their babies. Of course, Brady agreed as she was anxious to spend time with them and her great-grandchildren. As they walked through the local grocery store the girls enacted their plan. Paige (who had battled diabetes for most of her adult life) pretended to pass out in the aisle of the store and as Brady rushed to her rescue, Nicole went through her grandmother's purse and confiscated her bank cards, driver's license and social security card. By the time Brady had gotten Paige off the floor and back to normal, her entire identity had been copied down and stolen by her own grandchild.

A few weeks later, Brady received a call from Grace asking what she had been spending so much money on as she and Grace still shared an account. Later, she saw that her entire savings had been wiped clear. After the investigation revealed that her granddaughters, Nicole and Paige, were the culprits behind the scam, Brady decided (against everyone else's opinion) to drop the charges as she didn't want to put her grandchildren in jail (where they rightfully belonged). Though Jay felt badly about what her grandmother was dealing with and she wanted nothing more than for those two to rot in jail, all she kept thinking was "karma's a bitch." Just a few years prior, Jay had lost her entire savings, had been kicked out of her home, and was struggling to remain in school as Brady kept proclaiming that without the money she and Grace provided, she would equate to nothing. Now, how ironic is it that she and Grace's savings had been wiped away as though it never existed by the same kleptomaniac bitches that were the cause of her losing everything. "Everything happens for a reason," she thinks to herself because had Grace and Brady not kicked her off of their joint account, the little that she did have would've been erased along with theirs.

As Brady called Jay pouring out how disappointed she was with Nicole and Paige, all Jay could say was "well" and carry on with her day. Oh, how the tables turn as they would now feel the pressure of losing everything at the hands of their own blood. Nonetheless, they were still in her bloodline, but Jay didn't consider them family at all. Her cousins were just people she knew. Jay would often compare them to animals rather than humans as she would say "Humans are the only species on earth with a conscience, and clearly their conscience was nonexistent." As Jay had always believed in karma, it was Nicole's turn. A year following her stealing the life savings from her grandmother, aunt Grace and Brady's sister Brenda, Nicole passed away "mysteriously" a day before her thirty-third birthday.

For Jay, the saddest part of her passing was not her death, but rather the lives of her children who were now left motherless. She had three children, a fourteen year old son and two and three year old daughters. Still, with no pity in her heart for the miserable mother, daughter, granddaughter, niece, big cousin, family member and overall person she was, Jay never shed a tear as karma had simply made its way back around to her. Just as she had claimed the savings, identity, belongings and security from everyone around her, death finally came knocking on her door to claim her life. No one in her family could understand Jay's nonchalant attitude about the incident but Jay was far removed from having any emotions toward most of the members in her family that had wronged her or especially her grandmother. Jay's perceptions or feeling toward her were not changed just because she passed; Jay wasn't going to pretend or lie, if it wasn't about the babies or her grandmothers, Jay didn't care about "family". Jay loved the children, because they were children, but adults received no tolerance. Besides, the family that she was planning to build with

Chase was beginning to garnish all of her attention and emotions (in the most negative way).

The first incident with Chase happened as they were celebrating Jay's birthday weekend. At 3:42 AM, Jay heard his phone ringing repeatedly. She immediately began to think it had to be some type of emergency for whoever was trying to reach him, she answers sleepily "Hello, this is Chase's phone, how can we help you?" She was completely shocked to hear a woman's voice going off on her as if she had done something wrong. "This is Jazz, why are you answering his phone and who are you?" Jay responded, "This is his fiancé Jay, now who are you and why are you calling him at close to four in the morning." After a little of the back and forth with this unknown woman, Chase had awaken and taken the phone away from Jay. Upon questioning him about the woman, his mouth filled with lies and her heart broke more and more with each discovery.

Eight women, a phone call from a random woman saying that there was a strong possibility of Chase being the father of her child, a potential sexually transmitted disease later, and one of her best friends telling her that he had made advances toward her in Jay's absence, she called it quits. From the very first phone call she received from the woman that night, up until she was told by Chase to be checked for a sexually transmitted disease, everything in her relationship was a lie. Though she kept turning a blind eye to the many "female friends" he had, the number of times he would tell her that his connection with other women was because of her incapability of supporting him, never would she have imagined she'd be sitting in this clinic praying that the results come back "negative." She thought how disrespectful he was as she sat there "If you're going to cheat, at least use protection. You don't bring your dirt back home with you," she thought. She had given everything to him; she had built him into a man that she thought she would be with forever. Little did she know the creature she was fostering was a monster and deep down inside, she knew it all along. Jay was the reason he got that new five-figure job from where he was originally making minimum wage at the bakery shop. She had found his father and held his hand as he called him for the first time since he had last saw him at age thirteen. She had agreed that upon marriage they would have a child despite her never before wanting children. Just so that he wouldn't be deprived of fatherhood, as he repeatedly expressed how badly he wanted a daughter, she agreed to conceive when the time was right and he'd just have to hope he implanted a little girl because she had a one child limit. She opened his world to new experiences; she comforted him in his darkest moments. She did everything in her power to uplift him regardless of how low she was herself. They had struggled together as she worked two jobs to put herself through school; he worked two jobs as well attempting not to have to sleep in his car as he had done so many times and to give her the wedding she wanted. They were both familiar with hardships but their love outweighed (or so she thought).

Jay blamed herself the most for two reasons. Firstly, because she was the one who had seen him first. Though he approached her, the first move was technically hers. Secondly, she chose to love him. She wanted to love him. She wanted to show him a world that he didn't know existed. What began as sweet eye candy ended in bitterness. She thought her match has been made. After all, he knew the value of work ethic; he knew what it meant to struggle, to grind, to provide. There were days where he'd buy one meal and give it to her because that was all he could afford and when she offered to share, he'd say he'd already eaten when he really hadn't. There was never a time that she would call him, and he wouldn't answer, even if he was at work. They attended his mother's church together regularly (his mother was a minister whom loved Jay like her own child). He was a god to look at; very appealing to the eye and his manhood felt even better. She thought that she was blessed to be in his presence. She thought that she was blessed to have found love. Before Chase, her toughest situationship was with Xavier. Jay thought the love she had for her first could never be topped and though Xavier will always be a fond memory because he was her first it had been topped in every capacity, including how much harder she fell from cupid's arms. He was an amazing man to her, and apparently so to many other women simultaneously.

As she was giving every bit of herself that was not taken, to him he was taking from her with no reciprocity. She had given her time, she had given her love and was soon to be giving up her last name to take on his, but she refused to give her sanity. She hated herself more than she hated him. "How could I ever get to a point in my life where a man has jeopardized everything in my life," she'd ask herself often. She picked up the pieces of her heart that was left and though it was one of the hardest things she had to do, she had to let him go. She couldn't keep allowing Chase back in time after time; but especially not this time. Every time he got caught cheating (and he got caught every time), he would beg and plead as he watched her cry countless tears. Just as she thought of her cousins, she thought that you have to be some kind of animal to be able to sit with a straight face and watch someone (that you supposedly loved more than life itself) cry so much from actions that could have been easily avoided. She thanked God that she had dodged a bullet and that disease.

Even in the midst of another low, God revealed his face. She was scarred from the emotional abuse but her body was healthy. With negative results, she became more thankful that her life had not turned into what it could have been. She was about to face a lifelong path of infidelity from a weak-willed man that would only weaken her spirit until the day she died. She was one unprotected encounter away from having a disease that would dwell in her body eating away at her flesh and down to the core of her soul until she died. What hurt the most was that she knew better, fiancée or not, she knew better than to leave herself that opened. God spared her, but that was one of life's most brutal beatings.

Though she struggled to keep herself from falling into dejection, she made some more life changing insights. She realized that no matter how much Chase projected her as being the problem, she was not the issue. He would often say that he found his solace of manhood in different women because she was a dominant woman and would not allow him to be a man. She had stroked many parts of him in that relationship, but his ego was not one of them. She fed into that being the cause for his first couple of mishaps but never should an un-stroked ego lead to children from another woman whose last name he didn't even know. All along while thinking she would soon be a wife, she was reminded in an instance what her grandfather James had once told her. "No man would ever want to marry you." It hurt to see those words coming into fruition. Despite the pain and carrying a bit of those insecurities into her future relationship (that also failed), she knew who she was and decided that never again would she change that to fit the mold of a damaged man. His karma had been long destined as she said goodbye to the most dangerous species known to woman; a broken man.

Maybe that relationship was her karma; karma for her bad decisions, for giving in so easily to what she thought was love without questioning its validity. She hadn't considered that maybe Chase's entry into her life was karma for trying to pull someone else up while allowing them to drag her down. However, the vital karma was trying to love a man before learning the art of first loving herself completely. The message was loud and clear and though fate had brought her down to her knees, good karma was headed her way and when it was her time she arose.

For two years she had struggled more than she ever had in her life. She had no money. She went without meals, she'd been attacked by strangers, and she had permanent callus on the bottom of her feet from standing ten to twelve hours a day as she worked both jobs from shoes that had lost all of their arch support because she didn't want to buy new ones. She had stress related health problems as she had also learned of cancerous fibroid cists now growing on her uterus. She had been in a relationship that almost cost her life through an incurable disease, she was watching her grandmother die before her eyes and she'd been told that despite her best efforts, she wouldn't graduate on time with her 2015 class.

However, after living on bags of chips and cold sandwiches, and a few caffeinated drinks a day for two years, after fighting off her attacker with nothing more than a key and will power, after continuing to stand regardless of how tired her feet were, after the cists disappeared, after failing at love yet again, after overloading in her classes; taking twenty-one credit hours until the last semester of her senior year, the ultimate karma knocked on her front door.

Battle Twenty-Three

Goals to Success

On May 17, 2015, Jay walked across the stage and looked out into a cheering audience at such an auspicious occasion as the dean called her name. She was presented with her Bachelor of Arts degree in psychology. People gathered from wall to wall forming a sea of many colors filling the space. She could make out some familiar faces from a distance. She shook the hands of the dean and president before snapping a mental picture of what would be her highest esteemed honor and most sought after reverie. In that special moment, she paused and took a mental note of the thousands of people in the room smiling at her beaming with delight. She had graduated from the internationally recognized and highest ranked Historical Black College, Spelman College. There were so many people present to celebrate her successful milestone, yet none of them truly knew the person they were celebrating. This caused mixed emotions of pride and emptiness overwhelming her as she stared back into the crowd. She was proud because she was the first in her generation to earn a degree on both sides of her family, but also empty because two of the three people whom she had done it all for were not there to witness the spectacular feat; Lillian and her mother.

She had done what seemed to be impossible in her family; to graduate with a degree in four years. Not even her childhood friends had yet to accomplish this as they had all fallen by the wayside of the south Memphis tide. She, Mitch, Morgan, Amber and Xavier all went to college in 2011. In 2015, she was the only one left standing on a stage accepting a degree. She sat there observing it all as a part of her felt that this experience was so surreal and the other part of her knew all along that she would someday be in this place. Nonetheless, there was no such euphoria sweeter than the one she was carrying in her heart. There was no pleasure, no pain, no relationship, no fight, no accomplishment and no failure that had ever elicited as many emotions at one time that she was feeling in this moment. As she had returned back to her seat with a degree in her hand, and the tassel had been turned to the left side signifying that indeed, she was a college graduate, she bowed her head in gratitude. Nothing felt more esteemed than being an educated woman who knew the value of struggle.

Spelman had taught her so much as it brought forth a multitude of opportunities for growth. She had ultimately declared her major in psychology to be able to diagnose herself; to identify who she was and why her mind functioned in the way that it did. She faced so many challenges throughout her life beginning with her attachment issues that she still fights daily to overcome. She was so afraid to be left alone and to face the quarrels of life by herself. She wanted the gratification of someone constantly being by her side to shield her from those who wanted to hurt her. She had been so overcome with thoughts and feelings about bad decisions and disappointment that she had dealt with alone (for the most part).

Until joining Spelman's psychology department, she had been instructed by her grandparents, church members and so many others to "Just pray about it," in regards to her feelings of depression, so much so that she stopped entertaining the "mental health" conversation with Christians (despite being a Christian herself). All of them were ignorant to the fact that depression doesn't go away with a prayer and it was beyond annoying to have religion thrown in her face as if their symbolic reverence/referral to a Bible story would suddenly end a person's thoughts of suicide.

Most of the time, it doesn't. They failed to realize that sometimes, all a prayer does is anger a deranged person even more because there is a believed "higher being" that is allowing this pain (for whatever reason). Religion/God/prayer does not dismantle mental illness and black people need to stop dismissing mental health issues through religious sentiments or shunning those who've admitted to not being okay. Spelman encouraged opened communication; where the victim speaks and listener listens (this is a much better method than repeating to someone "God wouldn't put more on you than you can bear." Some things are unbearable and just because it doesn't kill you, doesn't mean it doesn't weaken or permanently alter you.

Within her community, black women didn't have the time to grieve, mourn, suffer, withdraw or go on strike because in a black household, everyone is dependent on the woman (because far too often there is no man in the house and if there is, he is still dependent on the woman as well). As a little black girl, she noticed how all the women around her were always seemingly angry and as she got older, she would hear it referred to as black women having an attitude problem. But how can a woman carrying the weight of raising her (broken) family, dealing with financial burdens, being body shamed because of her melanin and natural curves (yet it's acceptable and glorified when imitated by "others" through tanning and surgery), and then having the men that she's defended, supported and raised choose the cloned version of herself be anything other than angry? She works a job(s) to support her children and self and is utterly disrespected and abused, often by the men she has held down. In actuality, black women and women of color have more of a reason than anyone else in the world to be angry. Yet, no one talked about it.

Black men have been the most sought after commodity since the beginning of slavery in the worst ways. They are trapped in situations with no plausible escape as the government and world around them continues building ruses for them to fall into. Once they are in the system, their rights are stripped away, their mindsets are trained to be like the minds of confined animals and then (if released) they are told to act as normal citizens of society. How? They have been ruined, their minds have been ruined. Many are grown-boys because there were no men in the house to set forth an example of black manhood (because their fathers were too trapped in the exact same system). The black men that successfully dodge the sparrows of the enemy through education face one of two battles. Either realizing that regardless of the feat, their skin is still black and that will always be the number one descriptor or they indulge "others," forfeiting any chances of giving back the unwavering love given to them by black woman and eliminating portions of his relatability to the black plight. Yet, no one talked about it, until Spelman. Though she appreciated being raised as a black woman to be strong, she was angry too. She had a right to be angry.

However, along with the knowledge gained from earning her degree, she also knew that everything that was once poured into her will always be the only solace she needs to get through life as she remembers her grandmother's words, "You were born equipped with everything you'll ever need for survival." Now she knew methods of accessing and applying those survival skills. The prognosis all along was that her true fear was of herself as she realized that the company of others quiets the demons running wildly in one's own unconsciousness. After facing those demons, she finally diagnosed herself, "schizophrenic and bipolar; ultimately insane." She was schizophrenic because her reality was distorted by the multiple compilations that created her. She was produced in a world of affection but tiredness from Lillian, sternness and disappointment from Brady, honesty but non-relatability from Curtis, lucrativeness but hypocrisy from James, friendliness but distance from Grace, and love but demolition from Jane. She was a concoction of everyone in her life and that mixture created a cypher of insanity that she learned to embrace.

However, her education extended far beyond any book that she had read, any class that she attended and any grade that she had earned. In depth, she learned of will power, friendship, spirituality, confidence and love of self. Above all the grandest of her lessons was struggle. She had truly learned how to struggle. Though to most of those around her, learning to struggle is not a profitable lesson but to Jay, it was among life's best lessons. Her struggle taught her how to stretch a penny. It taught her how to pull herself up when no one around her extends a helping hand while putting her pride aside when those people who are willing to help come along. It taught her to always have her own back when there is no one else to lean on. It taught her to fight for her life and to survive. Without her struggles, she would never know how to appreciate her successes. She knew who she was, she had finally gained herself.

Even as she stood there captivated by pride of her newest achievement, still two parts of her were missing. Everyone other than her grandmother Lillian and her mother were there. Brady was there and had brought with Grace, James and Ms. Gardner from their church. Curtis was in attendance with his dreadful wife and step-daughters. Her two mentors, Morgan, Amber, Kenya, Kenya's two younger siblings, Lenzie and her sister Lea were all present as well. Lillian was not able to come because of her health conditions as there was no way that she would be able to withstand a six hour drive and the doctors advised for her not to travel on a plane. Even though her predicament was understandable, still, there was an empty seat left for her and an empty place in Jay's heart. Her mother's absence was gravelling, she just simply expected her to be present for once. But it should not have been a surprise.

Over the course of Jay's life, she was constantly in a mental battle that she believed was caused by her mother. "Why doesn't she want me?" seemed to be the question of a lifetime up until this point in her life. Broken homes were a common phenomenon in the neighborhood that she had grown up in as well as within her own family. However, that brokenness was usually derived by the father's absence. Jay had always felt that the absence of a father and the absence of a mother were two completely different realities. Neither parent's absenteeism is acceptable, but there is a much deeper pain experienced when it is a mother. Jay's logic was "Here's a person who carried you for nine months. Each breath that she took was the only air you survived on. She felt a life growing inside her and seeing a tiny body move inside hers. A mother feels the babies' heartbeat growing stronger by the day until the baby can breathe on their own through birth. As a mother, how can you bring forth a life, only to abandon it once it arrives? However, putting her pride and selfishness aside, she began to think selflessly in that moment.

"I can only imagine the hardships my mother had to face. If I extract my own pain to think about the pain that she endures, her absence becomes crystal clear." She had made it to her senior year of college, only three credits away from her degree when her father was killed and she dropped out. She met this man that paid her more attention than she'd ever garnished at home throughout her entire life. She falls into the traps of his lifestyle, losing everything that she had worked so hard for including each of the five babies she'd lost before birthing Jay. Finally, she has a child and miraculously everything about Jay is the spitting image of her. She looks just like her; she acts just like her, their handwriting is even identical.

Now, she faces the fact that her most beloved has suffered by the mistakes of her addictiveness. She now has one daughter that she never experienced anything with and that has turned out to be everything she once wanted for herself. Many judge her, thinking that each high was a choice. When the first high was the only choice, the addiction was the life altering effect of that first choice; an illness. She missed every event because she chose not to embarrass Jay because even on her most sober day, anyone could tell that she was an addict. After getting sober, she was constantly overwhelmed with guilt for the pain she caused, the things she allowed to happen and the decisions she made and thought, "it's just better to stay away." It was then that a peace she'd never experienced before when thinking about her mother came over her.

Her entire life, she'd lived with this desolation, bitterness, hatred and depression because of her mother's absence and the bad things that happened in her mother's presence. She had gone through every emotion fathomable at the thought of her mother. Living each day with an attempt to be nothing like her mother and hating herself because everything from the shape of her own body to her temperament was an exact replication of Jane. Finally as she looks at her name written on this degree and she clinches it tightly, the warmest feeling regarding her mother consumes her spirit.

"The best thing Jane could have done was willingly give me to Curtis, and then him giving me to Lillian, who then became best friends with Brady whose youngest daughter, Grace loved me like the daughter she never had. That was the most selfless act that she could have done. Her absence in my life was a blessing because with her presence, I would not be the woman I am right now. Without the decision to give me a better life with someone else, I'd probably be dead. After all, she had no one to teach her what it was to be a mother, just as Brady had no one to teach her (as she too was raised by her grandmother) and had they been raised in love rather resentment and feelings of inadequacy, the entire lineage may have turned out differently. Brady didn't want children after raising her siblings and neither did Jane, now neither do I. Though my goal all along was to be nothing like her, her goal was to shelter me from the lifestyle that claimed her life, to ensure I'd never go down that path. I believe it was her goal for me to be nothing like her as well.

I am her only child and even my life wasn't supposed to make it, and I know that she wanted the experience of being a mother once she became one because it was the only chance she would ever get. Never had she heard the words "mother, mama, ma or mom because I always called her by her name; Jane. In my mind, she didn't deserve to have that title as she was nothing more than an egg carrier. Just as Jane would never get another daughter, Jay will only have one mother (and Lillian/Brady) and after realizing that she had made the choice to put Jay's life before her own by giving her away, she had acted as a mother and with or without the title, she would forever have my respect. Mother, I thank you."

Weeks after graduation, Jay traveled over three-hundred miles just to allow Lillian to see and touch her degree. Not aware that she was coming and with full blown Alzheimer's, Jay walked through the door. "Hey Jay, how are you?" Lillian asked. "She recognized me, she knows who I am, she's having a good day," Jay thinks to herself elatedly. "Hey grandma, I brought you something," she says to Lillian. Lillian had completely forgotten how to read and write, she couldn't even spell her own name anymore, but what was about to happen proved that Lillian still carried Jay in the crevices of her heart and at the top of her mind.

Jay handed over her degree to Lillian. Tears welted up in her eyes as she said to Jay, "You did it. I prayed your entire life that I would live to see this day. God can open the gates of heaven for me now, because my prayers have been answered. I can leave this world knowing I've done something right, I got one chance to raise a little girl into a beautiful, educated, strong and God-fearing woman, and I thank God that I got it right." Lillian sat there in tears clinching Jay's degree tightly in her hands and holding it up to her chest. She didn't want to put it down but she sat it on her nightstand and grabbed Jay's hands. Without any warning or tune ups she looked Jay directly in the eyes and began to sing "♪*If it had not been for the Lord, on my side, tell me where would I be, where would I be*♪. Her voice was weak but was still the most beautiful sound Jay had ever heard and would never forget.

Jay thought, "It was all worth it now. Both grandmothers had given up their lives for mine. They had polar opposite views on raising me, but they are the reason why I had come thus far. The lessons I had learned from them were influential to my entrance into adulthood as I grew from the experiences they shared with me." They had struggled in so many ways to raise Jay from the very start and her success was derivative of their prayers. So many things they sacrificed and endured to ensure that she'd never have to fight the battles that they or members of their family faced. For their sacrifices, she was so thankful.

Lillian quit her job and opted out of a path to earning a retirement income to stay at home to raise Jay. Lillian had wiped the tears Jay cried as a child over her mother and then as an adolescent, over her first lover. Lillian had dried all the stuffy noses, and she had changed the diapers. I wonder how tired her arthritic knees must've been Jay's entire life to have rocked and bumped her on them anytime Jay needed to be comforted (as she didn't stop sitting in Lillian's lap until she was well over eighteen years old). She had taught her through conversations about life, about love and about her blackness. Jay reflected on all the songs that Lillian had taught her, and the spiritual guidance that she had given her. Jay remembered the five star meals she had made with government cheese and loafs of bread, the stories she had told to get her to this point including stories of misfortune and disadvantage. Her constantly pushing Jay to keep reading, keep writing, keep going because an education (especially to be able to attend integrated schools) was not an opportunity available to her.

Brady had still not retired in order to cover all the expenses of raising a child. Serving as a maid/nanny for her entire life, one attorney after the next she'd often say that "lawyers are the laziest people on earth" and though she had worked for some really great people that treated her like she was their own grandmother, she had worked in the past for some who thought nothing of her other than being the negro servant. She had prepared meals, cleaned dishes and washed clothes for people that thought of her as disgusting. She had made the husbands their cups of coffee before they left for work while sewing up the wife's dress for balls and galas that she was never invited to. If she were invited, it was only to be the "on the road nanny"; babysitting the children, ironing the tuxedos and making last minute alterations to the gowns. She had scrubbed scum off the floors of mansions with toothbrushes on her hands and knees despite being a brittle old lady never to receive a "thank you" or even acknowledged with eye contact. She had cleaned up messes purposefully left behind, yet through it all, her demeanor of having high standards never changed. She taught Jay that she was a queen and that she didn't have to take shit from anyone. She taught her the meaning of "by any means necessary" because that was her motto when raising Jay.

As a child, even while living in the hood, Jay didn't think she was poor. After all she wasn't; she was rich in love, rich in ancestry, and rich in literacy. Brady made sure that from each dish she washed to every attorney she worked for that Jay had the best view of south Memphis that she could possibly have. This view didn't shield her from the surroundings and regardless of her parenting style being extremely strict, Jay knew now that it was all worth it. She looked back on all those slaps and punches to the face and sometimes harsh words with understanding and resolve. It was not out of negative intent but out of love. Brady loved Jay more than life itself though she never understood the depths of her love until adulthood. Brady's rules of "no tight clothes, no red fingernail polish, respect for elders and no boys only books" was for a reason. "I get it now", Jay thought.

Jay gathered herself and decided to go by her old neighborhood before returning to Atlanta where she was building a life with her newest found love who just so happened to be a Morehouse graduate. She noticed the now vacant and abandoned house that she was raised in. After Lillian was taken to live with Leon, and James moved in with his sister, the vacant house still had warm memories and because of that, felt like home. She sat on the porch holding her degree and looked out into the street. This was the same street that she had witnessed a murder on, seen men on the corners selling drugs, and women prostituting their precious bodies. This was the same street that she took off running down as a baby afraid that her grandmother had left her. This was the same street where she threw her first punches and ultimately learned how to fight for her life. She had done it; escaped the grasp of poverty. Jay has now left it all behind to start a better life.

Sitting there on the front porch, she realized that she had a story to tell and so she wrote. She wrote about the many times she should have died. First, beginning with her conception and birth, she had fought to survive the effects of being exposed to drugs in utero. Of the many things she was exposed to at such an early age, she only saw visions of herself one day becoming something better than what was expected of her. No one would have imagined (not even some of the people in her own family) that she would make it out in the way that she did. No one would have thought that she'd graduate from high school without a child and furthermore college. Or maybe all along, they all knew that she would. On the contrary, maybe everyone saw from the beginning that this was the destined child. The journey that it took for her to arrive to this place in her life was a long and tedious one. She had learned to be resilient. Of the hundreds of people, places and things that tried to fill her life with tranquility, she was the one-percent that fought back and survived.

There are some that are among the more privileged that attending college and receiving a degree and striving to be successful is second nature. Then, there are others within that one-percent who were always told, they'd never amount to anything and have to fight for everything they have. Here are a number of the underprivileged, broken and defeated one percenters like herself:

Grace, *Jay's aunt,* was born the youngest of three living in the shadow of her older siblings who had learned to escape the austerity of their mother Brady. She was born dead as the umbilical cord was wrapped tightly around her neck as she laid there lifeless almost claiming the life of Brady as well. Within minutes, she was revitalized and grew to be a successful ballerina, graduating in six years as the first African-American ballerina/majorette at the University of Memphis and is thus far the most successful member in the family: first and only in her generation.

Lea, *Jay's older sister*, was the second of three children born to her father, Curtis, and the third of five born to her mother. Though she and her mother never got along, she had a close relationship with her father and step-mother (Jane). They hid their lifestyle from her for as long as they could until one day, her father disappeared from her life without returning for about four or five years. She filled that void in her heart with men and became pregnant with her first child at age fifteen with six more children to follow. Despite being looked down upon for not having an education and house full of children, she still succeeded and proved that a degree doesn't mean everything. She loved to cook and started her career as waitress. She is now the head chief of two nationally recognized restaurants in Memphis. She holds the embodiment of a mother as she has raised all seven of her children alone. Her oldest son is currently a freshman at Lemoyne Owen College (following in his Aunt Jay's footsteps). She was the first successful mother, the epitome of all a mother should be that Jay had ever witnessed.

Kenya, *Jay's second cousin/best friend/baby sister*, was the first born of three to a sixteen year old mother (Lenzie) living in south Memphis and has instead of being raised, has raised herself. She is the second in the family to graduate from high school with no child and is now a sophomore at the University of Vermont majoring in psychology (as she too has followed the footsteps of her older cousin, Jay) and will graduate as an officer in the U.S. military which is first in her generation.

Amber, *Jay's first best friend from her church*, born the second of four children has achieved the most out of her family. Though she became pregnant (with Jay's god-daughter LA) as a freshman in college, lost her second child, was forced due to health related issues to take a year off from school, she has overcome the torment of being sexually abused repeatedly, she has faced her biggest fears. She has now graduated with a double-major in Spanish and International studies from Murray State University and is currently in graduate school earning her masters with hopes of becoming a U.S. Ambassador: second in her generation.

Mitch, *Jay's 2nd best friend from fifth grade,* adopted and was the victim of bullying for most of his childhood life until befriending Jay in the fifth grade. He was originally born to a prostitute (who he's never met) and has several siblings by his mother which he never garnered a relationship. Due to the conditions of his conception, he will never know his biological father either. He relocated with his adopted family to Miami, further pushing back his education, he is now a senior in college with a major in environmental science and plans to become an environmentalist: first and only in his generation.

Morgan, *Jay's 3rd best friend from seventh grade,* the youngest of three girls was born into a family of resentment and confusion. Though she was raised by both parents who were married her entire life, she struggled with having a healthy relationship with her father, who'd she'd witnessed abuse her mother physically and verbally. Though she attended college for two years, she decided to take a break and do what she loves best, work with animals. She too has proven that even without a degree, success is obtainable as she has relocated alone to Orlando, Florida, working for Disney and doing well for herself. She has just welcomed into the world her first baby boy, and she is wearing motherhood like an evening gown.

Kelly, *her college roommate,* was born the youngest of three from Lumberton, North Carolina. Besides being a loyal friend and roommate to Jay from sophomore to junior year, she too graduated from Spelman College as a drama major. Despite facing the challenges of being verbally and physically abused by her older siblings because of her weight, being overlooked and told that she would not make it in the industry for being a plus sized actress, she has grown to dominate the stage and is traveling the world and working as an actress: third in her generation.

Tonya, *her college friend,* was born the third of five siblings in Omaha, Nebraska suffered from the "middle child syndrome" and had to learn to live life independently. She survived sexual abuse from her own father as a child and an abusive relationship by her first true love as an adult. However, regardless of the challenges she faced prior to Spelman and in the midst of earning her degree, she too graduated with a degree in psychology and with honors. She is now aspiring to be a child psychologist to help other traumatized children like her: first and only in her generation.

Lastly, is **Norma** *college best friend*, born the third in her family of eleven in Atlanta, Georgia. She and her siblings were in and out of foster care her entire life due to her mother's negligence and mental health problem. Among dealing with the instability of her home life, she worked tirelessly to provide a better life for her younger siblings. Through the responsibility of becoming a caregiver to her mother and adopting six of her younger sisters and brothers to keep them out of the foster care system, she is the only one in her family thus far that has graduated from high school. Furthermore, she attended Spelman on a full ride scholarship and graduated Summa Cum Laude earning her degree in early childhood education. She is in the process of becoming an elementary school teacher: first and only in her generation.

Each of the aforementioned people, are Jay's dearest friends and family members. Ironically, as Jay grew up with feelings of isolation and loneliness, it wasn't until the aftermath of her own struggle that she understood she was living amongst amazing other one-percenters. All along, while she was telling her own story, she was telling the story of everyone that surrounded her as well. Each of these women (and Mitch) is the compositions of her heart through friendship. Remarkably, each of them has faced the same battle of being a deviation from the rest. The energy that she put out into the universe attracted people who were struggling just as she was. Through their struggles, they uplifted one another. Each of them have stories of sadness, anger, bitterness, love and success as each of them have escaped the perils of their circumstances and environments including neighborhoods, their relationships, their unhappiness, their situations; just as Jay had done. These are the members of her chosen family that share in her experience of being the one percent.

Thus are the detailed composites that garnished her within the single percent. Though this young woman has gone through a number of challenges and still faces them, she wanted to reveal to others the power of believing in one's own capabilities. She reminds us all that within life, we are guaranteed to encounter some turmoil and those situations are not in our control. However, life is about the choices you make, the people you love and your spiritual oneness with a greater being. Her life transcends beyond the typical day to day lifestyle of survival but into a world that few are called to be a part of. Her life was chosen to exemplify both the negatives and positives of humanness. She is a compilation of past mistakes and present strength that is more than a fable of tales of unrealistic matters. Her life is real, her issues are real and her message to you is to believe that the impossible is only a stretch out of your comfort zone.

To those of you who are looking from their porches with hopelessness in their minds and defeat in their heart, she reminds you to take the first step. Move from your porch and into the arms of gravity. Allow yourself to dream, it distorts the reality surrounding you and places you in a space of infallibility. To those out there struggling to have their dreams come into fruition and want nothing more than to give up, I beg of you to fight: Whether your goal is to make it out of your neighborhood or get out of an abusive relationship: Whether your goal is to get a better job or buy a car. Whether your goal is to graduate from Spelman College or write a book, it can be done.

You ask how do I know? ....

Because "J" is my middle initial and **I am that One-Percent!**

Aerielle J. Tuggers

What's Happening Now?

The Battle Continues

Though *One-Percent* concluded with graduation, it was not the end of my story as I continued to face challenging battles daily and discovering more about myself. After graduation, I decided to reside in Atlanta and gain more experience in the field of law until law school despite the persuasion of my family to move back to Memphis, which too warranted unforeseen struggles.

My first post-graduation job offer was a promotion from my sales associate position at the airport to the lead human resource managerial position. However, two days before I was scheduled to begin work in my position, the offer was rescinded and extended to an older and more experienced candidate. Having the offer retracted was a major set-back as my livelihood and plans to remain in Atlanta were all dependent on that job. Murphy's Law "Everything that can go wrong, will go wrong" seemed to be the story of my life.

A few months later, and exactly one week before I was to be evicted and headed back to Memphis, I was offered a position as a legal assistant to two attorneys in the Atlanta/Decatur area. The job was nowhere near the salary I would have been making had my original plan gone through, but it was a job that would get me one step closer to my dream of becoming an attorney nonetheless. The position offered no benefits; vacation time was earned at 3.3 hours per month (meaning I would have to work two and a half months straight before earning one vacation day even after the 90 day probationary period). There were no sick days, no healthcare coverage and the amount of my earnings left me with approximately twenty dollars to live on after paying rent, food, and transportation expenses (regardless of the fact that I was living in the cheapest apartment complex I could find in Atlanta). Still, I was determined to make this work and for the first time, I was working for two African-American female attorneys: one, a personal injury attorney and the other, a civil rights attorney.

Three weeks into the new job, my views about working for black women began to change and a whirlwind of bad luck graced my path even further. My maternal grandmother had been hospitalized again for congestive heart failure, my companion at the time was forced by his parents to move from Atlanta to Washington, D.C. for graduate school and the two women I worked for were the worst employers imaginable. While one was the most incompetent lawyer anyone could ever hire, the other was frankly a bitch.

The civil rights attorney decided that she would move to Cayman Island while still running a law firm in Atlanta. Every day, clients called with no response from her and some even came to the office looking for the attorney they had hired only to be greeted by me. The personal injury attorney was condescending. She had the most disgusting disposition of anyone I had ever met in my life. She was extremely rude as she would address most of my questions regarding legal filing with, "There is a such thing as a stupid question, and I'm going to just let you sit there and process that stupid question and figure it out yourself". Of course when the document came back errored, I was held accountable for it when the discrepancy could have been corrected by a simple, "yes" or "no" answer.

It was miserable being their legal assistant because I was never properly informed of the progress of cases, it was impossible to give clients any updates in either of their absence (which the civil rights attorney was absent every day). The personal injury attorney was repulsed by the thought of having a conversation with me unless it involved depreciating my intelligence, my womanhood or my alma mater (usually nothing positive or related to her clients).

The final straw came after the civil rights attorney called and told me that as of the very next week she was no longer able to pay me. This came as no surprise as I thought all along "They both should be disbarred." However, when I accepted the job, it was understood that I would be working jointly for the two attorneys (who were two separate law firms sharing one space). It was a combined package as I worked for one attorney for the first part of the day and the other during the latter part of the day. So ultimately this would mean that my pay would be cut in half within a week's time. As if not being able to pay your legal assistant (the very minimal amount that she was already being paid) isn't tacky enough, she then called back and asked if I would be willing to work as an errand girl for twenty dollars a week; picking up her mail, making bank runs and still minutely handling her clients. Completely offended by that question as twenty dollars wouldn't even fill up my gas tank to get to and from work from my house and revolted by the thought that I had earned a degree only to be someone's errand girl, I respectfully declined and began looking for employment elsewhere.

Throughout the nine months that I was working there, the personal injury attorney would often vent to the two other attorneys that had firms in the building, instead of addressing her issues directly with me. Little did she know, my networking skills outweighed her gossip and I had built relationships with the outside attorneys too and they were very well aware of how I was being treated at work.

After nine months of being verbally abused at work, crying in the bathroom on my lunch breaks, being hospitalized twice for my asthma, being placed back on six month watch for my reappearing cancerous fibroid cists, my depression had reached the lowest level that I had experienced in years. It was time to move on and ironically the main two attorneys that the personal injury attorney worked with and vented to negatively about me, were the two people that served as references for my next job opportunity. They even forwarded my employers negative emails to me.

While it was a rough nine months, I was grateful for that experience. As a freshly graduated student entering into the professional world, my skin needed to be thickened. I needed to be taught patience and humility. I needed to know the difference between handling conflict in the hood and in the corporate world and that knowledge was definitely needed in order for me to be mentally prepared for any future job.

The following job (though it was the complete opposite environment of working with the two black attorneys) taught me that sometimes people will walk in and not even acknowledge my presence (no good morning or hello), and that is okay. People will toss me their work to be completed without even really acknowledging me with eye contact, and that too is okay. What is not okay and never will be for me, is being greeted first thing in the morning with a command like "Make sure those dishes get out of the sink and into the dishwasher" as if I am the custodian and they are not able-bodied adults. What is not okay is being followed around the office as people pry into any general conversation I may be having (as if I am conspiring against them) while "others" are able to stand around gossiping (usually about me) for thirty to forty minutes at a time. Even noticing them making out-of-the-way trips just to stand behind my desk to see what's on my computer screen. It is not okay to be hired to do one job with strict compensation that matches that specific job description to a month or so after being hired being given the ultimatum to (along with what you were hired to do) take on duties of another role without the job title or compensation being changed. Though I say little, I am not blind to the foolishness nor am I stupid in either of these situations. Upon voicing that I would not accept this, I was responded to with the following: "I am not big on titles Aerielle, they really don't mean anything."

Well, to clear up any discrepancy, "I am big on titles." Not for braggadocios reasons per se, but for no greater reason than, I've earned it, along with the money attached to it. Everything I ever had was worked for and taken. So, I'll be damned if I just give up a piece of my worth without proper compensation just because someone asks for it. I know my worth and am no longer accepting anything that compromises my peace and anything asked of me on a mid to long term basis, (that does not fit under the realm of volunteer work) compromises my peace. Never would I allude to not being a team player, but I have been taken advantage of my entire life and I refuse for it to continue in my personal or professional life.

It has been rough, but I have learned through these job opportunities that neither companies nor people are loyal to me. I have learned that co-workers are not my friends as they can be smiling in my face and asking me very intimate questions about my personal life yet feel the need to go to my employer behind my back or have demeaning conversations about me amongst themselves when they have an issue with me that could be cleared up by talking to me (and no one else). They don't care about me and as long as I am not the owner of the company, I am disposable at the drop of a dime. I learned to always protect myself because as a brand, it is not in the shareholder's interest to protect me, but their company. I have always committed myself to diligent work, but never again will I be stretched out of my capacity placing my physical or mental health at risk for a company or brand that is not my own. I made a promise for my sanity to do what I was hired and paid to do, because any added stress lands me in the hospital, which no one is footing that bill nor will they be by my side when all things fall south. Thinking of how assiduously my grandmothers had worked their entire lives as a janitor and housekeeper; raising other people's children, cooking for them, washing clothes and cleaning up after them daily with nothing to show for it has left me bitter. Conversations with my father who watched his mother work as a janitor and having conversations with my grandmother who was still working as a housekeeper until she was eighty-four years old led me to promising both of them, that all of their hard work would reap great benefits for them through me.

I have learned as a black woman, I am a double minority and in any profession I enter, there is no room for error because I automatically represent my alma mater, African Americans, women, Memphis, my family and then myself. I am human and I will make mistakes, but I now know that my mistakes will carry greater bearing and will be handled differently. I will never walk into a room of the privileged and solely represent Aerielle. Before walking into that room, all of my social media has been accessed, phone calls of references have already been made, all to associate me with something or someone because my mere existence is not valid without an accomplished connotation and that is to be expected.

Now that the lesson of what I am worth within the workplace had been taught, the all-time test of strength was given on Tuesday, August 2, 2016 at 1:30pm. Rushing home from Atlanta at a moment's notice, I raced down highway 78, shunning the voices that had been lingering in my ear for about a year now, saying to me "Prepare yourself." Knowing that it was the voice of God warning me, I kept saying "No," until God finally responded that there are only so many times I could say "No." Tears of anticipation rolled down my cheek as I sped through the city limits of Alabama in a rain pouring like I had never driven in before. Finally as I exited Jasper nearing Mississippi, another voice said to me clearer than the sky that had begun to gleam with the rainbow that followed the storm, "She's gone." The car began to swerve uncontrollably as I sat there praying that my car would just flip over the embankment. But it wasn't my time to go.

As a child, I often prayed that God would take me before taking one of my grandmothers because I didn't think life was possible without either of them. Anyone that knows me knows that I loved my two grandmothers more than anyone else in the universe and if I could have had it my way, I would have easily given my own life for either one of theirs. Despite my best efforts, I didn't make it in time; through all of the speeding, the many prayers and the constant battles with God, I still didn't make it in time. Hours before making it to Memphis, at exactly 1:30pm, a half of my heart was ripped from my chest; one of my grandmothers was gone.

Though the thought of losing either of my grandmothers was unbearable, I never imagined that this one would be first.

After all, she had survived a brain aneurysm, brain surgery, a total of thirteen heart attacks, congestive heart failure (twice), opened-heart surgery, was widowed twice and suffered from a broken heart because out of her three children, the only one that she knew was there for her was the one that was the furthest away, her youngest daughter. Of her grandchildren the only pride she had was in her youngest granddaughter, me. And she had five young great-grandchildren that she hadn't seen grow up yet. But to me, my grandmother was invincible, she lived through everything. I thought she would live forever and within an instant, she let go of all the pain that she had held on to in her lifetime and proved her invincibility to be false.

I began to think of one of our most recent and consoling conversations about a week prior to her passing. I called her one afternoon on my way home from work as I did just about every evening and my grandmother began to tell me how proud of me she was. It was a significant moment in my life because her pride was always shown through her bragging about me to other people, or carrying around my Spelman graduation invitation in the left pocket of her purse to show whoever inquired about her youngest granddaughter, but was never expressed explicitly to me.

"I am so proud of you, now you keep going, don't you ever stop. And don't you dare let any of these knuckle head, good-for-nothing boys get you off track. As women, men are our biggest distractions and in most cases, our downfall. Don't you dare let anyone trip you up. God has blessed you with a brilliant mind my child, so don't you trade your common sense for love, you'll end up on your ass every time. Your mind is your power, don't give up your power, I know you won't" rang loudly in my ear; my consolation in my lowest moment. It felt as if she knew her time was coming and she needed to leave one last life tip for me to live on. In that conversation, she told me the reason why she was so hard on me for my entire life. Though I know that a part of her resented my mother and being that I was the only seed my mother bred, I was the recipient of her misplaced aggression. However, I also knew that she loved me unequivocally. She told me, there was something inside me. She told me that I was a fighter and that she knew I would never give up on myself. She told me I was like her because my beliefs, my pride, my consciousness was unwavering. She knew the one strike that would make me prevail, was doubt. She alluded to doubting me, and proclaiming that I'd turn out like her least favorite and in doing that, she knew I'd prevail.

"But how could she leave me now, what am I supposed to do without her? She hasn't seen me graduate from law school or become an attorney (or whatever other career path the universe leads me to). She hasn't seen me get married and (possibly) have my first child. She hasn't read this book that I began writing therapeutically three months before she passed (how ironic). Grandma, I wasn't done making you proud" I thought to myself for a while. I found solace in the fact that I had spoken to her on August 1st to wish her a happy birthday and the last words I said to her before getting off the phone was "I love you Bobbie Nene" to have her respond coherently "and I love you." Not then knowing that that conversation would be the last I would have with her and that the very next day, she would be gone away from me forever. There is not a day that goes by that I don't think about how blessed I was to have my last words to her be "I love you" and due to that I now take every opportunity to show and spread love to those I can't imagine my life without.

Upon my arrival into Memphis to lay my grandmother to rest, I was greeted by family members (some I didn't even know) standing in every corner of the house, people were walking out with bags of my grandmother's belongings and saying to my aunt and I "She would have wanted me to have it." On the day that she died, people were already claiming dabs on what they wanted, from the house to the car. Family members who were unaware that she had even been sick crowded around asking to help get rid of her furniture and personal items. Among hiding my grandmother's valuables from family members who were trying their hardest to gain access to her house just to scope out what she had and what they could take, I along with the help of my aunt and the only uncorrupted cousin in the family chose the outfit that my grandmother would be buried in, wrote the obituary, chose the casket and the floral arrangements. There was no time to even grieve.

On the day that I buried my grandmother, tempers arose and fists were drawn as I and my aunt placed a divider in the house blocking off access to the bedroom and personal space in the house. Close family members again asserting how I thought myself to be so much better than the rest of the family by not allowing everyone equal access to the house. Nonetheless, I carried on handling my grandmother's business because she had made a will and intentionally left everything for the person who she thought deserved it. After completing a funeral in only three days and dealing with the quarrels that come along with a drug addicted family, I broke down. Every time I looked down the hallway, I imagined that my grandmother would be coming up the stairs and knowing that she wouldn't broke my heart. Knowing that I would never again be able to call her and hear her voice on the other end of the receiver garnished a pain that I had never before fathomed.

My heart hurt, there were moments where I couldn't even catch my breath, and there were times that my limbs remained stiff regardless of how much will power I put forth to move them. However, one day soon after, my perspective was altered a bit.

My younger cousin walked in to see me in fetal position sobbing on the floor in my grandmother's room and said to me "This is your test Aerielle" before turning and walking away. I then got off the floor and began to repeat those words "This is my test." I was fluttered with thoughts of my mother in that moment, remembering just how parallel our lives were. When my mother's father died, it came without warning and with much pain, however, that pain is what led to her attempted suicide and furthermore, her drug addiction. That was her test, of which she failed. Though my mother's choice all made sense now as I understood how losing a piece of myself could make me contemplate what I have to live for, I realized that sometimes being strong is the only choice I'd have. I realized that even at my worst, my grandmother's spirit was within me because no matter how bad the days got, I refused to fail this test. People often said that though I was the youngest grandchild, I was the most solid. Ironically, the very same thing was said about my aunt who is the youngest of my grandmother's children. And though in regards to my mother's side of the family, I thought I would never be a family oriented person, I had found my ride or die for life; my aunt/god-mother. When being strong was our only option, together we stood; fierce.

Through my grandmother's death, a part of me has died and can never be revitalized, but another part of me has been taught how to live. Knowing how proud of me she was has sparked the attitude of invincibly that I thought she had all along. As I remind myself that "The only failure is failing to try." So I have begun to try. I try to cry loudly, releasing the pain that I often quieted to the ears of others, in attempt not to show weakness. I try to laugh more to soften the stones of hatred I still carry for a select few that have built up in my heart. I have taken the chance on love again and failed with a man that is the complete opposite of myself (as he belongs in the ninety-nine percent of the privileged people). I still think of my male best friend's and grandfather's words, hoping to one day defy their proclamation that no one would ever love or marry me. Still, I struggle with trust as certain scenes in my life constantly replay in my mind, yet I have dreams of the future that the demons of my past could never cloud. Traveling the world while still remaining close enough to Memphis to be with the other half of my heart (my living grandmother) has become my number one hobby and the erudition of self is becoming more vivid with each passing day as I continue to allow difficult experiences to mold me into an even better woman.

Shortly following the death of my grandmother, I lost two of the other one-percenters that were mentioned in *battle twenty-three*. Two women who I thought would forever be my friends and that I considered my (chosen) family broke my heart worse than any boy or relationship had ever done. One of them left me hanging for the last time, in a financial situation that literally put my account in overdraft that was all her fault in the first place. She took no responsibility for the action that left me in debt. Each time there was a quarrel between us, I was always the one to mend the relationship, wanting to hold on to the friendship. I decided at that point, if she or anyone else wanted to walk out of my life or did anything to exclude themselves from my life; I was no longer going to stop them, especially if they have tried to do so on multiple occasions. It hurt me to the core to see the friend that taught me how to live in the moment go, but such is life.

The second was an even dearer friend. This was the sister that protected me from losing everything in college through helping me to avoid eviction until I could better my situation. Prior to being diagnosed with bi-polar disorder, she changed in the blink of an eye. I was one of her most beloved friends but through her illness and over-doing it on a certain natural remedy (hallucinogen), she accused me of betraying her. She slandered my name by spreading lies to everyone we mutually knew, she wished death upon me and members of my family, she falsely went to the police on me, of which no action could be taken because I had done no physical (or even verbal) harm to her. It was all because in her mind due to her mental illness I had become a threat. I never saw it coming and I did absolutely nothing to deserve it. Having a degree in psychology gives me some background knowledge of her illness, but it's easier to handle when I am not the recipient of her episodic antics. I have been encouraged through a mutual friend to try to get past it because she can't control it, and that I shouldn't just end a friendship when it's clear that she needs help. However, every time I hear her say something of that nature I have to bite my tongue. I could be screaming to the top of my lungs for help and that particular friend (along with quite a few others) wouldn't give a damn about me but I am always the one who is told to basically "Get over it." I won't get over it, my peace was compromised and she was deleted from my life, instantly.

So, I choose not to again attempt to pull someone up leaving myself vulnerable to be dragged down, like I've been so many times in the past, all by family or friends. It's so ironic to me that I have never been hurt by a stranger; it's always someone I know. Yes, I will always love them for the women they were to me during those seasons in my life; however, while one of these friendships lay dormant, the other is completely dead. I still struggle severely with attachment (especially towards my living grandmother), but losing one grandmother, ending a close to three year relationship because of the distance, and losing two women who were literally my rocks while I was away from home all within months apart from each other has loosened my grip on people in general. I am an extroverted introvert; I'll converse with anyone who converses with me, I love conversation, it enthuses me, it educates me. However, every battle I've faced lately, I have again been doing it alone, without sharing with anyone my sporadic feelings of depression, my failing health predicament, irritation with love as my grandfather's words that "No one would ever love or tolerate me intimately" are reining true thus far. At the end of the day, all I have is me, and I've figured that maybe I wouldn't have all of these issues if my attachment were to a higher being and to myself only, but that's easier said than done.

Currently, I am learning through mediation, how to become one with the universe. I am being taught the strength of vibrations through stillness. My peace (though is still often disturbed by distractors), is being centered and will soon be an accomplished state of being that I have never before experienced in its entirety. I am being rooted in my identity as a woman; I am being grounded in my blackness. Ultimately, I have gained the comfort of opaqueness. Where I was once shunned, mocked, fought and abused for standing out, I am now celebrated for it. I now celebrate myself for it. To a world that thought I was normal, I reveal my differences and embrace all of my insanity. Though the conditions of my birth were deadly; leaving me within inches of my life; I lived. Though the balled fists and harsh words over the years pierced deeply; I've fought back. Though everyone I have loved has left me in some way, my love is everlasting and I am channeling that love back into myself.

I am now doing what I love the most; being an author and touching the lives of people that are most similar to me, while also providing a clue to the clueless. Of the ninety-nine percent, I still stand outside the realm, and in all honesty I am beginning to love it. Since my grandmother has passed, I live freely, saying what I want and doing as I please…what do I have to lose; my job, a relationship? I could care less, my peace is pertinent and I have learned that if it vanishes, it wasn't meant to be and I'll never implore to keep the presence of any entity that the universe is stripping me away from (people or situations). I am in love with the woman I have become and am more in love with the thought of who I will be in the future. I am grateful, I am whole, and I am happy in this moment; flaws and all. Through it all, I'm still figuring out this thing called life and thus my journey is not over, but just beginning!

~ To my living grandmother, I thank you, for you have been the pillar of my strength. You have taught me to fight for what I deserve regardless of the costs, and though your memory is faint, I'll always remember your words of wisdom, your love and I'll always hear your melodic voice singing songs of resilience in my ear in the moments that I want to give up. I owe you my life and for you, I will succeed.

~ To my father, know that I will always be your babygirl; I'm a daddy's girl forever and never will that change. You have taught me the definition of sacrifice. You bettered yourself; completely gave that lifestyle up so that I could have a chance at life. Now I work to make you half as proud of me as you have made me of you. I am beyond blessed to have you as my dad and friend. I love you always and forever Pops.

~ To my grandfather, I thank you for taking on the challenge of raising a baby girl to be the independent woman you had planned for her to become all along. You have instilled in me the value of work ethic as I saw you leave for work every morning for the sixteen years I lived under your roof. You have implanted in me the attitude of non-dependency on any man: but rather to get an education and to do for myself. Thank you for your solidness, I love you with my life grandpop.

~ To my mother, know that I will always love you, for you are the alpha to my existence; I am you and you are me. I accept that God didn't match me with you without intent and I am proud to be your only daughter. Because of you, I have a story to tell. I cherish you, I admire you and I understand you. Remember, "You die, I die; a love so connected we hit rock bottom together with our highs." Forgive yourself, I have forgiven you; I still need you and I love you, always.

~ To my aunt/godmother, you are everything beautiful about life! Thank you for the example of love you have set forth. You have taught me how to wear the toils of life gracefully. You have shown me through your example, the meaning of success. The warmth of your spirit, your elegance and your grace shines onto our family as God's light. I love you with my whole heart godmommy!

~ To my younger cousin/baby sister facing adversities in that new environment in Vermont, you are a true queen and my journey has been made worth it to see you become 2nd in our family to escape. You have a story to tell, write it down and show it to the world; show it the two younger ones coming up after you. We can all make it out. I love you baby sis!

~ To my god-daughter LA, know that I love you little girl. You entered my life when I was just nineteen and you are the closet to making me a parent that I have experienced thus far in life. I thank your mother (one of my best friends and other one percenters), she has given me the ultimate gift of love through you.

~ To my grandmother watching over me from above, I dedicate this book to you. Thank you for your tough love. You have taught me through the essence of your being not to ever give up on myself and in all things, to remain focused on the overall goal. Well, here is another reason for you to be proud of me and be sure to read it to everyone in heaven, I miss and love you, always.

~ In Loving Memory of my grandmother; the most beautiful,

spirited and strong-willed woman I know…

Bobbie Jean Brown (aka Bobbie Nene)

August 1st, 1932 – August 2nd, 2016

Your tough love built me and gave me the strength to get to this point!

&

~ To my own personal angel and reminder that my grandmother's spirit is alive and well…

Little Ms. Riley Renee`

Born on August 5th, 2016, the day my grandmother was buried.

Your smile warms my heart and gives me the hope to keep going!